B A T T L E

JUSTICE FOR KIDS WITH SPECIAL NEEDS

BATTLE CRIES

JUSTICE FOR KIDS
WITH SPECIAL NEEDS

by

Miriam Edelson

SUMACH PRESS

LIBRARY AND ARCHIVES CANADA CATALOGUING IN PUBLICATION

Edelson, Miriam, 1956-
Battle cries : justice for kids with special needs/Miriam Edelson.

Includes bibliographical references.
ISBN 978-1-894549-42-4

1. Children with disabilities — Services for — Canada. I. Title.

HV890.C3E318 2005   362.4'083'0971   C2005-904728

Edited by Lisa Rundle & Jennifer Day
Designed by Liz Martin

Cover photo: *Enosh at age 12 enjoying a school trip
with friends to Flower Pot Island near Tobermory, Ontario.*
(Provided by the Gaster family)

*Sumach Press acknowledges the support of the Canada Council
for the Arts and the Ontario Arts Council for our publishing program.
We acknowledge the financial support of the Government of Canada through
the Book Publishing Industry Development Program (BPIDP)
for our publishing activities*

ONTARIO ARTS COUNCIL
CONSEIL DES ARTS DE L'ONTARIO

Printed and bound in Canada

Published by
SUMACH PRESS
180 Bloor St W #801
Toronto ON M5S 2V6

info@sumachpress.com

To my parents

*

HIS LAUGHTER

The first time
his laughter
unfurled its wings
in the wind, we
knew that the
world would
never be
the same.

— *Brian Andreas*
ARTIST, SCULPTOR
AND STORYTELLER

CONTENTS

II: PORTRAITS

THE POWER OF NARRATIVE 107

MIRIAM, COLLEEN AND JOHNNY, AGE 13, IN CONVERSATION
AT THE FAMILY'S HOME IN ST. JOHN'S, NEWFOUNDLAND.

INTRODUCTION

WHILE I WAS IN THE MIDST OF WRITING this book, my son Jake died. He was born in 1990 with a serious neurological disorder and was not expected to live more than a couple of years. He overcame many severe bouts of respiratory illness — oxygen delivered through a pint-sized mask. An arsenal of antibiotics and other medications were shot directly into his stomach, pumped through a tube that sustained him, with baby formula and juice. Frequent seizures caused his limbs to jut abruptly akimbo, like a toy soldier stuck in freeze frame.

In the prime of his life, Jake offered smiles and quizzical looks to those around him. He was a handsome child, strawberry blond hair and sea-blue eyes with long lashes. Although his ability to communicate and to reach out to his surroundings was severely limited, we learned to bring the world to him.

A flicker of light would almost always kindle a smile. In warm weather he enjoyed the tickle of a breeze on his cheek. We loved to nestle in together, his head resting on my chest. When sensing the constancy of my heartbeat, Jake was uncharacteristically calm. One month short of his fourteenth birthday my young man went gently in his sleep, claiming a peaceful death.

I loved him to the moon; no holds barred. Jake's father snapped many photos of our boy, and the wonderful memories of his deeply expressive eyes and the cooing sounds he would make when I held him close will be ever-present. During all those years, he listened to me sing and rhyme words in his ear, sharing my most intimate thoughts.

Although Jake had hefty limits — he never learned to hold his head up, sit, stand or speak — he brought a great deal of light into the world. In his vulnerability, he brought people together, urging them to reach out and grasp life's moments. And he taught me to love with a fierce determination I had never before known.

Losing Jake left me rudderless. He was my muse. Emptiness moved in like a squatter, taking over the spot where my heart used to live. His birth and our struggles to ensure he had complex nursing care twenty-four hours a day affected my own equilibrium while we all rode the "red alert" rollercoaster. The entire experience proved all-consuming, and by 1996 my marriage had ended.

The original impetus for this book was very much wrapped in my love for Jake and a commitment to make the world a more welcoming place for young ones like him. Like so many other parents of children with disabilities, I envisage a society where children now most typically defined by their difference and discriminated against for it would instead enjoy lives characterized by comfort, dignity and child-appropriate physical, cognitive and creative stimulation.

When I lost my son I also lost, for a time, the passion that had propelled me to write about these issues. I stopped believing that anything I could say would make a jot of difference. Enveloped in sadness, I no longer believed that my words could possibly bring solace to any other mom who finds herself in frightening, uncharted territory when her baby is born, or that any kind of community action could truly transform the world into the place our kids deserve.

I am fortunate, though. I have another child, Emma-Maryse, just two years younger than her brother. She propels me ever forward, day after day, into the future. Her energy and hopes are a source of sparkle and comfort (as well as the usual frustrations that accompany raising an independent-minded adolescent!). The pleasures I reap from knowing her root me firmly in the present, in spite of myself.

I grieve and also keep going. Emma needs me not to lose my balance, and so I retreat ever so slightly from that precipice of pain, the abyss into which I am so afraid I will fall. At glacial speed I sift through fourteen years of accumulated sediment, a life lived in the shadow of my son's eventual death. The moraine left behind is rich, like the rock and minerals wrenched asunder by unstoppable masses of ice and snow. With time, the material of my life is deposited farther down the path. New formations emerge, my personal bedrock weathered and worn — but not without its core of hope. My arms reach out to embrace both the sweetness and desolation that embodies my experience as a mother.

What This Book Is about and Who It Is for

I interviewed eight parents of children who live with a variety of disabilities. The families, as well as their kids' challenges, were quite diverse, and so my dialogue with them portrays a small group — but one with a certain breadth. The interviews were grounded in principles of feminist qualitative research; the underlying premise being that by coming to know these parents, asking them to reflect and reach down into their core, one can catch a glimpse of how they interweave the many strands of their lives. This research methodology also seeks to embed personal experience in a broader social context. My purpose was to unearth information and insights that would help parents, policy-makers and health care professionals treat our most vulnerable persons in the manner they deserve. You will meet the parents I spoke with in the second half of the book — the section entitled "Portraits."

Two questions propelled me forward when I began my research. I wanted to know if the advocacy many parents perform on behalf of their children with disabilities led to a greater involvement in the life of their communities, as citizens[1] engaged in pursuit of a common good. I also wanted to know how mothers and fathers built community around their children and themselves.

I chose to interview predominantly women because I have a particular interest in the distinct experience of mothers — who are most often the primary caregivers. I hoped that their reflections would reveal the multi-layered texture of their lives, including the rough patches. I also hoped that by exploring how these parents fashion their lives, clues to fostering community action and political changes would emerge.

The first part of the book explores key themes that surfaced in the interviews, previous research and the experience of my own family. These themes include gaps in services and supports; a more humane foundation upon which to organize and fund programs; our fear of difference; mothers' unpaid work as caregivers; integrated settings versus segregated ones for children with disabilities; relationships between siblings; how aging parents plan for their child's future and how we engage as parents and citizens in active work to ensure our kids get what they need and deserve.

A common thread winding through the first part of the book is my view that families with disabled children need support at two distinct but related levels in order to manage well. The public/formal organization of services is the keystone, but the personal/informal means of support in which families engage are also vital. In day-to-day life these two levels interlace as a matter of course; both are examined here.

My hope is that this book will contribute to identifying best practices for these children and their families in an assortment of settings. A best practice provides a child and family with competent, therapeutic intervention in sufficient amounts and frequency and, further, is infused with respect for parents' knowledge about their children. A best practice seeks to empower these families in three ways: to teach them to perform essential caregiving tasks that promote attachment between parent and child; to show them how to successfully secure and apply assistance the child needs and to engage in partnership as advocates for services that are not easily obtained in a climate of scarcity. Moreover, a best practice is publicly funded and universally accessible — its delivery is not based on socio-economic standing, race, language, sexual orientation or religious background.

My Point of Departure

Some months after losing Jake, I returned to complete this book. A close and trusted circle of friends urged me to continue and assured me that the stories in this book would resonate with other parents. I was reminded that the light these parents' honest words would shed on the shortcomings of current supports for these families would be instructive. One of the women I had interviewed a couple of years earlier called me from Newfoundland when she learned of my son's death. She held me in generous spirit over the telephone line and urged me not to abandon this research. And so I continued to write, by times finding the passion to persist with purpose, more often just trying to roll with the waves of grief that, like the birthing of a child, generate their own unique rhythm.

My own experience as Jake and Emma's mom had taught me that making a family, especially a nuclear family, without a great deal of day-to-day assistance was an isolating and sometimes enormously draining experience. I know this is not every woman's experience, but I found trying to raise children in a conscious manner while also juggling full-time work to be a huge challenge. Giving up my work outside the home was never a financially realistic option. Becoming a single parent when my youngest was pre-school age aggravated the situation.

People I would never have imagined playing a part in the lives of my children and my own life in other circumstances became a kind of extended family — Jake's caregivers, Emma's childcare teachers and the families in our secular Jewish Sunday morning school community. Having children also brought relative strangers into my home, and when it worked, the boundaries between me and my co-workers, acquaintances and one-time strangers became more elastic. I could not go it alone. For very practical reasons, to keep my children well and safe, I required assistance. Previously quite a private individual, I was forced to crowbar my life open and sustain more scrutiny by professionals and other parents than I would ever have thought I could bear. Somehow, despite the occasional and quite overwhelming discomfort I felt at the intrusion into my privacy, we muddled through. On balance, stretching out the girding that encases our family unit has been positive, particularly for my children. From this community-minded perspective, I wanted to look at the supports in place in this country for families like ours and how they could be improved.

As I pursued the research, a fairly obvious point became a great deal more tangible. Where families have practical supports in their daily lives — from individuals and public facilities — the possibility that children will flourish is enhanced. It became clear that when a household includes a child with a disability, that support is absolutely crucial, particularly for families of moderate means. Well-to-do individuals have always been able to purchase services to ease the unglamorous chores of day-to-day living. Suffice it to say that most North American families do not find themselves in that snack bracket. Finding a way to increase necessary supports such as special education programs and opportunities for high-quality, reliable respite care constitutes a glaring and fundamental need.

In Canada, the political culture that spawned universal insurance for physicians' services outside hospitals in 1968[2] has resulted in the provision of a hodgepodge of services for children with disabilities. There is no comprehensive system. Rather, programs meant to assist families are bewilderingly fragmented. Study after study demonstrates the inadequacy of the support many families receive, especially those raising children with any type of disability. From expertise in physical and speech therapy to the cost of necessary medications to relief from the unrelenting care needs of our medically fragile children, few families can go it alone. We rely on our social safety net, despite its tattered stitching after many years of cuts by successive governments. Many families will continue to flounder without quality, regulated and reliable health and social services funded by the public purse.[3]

I am university-trained in the disciplines of political economy and sociology. My twenty-five years of professional work in the trade union and women's movements captures several related streams of experience as a union organizer, human rights advocate, negotiator, women's rights activist and communications specialist. As I was the child of politically and socially engaged New York City parents, striving for social justice was ingrained in me from the first civil rights rally I can remember being carted off to.

I bring that optimism for a better world and the belief in our collective ability to achieve improved living and working conditions to my careers as an activist and author. I try to integrate a critical social and feminist perspective into my political and personal lives. Of course I do not always succeed. I am human, flawed, full of contradictions and sometimes, just plain wrong.

Nonetheless, the skills I have learned in various arenas of political engagement provide a reasonable grounding in strategic thinking. In applying this experience to families raising children with disabilities, I attempt in the first section of this book, "Mapping the Terrain," to analyse the big picture and suggest where improvements in our lives can be made. This discussion focuses on both the macro level of how services are organized and the micro level at which families are impacted, including the particularity of mothering in this context, the role played by the disability movement in our lives and how the community functions — or doesn't — to connect parents to one another and engage them as citizens.

This study is informed by both my grassroots community organizing experience and academic training. In this era of privatization and global economics, a bold and sweeping transformation of Canada's social structure is unlikely. I remain convinced, however, that ordinary people who engage together in pursuit of a common good can achieve incremental and meaningful improvements in their lives and that these tiny ripples of hope can "… build a current which can sweep down the mightiest walls of oppression and injustice."[4] If we are to effect positive change, people such as nurses, neighbours, occupational therapists and physiotherapists, doctors, school teachers, policy-makers and politicians must understand the circumstances that shape the lives of families with disabled kids.

The second section of the book, "Portraits," contains stories about the lives of eight families in diverse situations. Most live in Canada; one resides in Stockholm, Sweden. Six of the children are Canadian-born. Seven of the eight now reside in various parts of the country: Ontario, Manitoba, British Columbia and Newfoundland.

The interviews conducted were open-ended, informal and based on the principles of feminist qualitative research — that is, data collected in the form of personal stories by a researcher who engages individuals in exchanges of various kinds as a means of understanding how they function and feel in their role as parent of a disabled child. The interviews are presented not as edited transcripts but as portraits that include my observations and the context of the interview. After I had distilled what I considered to be the most important points, each interviewee vetted his or her respective text for suitability. I have attempted to render their stories accurately and with respect.

I found these parents in various ways: Some were already known to me; I came into contact with a few through colleagues in the disability movement; I also contacted a couple of disability service organizations for help in finding individuals who would be willing to speak candidly about their lives. The portraits reflect a particular filter. I make no claim to objectivity. From the outset, I share with these mothers and fathers at least one life experience. We all parent outside the mainstream and this fact made our contact more intimate.

A central principle in my research has been to interview fathers and mothers in a manner that encouraged them to share their stories and reflect upon their own experience. I developed a series of twenty open-ended questions to guide our conversations. In most cases, a follow-up interview — in person, by telephone or via email — was required. Of course the questions I asked have, to some extent, shaped the stories that emerged. My relationship with these parents is also influenced by our respective roles as researcher and subject.

The chapters that follow explore parents' experience and, in particular, that of mothers, as told from their own perspective. My research does not interrogate or seek to present the voices of children or young adults. I suspect strongly that there is potential for conflict between generations, particularly when young people develop the capacity to assert their independence from parental decision-making and control.

Arriving at best outcomes in social policy means acknowledging potential conflicts between the needs of parents and those of children. It means working them through in a fashion that respects both voices. Living with a disability, except among the most vulnerable children, does not obliterate youths' hopes, dreams and indomitable determination to set their own course. And so, I am troubled that the distinction between these two separate (but related) voices is often blurred in disability rights discourse. Narratives of both parents and children are valid, even though they are not mutually exclusive.

In selecting mothers and fathers to interview I looked for individuals from diverse backgrounds. The purpose of this book, however, is most definitely not to compare a First Nations family, for example, with a Jewish family. Moreover, the interviewees do not present themselves in little boxes labelled *Aboriginal woman* or *Black woman, Caribbean background*. The men and women I met with reflect a mix of many influences. Not one would claim to be entirely free of dominant North American societal values and norms. Variations in approach to parenting and in cultural practice are a given, even within groupings that might appear the same. Real people are far more complex than any classification allows. In conveying their stories I am most interested to understand the coping strategies these families have adopted. Moreover, I wanted to discover in very concrete terms what would make their journey easier.

Six of the interviews in this book were conducted in person. Two were conducted by email. Each family interviewed is raising a child with a disability along with a non-disabled child(ren). These parents vary as to their class backgrounds. All are heterosexual. The parents tend to be well-educated, although not all work in professional capacities. Each is proficient in English. Seven of the interviews were conducted in English, one in French.

What the parents have in common, and this will become evident as you meet the six mothers and two fathers interviewed, is the absolute, determined love they feel for their children. Of course this lion heart of love is not exclusive to such parents; yet the attachment seems heightened with very vulnerable children. Not knowing how many more breaths the little girl in your lap will take is both wearing and, simultaneously, enriching. It seems to propel one's perceptions up a notch.

Also significant to note is that each of these families is "mothering [or parenting] against the odds," the title of an insightful anthology published in 1998.[5] While all parents advocate for their children at some point, the stories that follow illustrate how most of these families struggle and advocate routinely. Without constant and deliberate pursuit of just treatment, they simply cannot get access to the health, social and community supports their children require.

WINNING IMPROVEMENTS IN SOCIAL POLICY

Inadequate social policy and implementation for people with disabilities has a profound impact upon our families, so we are compelled to work for change on many levels. Insisting, for example, that our children be seen as individual, worthy human beings by all is one part of this struggle. No doubt a youth with a disabled sibling is also affected when one child in the family constellation has particular and pressing needs. Is it any wonder that struggling for our youngsters to be treated justly is so integral to the territory we inhabit?

I do not presume that every parent will become an active participant in a battle for better education or therapeutic interventions. Many are too busy just trying to keep a household running. Rather, I am advancing the notion that the overarching conditions contain potential to spark resistance. We can make common cause to improve our children's chances in life.

None of the mothers or fathers featured here is extraordinary — there are no saints or martyrs. They are simply people doing the best they can with the cards they've been dealt. I firmly believe that those in this situation — perhaps more than ordinary families — must never think they are alone. Listening to their personal stories resonated deeply with me, giving me further insight. I hope that families facing similar challenges will derive ideas, vision and energy from reading these stories and that health care professionals and policy-makers gain deeper knowledge of the people their work affects. Beginning with feelings of empathy may spur us to act together, to forge ahead and win meaningful improvements so needed by so many. My son Jake's life and the welfare of all our children demand that we recognize the potential of our own power as citizens and act collectively to secure the quality of life every child deserves.

I

MAPPING
THE
TERRAIN

CHAPTER ONE

MEETING THE MAIN CHARACTERS:

A COLLECTION OF SNAPSHOTS

THE PURPOSE OF THIS CHAPTER is to acquaint the reader with each of the families we meet later in the book. I spoke to one parent in each family: Mary Ellen Jones, Sharon Daniels, Lillian Bayne, Mathieu Joly, Colleen Fitzpatrick, Julien Lee, Cheryl Gaster and Dave Lewis. The interviews with Lillian Bayne and Dave Lewis were conducted by email.

Both Mary Ellen Jones and Cheryl Gaster were casual acquaintances of mine before we met for the purpose of my research, people whose stories I knew something about. Lillian Bayne resurfaced in my life quite unexpectedly twenty-five years after we had known one another in university. Mathieu Joly and I have been friends — although at a distance and not on a consistent basis — going back twenty-two years. The other four parents were unknown to me prior to embarking on this project.

I was not acquainted with most of the children and young people in the book, with two exceptions. I have met Mathieu Joly's children on a few occasions and, as Mathieu's sister Dominique is a close friend, I like to keep tabs on how the young people are doing. I met Mary Ellen's son Jeremy when he was about seven years old and attending the same daycare as my daughter.

Who are these parents? What issues do these families deal with? These snapshots offer a glimpse into the challenging situations faced by the members of their respective households. In the rest of the book, I take great pains to introduce people first. No child or young adult is ever to be reduced to his or her disability. Medical diagnoses must take a back seat to the experience of flesh and blood human beings. In this preliminary section, however, details of various disabling conditions become a focus in an effort to acquaint readers with each family and its particular challenges. With that caveat in mind, allow me to make some introductions.

MARY ELLEN AND JEREMY

When I first interviewed Mary Ellen, her son Jeremy was sixteen years old. With the help of an educational assistant from his high school, Jeremy was learning to take public transit to and from school by himself. It would be another step toward his independence which, just as each life skill he has developed over the years has, required Mary Ellen's mindful coaching and the help of others versed in assisting special needs children.

Mary Ellen lives on Toronto's east side and works there as an early childhood educator. She grew up in Midland, Ontario, a town on Georgian Bay northwest of Toronto and was raised in the United Church. She has a daughter, Katie, who is three years older than Jeremy. Mary Ellen and her husband separated several months after our conversation for this project.

She describes her son as a happy young man. He was born with Down Syndrome, the single most frequent cause of so-called human birth defects. Medical texts suggest that Down "usually, although not always, results in 'mental retardation' and other conditions."[6] There is, however, a broad range of intellectual capability among those with Down Syndrome and some adults are able to live independently and work in the paid economy.

Due to her work with children, Mary Ellen was well aware of the developmental milestones infants and toddlers are expected to reach. She described working hard with Jeremy to learn new skills and how wonderful it was when he achieved them. She had no doubt that the stimulation he received during his very early years would be crucial to his overall capacity to learn.

She firmly believes it is not only possible but essential that parents learn to advocate effectively on behalf their children. A first step is coming to grips with the truth that only they as parents (and sometimes, the professionals with whom they come into contact) will stand up unreservedly for their child's extraordinary needs. Her own efforts to secure speech and other necessary therapies for Jeremy illustrate how difficult it is to access adequate publicly funded services.

Sharon and Shannon

Sharon Daniels is a mother of three living in Winnipeg, Manitoba. She is an Ojibwa woman and is trained as a social worker. Her eldest child, Shannon, lives with a disability. Shannon and her sister Sherri are just sixteen months apart and they're very close. Their brother Shawn is nine years younger. Clarence, Sharon's husband, works as a long-distance trucker. Like most of us, Sharon has always tried to balance her time and energy between the children. But it's difficult.

Shannon, now in her early thirties, lives with a form of cerebral palsy that severely affects her digestive system. She is mobile and her cognitive abilities are fully intact. Shannon has experienced several serious health crises during her life and has weathered them with fierce determination and spirit. A cardiac arrest and seventeen-day coma in 2000 related to her severe digestive challenges — she weighed only eighty-five pounds at the time — set her back, but not for long. She advocates on behalf of other First Nations youth with disabilities by volunteering with the Manitoba Chiefs Disability Working Group and Manitoba First Nations Youth Council.

Sharon was nineteen years old at the time of her daughter's birth. She knew from the first day that something was wrong. Her baby could not take in the sustenance an infant absolutely requires. It seemed she didn't have the usual sucking reflex — the muscle tone babies need in order to suck and swallow. The baby was often ill with bronchitis or pneumonia. Sharon became worried as she realized that Shannon was not reaching the usual developmental milestones, but she never felt that she was able to get an accurate picture of the parameters of her daughter's challenges. Shannon's challenges were not accurately diagnosed until she was twenty-seven years old.

During Shannon's early childhood, the family had moved from Winnipeg to their First Nations community in Peguis and found it beneficial for Shannon, but it became clear over time that she needed various specialized health services to flourish. At that time, the Band didn't possess enough funds to finance the various medical and physical therapies Shannon required. Eventually the family moved to Brandon and away from their native community. Sharon believes that her daughter lost a lot of ground as a result of this move. Not only did she lose her circle of friends, she was no longer among her own people.

High school in Brandon proved to be a discouraging time. Although there was no question about Shannon's intellect, her physical needs posed some challenges. Digestive troubles would sometimes cause her to vomit, and she needed help cleaning herself up. The school refused to accommodate her and insisted that she enrol in the Special Education classes. Sharon described this period as enormously trying for her daughter. Since then, Shannon has been accepted into university in Winnipeg. The Band in Peguis is now in a position to cover the cost, but Shannon is not yet ready to attend.

Sharon does not believe Shannon's disability to be a hindrance to Shannon or the family. She told me that her daughter's disability has taught her, Clarence and their two other children a great deal. Sharon wants her daughter to live a full and satisfying life, one that values her intellect and considerable skill as an advocate.

Lillian and Oliver

Lillian Bayne and her life partner Michael live in Victoria, British Columbia, with their two sons: Eliot, age fifteen, and Oliver, age twelve. Michael and Lillian moved to the west coast from Ontario in 1988. Lillian spent her formative years in Hamilton, Ontario, where she later began her university education. Michael's family originally hailed from Yarmouth, Nova Scotia.

Our paths first crossed while we were all attending McMaster University and were involved in various aspects of student activism. Michael now teaches at Simon Fraser University where he recently became Associate Dean of the new Faculty of Health Science. Lillian has held several senior positions in the Ministry of Health in British Columbia as well as in Health Canada. Before deciding to start her own consulting firm, she worked as Associate Executive Director for the Romanow Commission on the Future of Health Care in Canada. Quite out of the blue, Lillian and I met again in 2003 during a Romanow Commission consultation with stakeholders in Toronto.

Oliver (Ollie) was born in October 1993 with profound brain damage. His oxygen supply was cut off while he was in utero, possibly because the umbilical cord got tangled. The brain damage led to epilepsy, cerebral palsy and cortical blindness. Although his eyes are fine in physiological terms, he doesn't see like most people because the messaging to his brain is confused. Ollie requires various medications at regular intervals during the day.

Ollie cannot stand up without support to pull himself upright. However, he learned to walk at about seven or eight years of age and is becoming more accomplished every day. Last year, Ollie learned how to turn his body around while standing. Michael and Lillian are very proud of their son's accomplishments. He is now able to walk down the stairs without help. His big brother Eliot is a caring young man and very protective of Ollie.

Now at age twelve, Ollie is a handsome, spirited young fellow. He communicates in many ways with his voice and gestures, although he doesn't speak words. He relates specific desires, such as "I'm hungry" or "I'm thirsty" in ways his family and caregivers understand — he smacks his lips and makes little sipping sounds.

Ollie attends Victor School, one of the last segregated educational settings in the country for children with severe multiple disabilities and behavioural challenges. "It has a reputation for schooling the un-schoolable and the fierce devotion of parents of its students,"[7] reported an article on the school that appeared in *The Globe & Mail.* There are twenty-two students and a teacher's aide for every two children, in addition to classroom teachers. Ollie returns home from school by bus at about 2:30. Terry, his caregiver, meets him there, spends the afternoon with Ollie and gets him ready for bed.

Lillian is emphatic — Ollie should have every opportunity to live a happy and fulfilled life. Although she told me that resources for special needs kids are relatively available on Vancouver Island — at least as compared to other parts of the country — she does not have a great deal of faith that the services for special needs children will be preserved long-term. She and most parents at Victor School write letters to support the school's continued existence and also raise funds to help finance and improve its programs.

MATHIEU, AUDE CATHERINE AND VINCENT

Mathieu and his children Aude Catherine, age eighteen, and Vincent, age fifteen, hail from Ottawa, Ontario. He shares custody with the children's mother Suzanne, who also lives in Ottawa. Mathieu, who is French-Canadian with Québécois roots, has worked as a computer analyst at the House of Commons for the last twenty years. Although he and his four sisters were raised in the Catholic faith, the family (including his parents) is largely non-practising. Suzanne was raised on Montreal's south shore and has spent most of her career working in various national museums around Ottawa and Hull. The couple separated in 1999 and have continued to co-parent their youngsters in an amicable fashion since that time.

Not long after Aude Catherine's birth, Suzanne became alarmed that her daughter did not seem to react to sounds made around her. When she was eight weeks old, medical specialists determined that Aude Catherine hears virtually nothing without amplification. Mathieu and Suzanne scrambled (like most parents in this situation) to find out what resources existed in the community to help Aude Catherine develop her capacities.

As the family — including both extended families — conducts its life primarily in French, Mathieu and Suzanne needed to come to terms with the availability of French language resources in Ottawa, as well as to decide upon the most appropriate learning method for Aude Catherine. She was fitted with a hearing aid when she was ten weeks old, and in short order the family enrolled in an intensive program at the local children's hospital in which one parent and the infant go to the hospital at least once a week so that the primary caregiver can learn how to teach and work with the baby. The parent then works with the child daily. Suzanne, as primary caregiver, worked at home diligently with her daughter during the next five years with very positive results.

Vincent was born a few years after Aude Catherine. He also turned out to have a profound hearing deficit. He entered the same program as his sister, and Suzanne continued to work with both children at home. Both young people successfully completed public school programs; they each required a certain amount of speech therapy and other specialized tutoring. The relatively sparse availability of special needs resources in French has spurred Mathieu to become quite active in lobbying efforts to enhance services for all children with disabilities.

COLLEEN AND JOHNNY

Johnny Penney, age thirteen, lives in St. John's, Newfoundland with his mother, Colleen Fitzpatrick, and sister, Krystal. Johnny is an engaging child who loves to perch in his mother's lap. He makes sounds that Colleen and Krystal, three years Johnny's senior, seem to understand. Although Johnny is small for his age and does not walk, it is evident that he communicates in his own fashion with his entourage.

Johnny was born with Trisomy 18, a condition that results from an anomaly in an infant's genetic makeup. Johnny has an extra 18th chromosome in every cell of his body. The range of difficulties such infants and children face is extensive. Some of the most common symptoms are congenital heart disease, microcephaly (small head) and clenched fists. The baby's hands, with flexed fingers and, often, the third and fourth fingers overlapping, are a frequent diagnostic indication of Trisomy 18.

The vast majority of Trisomy 18 infants fail to thrive. Their lifespans are short, with 20–30 percent dying in the first month and 90 percent of those who survive longer passing away before their first birthday. At age thirteen, Johnny has lived years past his original prognosis. Early in her son's life, Colleen realized how isolated she could become trying to care for him twenty-four/seven. Her marriage fell apart under the strain, and her ex-husband is not part of Johnny's life.

Colleen is a friendly and outgoing woman in her early forties. She is a devout Catholic and a determined advocate for her son and other young people with disabilities. When we first met, she was organizing a campaign to win support in the community to keep the classroom unit Johnny attends Monday to Friday alive. Colleen spends most nights sleeping only very lightly, needing to soothe her little boy through seizures and a cluster of other troubling symptoms. Medications must be given at all hours and bedclothes kept dry from Johnny's unrelenting mucus flow.

When Johnny reached school age, Colleen was able to work outside the home for periods of time, managing retail operations. In the intervening years, she has found a neighbour who now cares for Johnny every second weekend. The break gives Colleen a chance to spend some time with her daughter and to rest.

The energy, humour and determination shown by Colleen indicate that she is a formidable force to contend with. And young Johnny, with his expressive eyes and face, reaps her love and radiates it to those around him.

JULIEN AND SIMON

Julien Lee, a nurse by training, works at the Canadian National Institute for the Blind (CNIB) in Toronto as a vision rehabilitation worker. After fourteen years as a geriatric nurse in hospital, she now performs functional assessments at the CNIB. Her work involves educating clients about how their particular disease is likely to progress and how to use the residual vision they have.

Julien, whose mother is a native of Trinidad, refers to herself as a Caribbean-Canadian and she is married to an African-Canadian man named Owen. The couple has two children: Jeremiah, age nine, and Simon, age six. Julien also has two adult children from a previous marriage. Now in her forties, she is an experienced mother and caregiver.

Simon was born with bilateral cataracts, which means the lenses on both his left and right eyes are clouded. This condition was diagnosed when Simon had barely reached one week old. Simon was born virtually without pupils: One was malformed and did not contract properly; the other was practically non-existent, meaning that light could not get into the back of the eye. The result is that his vision is blurry. He had surgery to remove the cataracts when he was six weeks old. Since that time he has worn strong contact lenses to correct his eyesight. His prescription is so strong that eyeglasses are out of the question. He also has glaucoma, a progressive condition that affects his peripheral vision. Increased fluid causes pressure within the eyeball that then damages the optic nerve. Glaucoma causes vision loss that can advance to blindness. Medication helps to reduce the intraocular pressure that frequently causes tearing, sensitivity to light and redness of the eye. Eventually Simon won't have any peripheral vision at all.

Simon experienced certain developmental delays as well. During his infancy and toddler years Julien worked with the help of infant stimulation workers and various therapists to help him cultivate his speech and reach physical and developmental milestones.

Since Simon's vision is so limited, he has learned to use a cane to navigate his way around unfamiliar spaces. This was an important achievement and contributes to his independence. Julien accompanies Simon, who is in Grade 1, to many appointments with specialists as well as hospital visits. She insists upon full explanations.

Simon's schooling, along with Julien's diligence, means that Simon is progressing steadily. He is learning to read Braille quickly, and use his computer with assistive software and zoom text — all of which enhance his ability to learn and function in a seeing world.

Julien is committed to helping Simon fend for himself and is confident that he will get an education and join the workforce when he grows up. For now, she is busy keeping a hectic schedule in her professional and personal life. It is a challenge she embraces with characteristic humour and a great deal of love.

CHERYL AND ENOSH

Cheryl Gaster works as a mediator for the Ontario Human Rights Commission. She and her husband Tzvika, an accountant, have had two sons: Enosh, born in 1974, and Jeremiah, born in 1978. Enosh was born in Israel, his father's homeland, where the family lived for a time. He was small at birth. He didn't immediately plump up, nor did he meet expected developmental milestones. It took a long time for him to smile. At six months of age Enosh became quite ill, but a full and accurate diagnosis was not made until several months later.

In 1975, the family returned to Canada, close to Toronto, to be near Cheryl's family and to take advantage of health care services. A geneticist at the Hospital for Sick Children in Toronto told Tzvika and Cheryl that Enosh had cytomegalovirus (CMV), a disease then only recently identified. CMV-related infection, which is a congenital (meaning, from birth) viral infection, is thought to be passed from mother to baby in utero. In 1975 there was not a lot of information about the disease. Life expectancy estimates were very guarded.

Enosh was able to say some words. He learned to use gestures and make signs to indicate his needs. Once they found an empathetic physician, the family was able to actively nurture their son's development through nursery schools and a very intensive physiotherapy program. Remarkably — and against medical predictions — by age five, Enosh had learned to move his body voluntarily and to walk.

Enosh had his bar mitzvah at age thirteen, as is the practice in the Jewish faith. When he was fourteen, his world changed dramatically. Repeated bouts of pneumonia assaulted his weakened system, and he began to experience frequent seizures. He could no longer pursue his usual activities. Up until that time, Enosh had always been cared for by family or close friends, except when he was in school or summer camp. As his health deteriorated, the family reluctantly engaged paid caregivers to assist them. There was literally no choice: two working parents and a young man in high school could not sustain the needs of their very ill loved one.

Cheryl and Tzvika had to lock horns with the school board and Ontario Ministry of Education to get Enosh into public school. This was during the 1970s, before integrated schooling became a desired and widespread goal. Enosh graduated from Grade 12. At age twenty-four, he died of natural causes.

DAVE AND LISA

Dave Lewis is a Canadian who lives in Stockholm, Sweden, with his daughters Lisa, age eight, and Linn, age six. He is originally from Hamilton, Ontario, and attended university in Toronto. After working as a social worker in various parts of the world, Dave settled in Stockholm where he now teaches political sociology. His older child, Lisa, lives with severe and multiple disabilities. Dave is Lisa's legal guardian; he and Anita, the girls' mother, separated when the children were quite young.

This portrait differs from all the rest as it reveals a panorama of programs and supports available in Sweden that are very different from what Canadians here have access to. Readers will not only meet Dave and his family but also be introduced to a system that is truly inspiring.

SERVICES AND SUPPORTS

LEARNING THAT ONE'S CHILD HAS special needs can be a frightening experience. For many parents it is like entering unknown woodlands without a map. Unfortunately, there is no map to be had. There are, however, markings you can spot along the way. Knowledgeable physicians and professionals trained in a variety of therapeutic interventions can help you get your bearings. Many parents notice signals that twig them to the fact their child is encountering difficulties — trouble breathing, moving or reading, for example. For some, identifying a disabling condition or conditions that hinders their child can be a great relief. Tackling a known adversary, rather than the one lurking in the shadows, is often possible in measured steps.

This is categorically not to say that a child who lives with a disability is "damaged goods." Absolutely not. But the situation facing this family is and will continue to be different from that of others. These parents usually need to develop — and fairly quickly — entire new skill sets. In addition to the emotional stretch many of us experience, there are very practical issues: uncommon feeding techniques; purposeful methods to stimulate an infant's sensory and cognitive development; techniques and exercises that enhance a child's chances for mobility, to name a few. These are specialized skills.

To better understand what our children need and how to access it, in the pages that follow I explore how social and health services are currently delivered in Canada and what supports, financial and otherwise, families can expect. Disabling conditions are unique for each person. Moreover, the contexts in which families operate differ greatly. Because of this, it is important to recognize that there is no one trail guide. There is an arsenal of tools families may use — as long as they can get precise information to access the support they require. Accessing this information, however, is not always easy; the current system of supports is constructed in piecemeal fashion and delivered unevenly.

Supports aimed at children with disabilities and their families vary from municipality to municipality and between provinces/territories. As delivery of health care and social services is primarily a provincial responsibility in Canada (although the federal government contributes the lion's share of financial resources), the organization of these services varies markedly across the country. Agencies at the municipal or regional level tend to carry responsibility for assessing individual cases and deciding upon the delivery of (limited) assistance. Parents usually need to apply for specific services. Often they are competing for placements or a spot in a given program because demand is greater than the supply.

The information families obtain about available programs ranges widely. The same is true of service quality. Health and social service staff in most jurisdictions carry enormous caseloads, and consequently there are discrepancies in the degree of attention and compassion clients command. Coordination of services is imperfect, at best; provincial governments perennially experiment with service delivery models. In nearly all parts of the country, private for-profit agencies are romping onto the scene as governments put contracts out to tender. Workers' wages and benefits are being ratcheted down, contributing to a significant breach in continuity of care. When one cannot access affordable assistance, the option of paying for private services usually exists; but specialized care doesn't come cheap, and many Canadians find such expenses beyond their reach.

Best-Case Scenario

In a best-case scenario, when a child's disabilities are identified, trained health professionals will rally around the primary caregiver, address the child's particular needs and convey more precise information to parents about the child's challenges. Again, in a positive intervention, the professional also gently instructs the primary caregiver (usually the mother) in techniques she may use to help her child experience the world. While learning some of these new skills can be daunting, it is through feeding and touching the child that we connect with our little person. In short, we need the science and clinical expertise professionals bring, and we need to know that we are engaged in a special kind of parenting.

A competent physiotherapist or speech specialist — especially one whose caseload doesn't have her racing between appointments like a Dash 8 — will demonstrate therapeutic techniques that also help parents to nurture their child. An infant sporting a feeding tube in his tummy, for example, is likely outside the realm of previous experience for even the most seasoned parents. I firmly believe that getting beyond a baby's mega-medical entrance into the world is learned behaviour. Unexpected birthing experiences tend to spawn bucketfuls of uncertainty. When young ones are "different," one needs to know many things early, such as how to hold them or what stroking will be right for them. An infant stimulation worker, physio or occupational therapist can show parents how to use different textures, touch or sound to bring the world to their baby and to soothe her/him. A respiratory therapist can show parents how to perform chest therapy — the gentle tapping over the baby's lungs from front and back — and give ventolin[8] masks to help keep breathing passages clear. Mothers, in particular, must be helped not to lose confidence in their ability to nurture, especially with a first baby. Everything they expected, from breastfeeding to baby carriers, may be out the window. Parents need to know they can rely upon care providers in the various therapeutic disciplines both to impart information about the baby's challenges and to commandeer necessary assistance.

It is useful to remember that just as in any other mother–child relationship, there are two people. Babies have wondrous means of letting us know what makes them feel good. Nonetheless, a young child with special needs might need particular help learning to roll over or sit up. A kind physiotherapist taught me to think about my body as a folding chair with umpteen settings. It meant my little son's head and torso could be supported in a therapeutic fashion and we could still snuggle up, notwithstanding his significant breathing and feeding challenges. I characterize this example as a best-case scenario. When this is the standard of practice we can all expect, better days will certainly lie ahead.

In the Hospital and Beyond

Infants with special needs are born every day. Mine arrived in a Toronto hospital following a glowing pregnancy in 1990. No advance warning. My son's birth sparked a specialized medical team into action. Its role? To breathe life into my struggling newborn. Jake sputtered, gasping for breath in the expert hands of highly trained physicians and nurses. Several long days later he was transferred to a different neonatal intensive care unit in a hospital closer to our home. Some days later, my then-husband and I brought him home.

The human and financial resources a hospital has at its disposal will differ between communities — rural and urban, remote areas or on-reserve. A child living at home may be brought in for a few hours to see specialists in any number of areas: respiratory, feeding or neurology. Hospitals are twenty-four/seven operations; each has its own shift schedules, protocols, staff rotations. An array of people carry out necessary tests and tasks, and the experience can be discomfiting for parents. Capturing an overall picture of a child's challenges takes a concerted effort. However, in the hospital environment whatever needs doing tends to get done — quickly and professionally.

Sadly, once a family walks out the hospital door, practical supports are in short supply. For many children, the full nature and extent of their challenges only become evident over time. A mother notices her baby doesn't react when she claps her hands in play. A newborn loses precious grams, unable to suck strongly enough to obtain sufficient nourishment; dedicated breastfeeding specialists with the finest accoutrements of the art cannot conquer the baby's "lazy" suck. Parents anticipating promised milestones during the first few months of their tiny daughter's life remark that she cannot hold up her head; even propped against pillows, it droops like a wilted lily.

Fuelled by founts of adrenaline, a mother might seek advice from her family doctor. Physicians meet new parents plagued more by worry than the usual bone-tired weariness. It is not unusual for mother and babe to return home with more questions than answers. "We'll test again in two months," says the kindly doctor, holding the baby gently under the arms, bouncing her little sausage feet lightly on the surface of his desk. "We should know better then how your daughter's muscle tone is evolving. Try not to worry. Some babies take longer to develop."

Tests may be ordered, a brain scan or feeding study. These investigations are necessary of course; turning our backs on science would be imprudent. Nonetheless, enduring any battery of tests is troubling. I watched in horror as my five-month-old son was strapped into a gizmo to check his ability to digest foods of varying densities. He nearly choked on the gruel technicians thrust into his mouth. I could barely contain myself. It seemed an eternity that he was tied up, with no one to soothe him as he struggled for breath on the other side of a glass partition. At the time, my gut told me to grab him and escape what seemed a hideous, heartless place.

Other families will recount their own thorny tales. Imagine: A baby's sweet face hurls into contortions. His jaw locks. His tiny torso becomes stiff as a board. Suddenly he resembles a bizarre reflection thrown by a midway mirror. When the family rushes the struggling infant to emergency, the doctor on duty tells his posse of medical students to "treat the seizure, not the parents." An intravenous needle is thrust into a tiny vein; medication shoots in to calm the electric storm in the baby's brain. No question, this is a rough and tumble induction into the ranks of active parenting duty.

I have listened to several mothers and fathers tell their story while still in the throes of anguish as they wait for a diagnosis (and prognosis) to be reached. "Nothing has prepared me for this," parents will say. "I have never felt so helpless." The wait is excruciating. One woman told me that when at four months old her daughter's seizures propelled them to Emergency at the Children's Hospital of Eastern Ontario, she remembers thinking, "What do you mean there are no firm answers? This is Ottawa, not Kabul. Certainly someone must know what's going on."

Interestingly, while it may seem counterintuitive, the number of children who need specialized equipment and intensive medical intervention at birth is on the rise in North America and elsewhere. Indeed the advent of new medical technologies and procedures means that the survival rate for children born with complex health needs is increasing.[9] The stakes are high and not just for health care practitioners. Increasing numbers of parents are compelled by circumstance to offer home, hearth and complex care to their vulnerable offspring.

Once a diagnosis is made, a treatment plan is put in place. Parents may adjust to the fact that the baby they have brought into the world is not the one they expected. Shock; denial; anger ... powerful phases of grief are triggered. Parents cry. Spouses collapse into the comfort of one another's arms. Or don't. In an ideal situation, the bonds of love that carry us humans through so many twists of fate are fostered.

My own sense during those first roller-coaster months of my son's life was that between the exhaustion, disappointment and bewilderment, I would have happily curled into a ball under his big metal hospital bed for weeks at a time, trying to breathe for him. Fortunately I was able to lie next to him and caress his head, his hands and legs — any spot that had no tubes or IV cables protruding. For what felt like an eternity, we seemed to live in a parallel universe; unfamiliar hospital faces and voices inhabited our days and nights. It took a conscious effort not to withdraw into sadness and confusion.

In these circumstances a new era commences for parents. Families are captured in a strange episode that resembles a novel with a poorly constructed plot line — exactly where is the story going? It is not that our babies are any less adored, but they are different than we expected. Unlike other members in one's childbirth class, these initial months tend to be wrought with more angst than awe. And yet most of these new parents share one profound realization: The little package in the crook of one's arm has enormous needs. We are her only chance in the world. When a child has special needs, this realization feels particularly onerous. It is like waking up against the ropes in a boxing ring as some contender suddenly delivers a powerful uppercut to your jaw. You just didn't see it coming.

ACCESSING SERVICES

A baby born here in Canada will most likely fare better than her counterparts in many other parts of the world. Why? In most of the country, with the exception of several First Nations[10] and some rural communities, access to creature comforts is high. With the exception, perhaps, of cases like the Walkerton, Ontario tragedy in 2000,[11] where E. coli was allowed to contaminate the town's drinking water, a parent preparing breakfast can distinguish easily between safe water and raw sewage. Children at play rarely stumble upon land mines or fall asleep to the pounding of bomb blasts. High quality medical services exist, however uneven their distribution.

Family physicians are generally a family's first point of contact for services and the first place they bring the questions. A family physician or paediatrician who is plugged into assistance available in the community may prescribe physiotherapy at three or four months of age, but many are not so connected. It's a crapshoot. Once a needed therapeutic intervention is identified even in large urban areas, the wait list for the publicly funded service is often months, not weeks. "What's next?" the mother might ask herself. "What more should I be doing for my little one?" Everything she reads and hears asserts that early intervention is critical to the child's future. Not only is the baby's developmental path uncertain, information and help are elusive.

Parents morph quickly into information sponges. The Internet provides oceans of material to cull through once there is a name for the infant's challenges. Websites crammed with information and support groups are listed. Parents unfamiliar with Internet research skills are at a definite disadvantage. A new lingo joins the family parlance — that dictionary way back on the top shelf is dusted off and pressed into service. Gradually one gathers the knowledge and confidence to navigate health and social services.

Further along in time, scaling the education system involves a new set of challenges. As parents confront an alphabet soup of programs, they master very practical skills. Learning to fill out government forms effectively becomes a precious, valued vocation. To advocate successfully for one's child means learning to categorize the extent and type of the child's disabilities.

Knowing how to present a child's capacities becomes central to finding and securing appropriate assistance. Scarce resources mean that families compete for placements. Some programs are open only to children with very circumscribed needs. The task becomes to fill in forms that best match one's child to, for example, the therapy or day program needed. It may be necessary to portray the child as highly functional if an ordinary classroom is the objective. If a particular behavioural therapy is needed, a less hopeful portrayal of the child's capacities will be more convincing.

The parents I interviewed told me they learned by trial and error how to express these nuances on paper.

Michael Bach, former Vice-President and Director of Research at The Roeher Institute (a Canadian research and development institute on public policy, disability and human rights) and now Executive Vice-President at the Canadian Association for Community Living, suggests that parents inevitably must learn to dissect eligibility criteria and how experts measure their child's capacities. For education programs, understanding this categorization is paramount. The irony is that promoting success by becoming adept at filling out government documents may lead to having

> ...a child labelled as severely as possible in order to gain access to supports, but then face the prospect that the child may not be placed in a regular classroom because those responsible for gathering knowledge to determine educational placements will likely find the child too severely disabled to benefit from, or to be accommodated into, a regular classroom.[12]

Often school board officials do not consider a family's knowledge of the child central in the process of determining the most appropriate educational path. In the absence of respect for the family and child's own telling of their story, best practices cannot occur. In the same report Bach argues for a shift that would require, as a first principle, that "... personal, narrative knowledge of a child's capacities, hopes, and forms of communication ... be granted priority status in educational placement status for children with disabilities." As we shall see later, Colleen's pitched battle with her provincial government to keep her son's unique educational program afloat speaks volumes to the pitfalls of ignoring parents' experience; it can result in a serious shortfall of good judgement.

How We Got Here

It is disturbing that in a country with Canada's resources the future facing children with disabling conditions, and their families, is far from satisfactory or secure. Several challenges exist. Policies sought and delivered regarding disability issues during the last twenty-five years have tended to focus on adults, with employability questions at the core. Critical programs and services that would assist disabled children and their families are not organized in any comprehensive fashion. Getting needed resources

— professional and financial — is further complicated as there is no single reliable point of access.

Kids in different provinces do not receive the same levels of support. Why? In short, the historical and political context in which federal and provincial governments operate reflects relations characterized by inter-jurisdictional bargaining, buck-passing and suspicion.[13] A long-standing squabble continues as to how much the federal government should pay into social programs generally and what, if any, conditions they should attach. In recent versions of this very Canadian contretemps, most of the heat has centred on health care. Polls indicate medicare is a value Canadians support.[14] In highly publicized federal-provincial talks conducted in October 2004, some progress was made toward parsing out who is responsible for what, but even casual observers will attest to the lacklustre pace of negotiations.

While programs and services aimed at children with disabilities have improved in some measure, the document that set out Canadian federal, provincial and territorial governments' priorities for children in 1999 originally made no reference to children with disabilities.[15] How could this happen? When the federal government launched a significant policy thrust for children's rights in December 1997, neither children with disabilities nor their advocates were at the table. That initiative had occurred in response to years of grassroots organizing and pressure from the child-care community, child poverty advocates, academics and social policy analysts. The purpose was to develop a shared vision, through public debate and research, toward improving the well-being of Canadian children. The document produced, *A National Children's Agenda: Developing a Shared Vision*,[16] made an important step forward by including focused research and consultation with First Nations organizations to ensure that social policy recommendations included an explicitly Aboriginal perspective.[17] The federal government did not, however, embark on a similar mission for children with disabilities.[18] As the Canadian Association of Community Living (CACL) observed, concerns were raised that "... the NCA did not include or reflect the reality of children and youth that have a disability."[19]

By May 1999, provincial and territorial governments set in motion a public dialogue about the earlier report. Disability rights organizations mobilized, calling for the perspective of children with disabilities to be included. The ensuing document, *The Public Report on the National Children's Agenda: Developing a Shared Vision* (2000) stemmed from this consultative process.[20] Despite these efforts, the situation facing families with disabled children remains well below any acceptable line, even that drawn by Canada itself as a signatory to the United Nations Convention on the Rights of the Child.

As of 2001, four provinces (British Columbia, Alberta, Quebec and Saskatchewan) had developed frameworks for social policy that emphasized inclusion and integration of services for these children. By 2001 four other provinces (Manitoba, Ontario, Nova Scotia and Newfoundland) had recognized the need for government ministries to approach and integrate these issues in a cross-ministry fashion.[21]

Interestingly, in Manitoba, Ontario, Nova Scotia and Newfoundland, where the need for improvement was recognized, considerable barriers remain. While some of these provinces have developed mechanisms to aid in coordinating service delivery, very little substantive action has occurred to develop genuinely inclusive policy frameworks. In spite of all the fine words and documents, children and their families continue to encounter alarming fault lines between their needs and the tangible delivery of services.

How Existing Services are Structured

What does exist? According to policy analysts (and some of the families featured in the second part of this book) discrepancies in service between jurisdictions are common, even within the same province. As health care is restructured, renewed and recast in tune with governments' platforms, these children and their families now face additional barriers. New layers of administration created at regional levels mean parents trying to secure programs must deal with ministry staff at the central and regional levels plus staff of the regional authorities.[22] Legislative frameworks allow each of the regional authorities to determine which services and to what levels a child with special needs and her family may be eligible.[23]

Not only is there a substantial variation between jurisdictions, the absence of adequate supports has a disproportionate effect upon certain populations. First Nation peoples both on and off reserve and low income families of all backgrounds are especially hard hit. Poor children, particularly those whose families rely on social assistance, as well as members of racialized communities, also encounter more obstacles in trying to obtain services. Children with multiple disabilities and those who require ongoing complex care encounter significant bureaucratic hurdles. As many experts attest, a patchwork of programs and band-aid solutions characterize the Canadian approach to caring for special needs children and their families.

This lack of organization and coordination contravenes every conceivable best practice model. It is neither cost-effective nor humane. As policy analyst Fraser Valentine points out:

> The policy sphere is complex, fragmented, uncoordinated and often underfunded. For parents caring for a child with disabilities, the situation is often one of frustration, disillusionment, and disappointment. The lack of concrete policy attention — and the action to achieve it — means that these children may fall through the cracks.[24]

In 2005, there is no national program to supply adequate home care services to seniors or persons with special needs. Each province writes its own rule book. Means tests tend to award services only to the disabled child or family considered deserving, a notion that contradicts the principles of universality enshrined in the Canada Health Act. Accessible supports wither against the pressures of fiscal restraint and program restructuring. Many Canadian provinces and municipalities are only just beginning to recognize the proportion of the crisis. Cities, in particular, are increasingly expected to implement programs downloaded to them with inadequate resources or accountability mechanisms.[25]

Even so, some specific measures of practical value to parents raising children with disabilities arose out of the continuing dynamic between federal and provincial/territorial governments. *Compassion care* is one such example. The federal government announced in its 2003 budget new rules that allow working people to use special employment insurance benefits to take care of gravely ill family members. Workers eligible for Employment Insurance are now entitled to up to six weeks of "Compassionate Care Benefits"[26] to look after children, parents, spouses or common-law partners or children of spouses or common-law partners. The program is far from perfect, but it reflects a measure of appreciation that many families are wedged between the competing demands of work and family.

THE FUNDING OF SERVICES

Until 2004, the federal government transferred a certain amount of money to each province annually in support of health care, post-secondary education, social assistance and social services. The Canadian Health and Social Transfer (CHST) which governs this spending came into effect April 1, 1996.[27] It was a single block fund, consisting of both cash and tax transfers to the provincial and territorial governments. These federal transfers were not tied to spending on the health and social programs mentioned above, although the provinces were obliged to abide by the Canada Health Act in order to receive medicare funding.

Political debates between provinces and federal governments have borne little assurance that equivalent standards of health care, regardless of geographic location, are on the horizon. Families raising children with disabilities are certainly in no better position. The highly touted health care deal struck by Canada's first ministers in October 2004 recognized explicitly the principle of asymmetrical federalism; that is, every province has the right to design its own approach to achieving good health care.

Accepting each province's right to do as it sees fit follows on the heels of the Canada Health Transfer (CHT), and its regulations were created by the federal government and came into force March 30, 2004. The CHT is a financial amount supposedly dedicated to provincial spending on health care and is separate from other fiscal transfers the provinces receive.[28] But the provinces still don't have to spend the majority of the money on health, and while there are some conditions attached to these dollars, they are very weak. Former prime minister Jean Chrétien's administration and current Prime Minister Paul Martin's administration also weakened the federal government's ability to enforce the conditions.[29]

In effect, the deal leaves the door wide open to private, for-profit care. The threat of privatization was never publicly addressed. While the agreement provides stable, long-term funding for health care, provinces like Alberta, British Columbia and Ontario have been given the green light to continue to privatize health services.[30]

Where does this leave special needs kids and their families? To have each province draft its own playbook means geography directly affects what assistance individual families can hope to access for their medically vulnerable children. Many hoped that the Romanow Report[31] released in November 2002 might lead to improvements for this population and all Canadians. It recommended a program to cover home care services under the auspices of the Canada Health Act. But no comprehensive, national home care program standard has been achieved. Instead, starting in 2006 governments will pay for limited home care services for acute care following hospital discharge including case management, acute mental health care in the community and end of life care. Sadly, it seems that for all the negotiations and new lingo crafted, neither the federal nor provincial/ territorial governments have come to grips with the harsh circumstances medically vulnerable children, the elderly and their families confront every day.

RACE, CLASS AND POVERTY

Achieving best practices for special needs children means acknowledging that class, race and disability intersect and come into play and can act as further barriers to accessing adequate support and care. These factors affect the bedrock of a child's life. Poverty can significantly reduce a child's chances to be included fully in society. Kids who have less than sufficient nutrition, shelter and clothing may well be at risk. Among children with disabilities, those from poor families are among the most vulnerable. The Canadian Council of Social Development reports that poor children are 2.5 times more likely to have hearing, speech, vision or mobility impairments.[32]

Canadians' definition and understanding of their rights are also far from homogeneous. Indeed for families with a moderate amount of education and the ease that class privilege entails, demanding assistance comes more easily. They may view help as a right, not a privilege. A Roeher Institute study cites research showing that poor families and families of colour have less access to caregiver relief,[33] a service from which most families would derive benefit. Similarly, recent immigrants who encounter language barriers or inaccurate assumptions about their cultural practices find it more complicated to access assistance. Not all agencies provide lists of interpreters who will accompany parents to hospitals and clinics. Members of immigrant and refugee communities are less likely to clamour for aid. Many individuals have already experienced dangerous, dehumanizing acts in the countries from which they fled. Uncertainty about their status in Canada may well stand in the way of seeking help to sustain their families.[34]

The lack of coordination between programs also increases the stumbling blocks parents experience. Finding out what social and health services are available entails a significant amount of research. It can easily turn into a hit-and-miss mega-project like drilling for oil off the Newfoundland Coast. Dozens of phone calls and dogged, just plain stubbornness are needed. There is no *Yellow Pages* on hand, and word of mouth becomes a treasured tool. This is genuine work, though unpaid and highly stressful. Studies document that this group of Canadian mothers devote approximately thirty hours per week to the advocacy, coordination of care and transportation for a child with a disability, in addition to the twenty to thirty hours of personal care provided in the home.[35] It is noteworthy, given the extraordinary demands made upon these parents, that the divorce rate among them is as much as 50 percent higher than in families with non-disabled children.[36] There is no doubt that the additional financial strain resulting from divorce is difficult for poor families to bear.

Parents' reluctance to ask for help is further reinforced by the extent to which Canadians consider internal family matters private domain. Most family groupings operate as relatively isolated units. The closest relatives may be hundreds of miles away. Some mothers fear they will be considered less than fit if they request assistance from public agencies. It is hardly surprising that this perspective shapes how families frame their needs. Of course the assistance parents think they should have — what they believe they are entitled to — is influenced by the broader socio-political and economic context.

TOWARD GETTING WHAT WE NEED

None of the health or social policy initiatives discussed above provide adequately for the long-term care needs of seniors, adults or children with disabilities — either at home, in facilities or in the community. A significant government commitment to spend on home care would create an enormous sea change and constitute a public acknowledgment that high quality, reliable and affordable home care is critical. At present, given the growing demand among seniors, adults and young children with disabilities, the Canadian home care landscape seems rather stark.

The situation need not be so dire. As will become evident in the second half of this book where we meet a Canadian family living in Sweden, the concept that disabled children and their families may enjoy a reasonable quality of life is entirely viable. It is a matter of political will. In the remainder of this book, I explore issues of concern to families with disabled children with the express purpose of contributing to the building of this political will through the application of political pressure. I believe these families can advance their children's safety, security and quality of life. It will require focus, leadership and partnerships between families and those who work to support them.

The portraits presented in section two illustrate, among other points, that there are many pressing needs. Successive governments insist that care in the community — rather than in large facilities — constitutes best practice. Families are called upon increasingly to meet their children's complex care needs at home, with shrinking reinforcements from public agencies. In October 2004, enormous funding cuts hit two major providers of health services to children in the Greater Toronto Area. Respite care was explicitly on the chopping block.[37] Compared to performing emergency heart surgery, caregiver relief might seem a frill. Not to these parents.

Spending a night awake to soothe a child whose tonsils are sore is never easy. The children and families we will meet are scaling qualitatively different terrain. When every night involves rocking a child afflicted with unrelenting seizures or holding a youngster sobbing in pain because a hip is turned akimbo, it is too much. Changing a blocked feeding tube or trying to catch forty winks while on call to suction a child who may suddenly gasp for breath is wearing over time. When the situation calls for giving medications and chest therapy at all hours, parents' energy tends to wane. A good coach knows when it's time to rotate the players. Society needs to provide other skilled individuals to step up and help meet the breadth of our children's needs.

Instead society relies upon the love, goodwill and sheer endurance of these families. A more logical approach would be to recognize that parents in such circumstances need scheduled relief to sustain the pace and intensity of furnishing care over the long term. Although much has been written about these issues, there is little evidence to demonstrate that the agenda for kids with special needs is moving ahead at more than a snail's pace.

A conscious and organized campaign is required to bring greater balance — and justice — to the lives of these children and their families. When people identify their own needs and calculate a net gain from taking action, it becomes possible to engage with them in powerful, creative community organizing. In short, the strategic challenge is to define the political space in which the struggle for improvements can be duked out. History teaches that when people can envisage a better way, they are more likely to hope and believe that change is possible. If they can pursue tangible goals, they are more likely to be spurred into motion.

Many of the families in question live on permanent overdrive. I will argue that a necessary precondition for this population to organize is that workers in the system also resolve to seek substantial changes in how their business is conducted. Leadership and focus are sorely needed. Social workers, psychologists, audiologists, physiotherapists, nurses and speech-language pathologists, for example, need their unions to put standards of care on the negotiating table. Instead of dampening families' expectations by administering program cuts made by people who are out of touch with front-line care, we need to create partnerships between committed health professionals and families that highlight winnable objectives.

During one very successful community organizing effort in which I was involved, paid staff at a facility slated for closure cared for the children free of charge one evening. It gave parents an opportunity to meet and discuss their options. A parents' advocacy group eventually emerged. With the support of these same paid caregivers and their union, families began to exercise their political power as a constituency. Over time, the partnership between staff and clients developed a powerful head of steam and the government was compelled to overturn its earlier decision to close the facility.

Under our current system, far too many families are in perpetual crisis. Their voices are rarely heard and their circumstances and struggles are largely invisible. My point is strategic. The ideal model, with all the supports our kids need, is not going to fall from the sky. But when families and staff that support them join together in pursuit of an achievable goal, hope can prevail over hardship. Personal health supports are a right for everyone in need, not simply a discretionary benefit. The potential exists to involve people who normally only connect to politics in a tangential way. Bringing them into the fray, sounding the battle cry, would represent a formidable step toward winning justice for our special needs kids.

CHAPTER THREE

MARGINS AND RESISTANCE

IT IS INCREDIBLY EASY FOR EVEN the most caring of us to be disrespectful toward someone with a disability. Perhaps it occurs when you are at a subway station during the frantic morning rush. Some slow fellow in front of you is very carefully depositing a token into the slot box to the right of the turnstile. It seems such a simple task; a child could do it! And yet, for someone who must concentrate deliberately to master fine motor movements, there is nothing easy about it. Similarly, if the side-effect profile of the powerful medication a person requires for a chronic condition includes tremors and/or blurry vision, getting through the turnstile may take a little longer. The hard press of commuter foot traffic, frenetic at the best of times, is annoying. And here's some bleeping slowpoke causing you to miss your train!

In this chapter, I explore the need for a critical understanding of how society thinks about disability. Discrimination is not simply bad manners demonstrated by impatient people. Discrimination toward people with disabilities (and all disadvantaged groups) is both overt and covert, the latter embedded in societal structures and institutional practices found, for example, in the delivery of health and education services. In the pages that follow, I will also argue that viewing disability as a negative is to fundamentally misconstrue the potential of diversity and difference and that the fear of difference has a profound impact on the families in question and, in particular, on mothers. Unless we find a way to lift the pernicious veil of prejudice, there is little hope we can fashion the array of humane services so vital to these children and their families.

Persons with disabilities, including children, are often perceived to be inferior[38] and certainly as differing from the norm. They are frequently excluded from mainstream activities such as the paid labour force, educational opportunities and housing. Individuals and society tend to fear someone they find different, deformed, dumb or disgusting, and this contributes to how persons with disabilities are marginalized.

At the core of this marginalization is our society's fundamental fear of "difference." Many people react with feelings of discomfort to seeing anyone who happens to look or sound different. For the child with a disability, his or her personhood is often invisible; the human being takes a back seat to perception of her physical or intellectual traits. These children remain socially invisible except when they come out of the shadows and into the community in search of education or housing opportunities. Or when we learn to bring the world to them, if their place of residence is a specialized setting geared to their particular needs.

Marginalization

Sadly, non-disabled persons frequently embrace attitudes that belie their fear of anything different or unexpected. It is that reaction, the labelling of another as "different," which is at its core disabling to the recipient of the label. Dealing with one's challenges may be a picnic compared to the negative or patronizing attitudes one frequently encounters. Unfortunately, but not surprisingly, discrimination occurs not only at an individual level, but underpins systemically many of the programs and services people with disabilities rely upon.

Mothers with disabled children tend to be marginalized by extension of this fear of difference. As their children are relegated to the sidelines, mothers also go along for the ride. They are expected to perform miracles with their children; to epitomize the "good mother," a paragon of virtue in a role characterized by self-sacrifice. What does mothering from this margin look like? It may be characterized by our absence from the habitual mid-morning coffee klatch with other mothers; the extra and complicated load of coordinating extensive appointments with doctors and specialists; feeling excluded from new moms' freewheeling conversations about the virtues of homemade baby food over Gerber's — because your baby receives sustenance through a G-tube inserted surgically in his stomach.

Parents raising disabled children often encounter troubling attitudes among their entourage, families and friends. More than most so-called self-sufficient family units, those with disabled children tend to experience even greater isolation from their communities. Combine the sheer exhaustion from the caregiving work involved with the fact that most families have limited resources at their disposal and is it any wonder many mothers experience acute isolation caring for their children at home? Taking a child for a walk in the mall with a suction machine fastened to the bottom portion of her stroller is a tad more complicated than bundling up baby into the car seat for outings. It's not a competition to ascertain which is harder, but acknowledging complexity is integral to understanding inclusion. The notion of the margin reflects that there is a centre at which a core of dominant societal values and economic power exist; a centre from which some are excluded.

INVISIBLE MOTHERING WORK

Exclusion can take many forms. It may result from the time devoted to making and keeping appointments with the medical specialists a child relies upon instead of more ordinary activities like taking her to "Lullabies and Lap Rhymes" at the local community centre. As previously noted, mothers of children with disabilities spend up to thirty hours per week coordinating services, medical and therapeutic supports and transportation. Carrying out these necessary tasks goes along with women's typical function as the "Executive" who manages the household. It is not unusual for this mother/case-manager job to become all-consuming. Who else is going to stand up for her child?

Nor does completing these necessary coordination and advocacy tasks bring any more status or economic return than the actual caregiving work. Mostly, this group of parents — predominantly women — provides free labour to keep their families (and our economy!) afloat. Their location on the fringe of society is reinforced by the fact that social and health policy in Canada — the practical supports needed — are inadequate to meet either the child's or the family's needs. The unavailability of childcare limits opportunities for mothers with disabled children to work outside the home. While this is also true of the general population, the situation is augmented for disabled children because they are not always welcomed in already scarce affordable care situations.

In 1991 (the most recent statistics available to the study quoted below, published in 1999),

> … Twelve percent of children with disabilities aged 0–4 needing childcare were refused the service: thirty-five percent by licensed facilities, thirty-eight percent by a caregiver in the child's home and twenty-seven percent by a caregiver in the caregiver's home. In addition, as of 1994, 9,550 children with disabilities aged 5–14 were neither in school nor were being tutored.[39]

Obviously, many such families must care for their children day and night. In the absence of a comprehensive policy framework for employment, family support and childcare, parents of children with disabilities are unlikely to be able to perform the added work necessary to support a secure foundation for their family's well-being.[40] What is the nature of that extra work? Several studies refer to caregiving tasks as demanding work that requires the combined professional skills of nurses, therapists, teachers and administrators. Mothers often have no choice but "to make a career out of caregiving."[41]

> In fact, they perform many skills that were formerly in the realm of paid professionals. Mothers manage complex intra- and extra-family relationships, monitor children's conditions, perform custodial, therapeutic and medial tasks; schedule appointments, act as advocates, and more.[42]

In short, it is the texture and breadth of responsibilities that seems to most distinguish these families.

In an insightful article, psychotherapist Miriam Greenspan suggests that these parents didn't sign up for an entire set of tasks they now perform that were not included in the job description they imagined when deciding to have a child.[43] As we will see in some of the narratives, these tasks can include anything from toileting a sixteen-year-old to sleeping with "one eye open" during the night to planning for a child's complex nursing care needs should she happen to outlive you.

Sharon Daniels, for example, who lives in Winnipeg, went through her pregnancy as a young woman, elated at the prospect of caring for her baby. The infant she gave birth to, however, was very different from all expectations. Could Sharon ever have envisaged that she would spend a significant part of the next thirty years interfacing with physiotherapists and physicians about her daughter's health? Understanding and naming this extra dimension is important, because it is at the root of why parents of these children are themselves invisible from the mainstream.

MOTHERS' UNPAID WORK AS CARERS

During much of the twentieth century and to the present, Canadian social policy has defined family in the most narrow sense, assuming that children are primarily the responsibility of their parents. Typically, it was expected that mothers care for their children (and elderly or otherwise vulnerable family members) while a male breadwinner worked outside the home. Feminist political economists and philosophers have critiqued these assumptions and examined classical liberal theory to ascertain more exactly women's role in society.

Women's work is largely ignored. Care of children and vulnerable family members is undervalued in economic and social terms. This point is well illustrated in certain interviews in this book. Sharon Daniels in Winnipeg and Colleen Fitzpatrick in St. John's, Newfoundland, both experienced first-hand how their intensive caregiving work is taken for granted by governments and agencies in the paid economy. How does this happen at a broader societal level?

In present-day Canadian society someone must bear prime responsibility to care for the disabled and elderly. This need is not just an objective reality; a powerful moral imperative is attached. Meanwhile their work is not compensated through payment, nor does it bring recognition as professional status. Women in this position are part of the invisible workforce. They are unpaid, considered unskilled, have no sick leave or health insurance benefits and are not covered by government-regulated safety standards or workers' compensation.[44]

The unpaid labour of women in the home is not considered a contribution to the economy, and although there is much lip service to family values and the role of motherhood in maintaining the fabric of the society, the work is not considered socially necessary.[45] Further, the work done outside the home by women in the paid economy caring for children, hospital patients and the elderly is low status, undervalued and low-paid. That work is viewed as an extension of work performed mainly by women in the home, an attitude which ensures a pool of cheap labour. It is cheap or unpaid labour which is required to prop up the rest of the paid economy.

Women's domestic labour and consumption of goods and services to support families is, in essence, part of the sub-structure that supports the operation of the paid economy. Women's work in the home caring for family contributes to the reproduction of labour power, as do education and the health care system, by ensuring that waged and salaried workers are sustained day to day. That caring work enables members of the paid workforce to earn wages outside the home to support their children, the next generation of workers. Mothers of children with severe disabilities probably suffer a longer period of marginalization than others, as their children are unlikely to be employed in the future.

This situation also "… tends to produce a policy framework that takes for granted the existence and privileges of heterosexual nuclear families where women are primarily responsible for caring for children."[46] Other family models are considered suspect, if not deviant. In this construction typical nuclear families are meant to function privately, largely in isolation from one another. Children are the responsibility of their parents, and intervention in the family is only permitted if children are thought to be at risk.

In Canada and elsewhere, policy initiatives based on these assumptions reveal fundamental flaws when looked at closely. The actual circumstances in which children and families live are often quite different from what is thought to be the norm. As early as the mid-1970s, some feminists argued that the largely invisible role women play in the paid economy had to be counted — not just acknowledged, but included in the statistics gathered by government bodies about the country's economic position. From this perspective, the raising of children and related tasks pulse at the heart of the economy; the social relations of reproducing labour power, of bringing up the next generation, are integral to both the economy and social fabric. And yet it remains unpaid and unseen.

THE GOOD MOTHER

The pressure many women feel to meet the impossible ideal of the good mother is heightened among those whose children are disabled. It is useful to deconstruct this notion of "goodness" as it may shed light upon the experience mothers (and some fathers) have. This value-laden goodness reinforces the sense of otherness experienced by parents of children with disabilities. Not only does society's perception and marginalization of people with disabilities affect this sense of otherness, it is intimately tied to society's treatment of women — in the family, in the workforce and as mothers and primary caregivers.

All mothers are subject to a certain amount of scrutiny in the community and this has some positive aspects. It can be safer for children if neighbours keep a watchful, caring eye out for one another's children. As Miriam Greenspan writes,

> If as the saying goes, it takes a village to raise a child, then special-needs children need that village even more than others do. The absence of that village — of community supports and of an honest, balanced, informed, communal understanding of the joys, challenges, and difficulties of raising a child with disabilities — not only contributes to what's disabling about disability, but is at the core of what perpetuates a sense of mothering at the margins.[47]

Clearly, the point is that few can manage all of the tasks involved without concrete, practical supports. Unless you have a nanny or can afford to buy required services on the private market, options are limited. The dilemma remains so long as family households are private, atomized entities and children are not embedded in networks that provide broader sustenance. Atomization refers to the separateness and isolation inherent in domestic labour carried out in private homes; the very character of this work today is that it is largely solitary. For those carrying out a range of daily domestic tasks inside the home, including furnishing personal care, contact with others is minimized.

What are the qualities the "good" mother of a disabled child should display? One is meant to be silent and indeed, stoic about the more demanding (or objectionable) parts of caregiving. Anything less could be considered complaining, a major no-no because it calls into question whether or not you truly love your child. In this mindset there is nothing, no amount of self-sacrifice — up to and including one's own health — that will suffice if we are genuinely filled with love for our children.

Due to the amplified contact one has with child development professionals and medical specialists, there is a tendency to feel under scrutiny a lot of the time —— because you are! As we will see in section two, when Suzanne, Aude Catherine and Vincent's mother, took her profoundly deaf children to the hospital frequently to have their learning progress assessed, such scrutiny was *de rigueur*. Spending five years at home to teach these two extremely sweet, lovable children was not an easy row to hoe. No doubt the rewards are rich, but I suspect it might also be tough to separate one's adult sense of self from the progress one's children are making in a very challenging program.

For any mother, but especially where parenting presents unusual circumstances, it can be difficult to find a safe place (outside the privacy of a therapist's office) to let off steam. Some mothers may do so together over a cup of coffee or on the park bench, chatting about their weekends while supervising their children at play on the swings. When one's child moves in and out of health crises frequently, the challenge is qualitatively different. You can be reasonably certain that the informal, light-hearted coffee group that gathers Monday mornings to debrief from the weekend and to share concerns about bedtimes, homework, teachers and nitrates in luncheon meat is not going to "get it" when you blurt out the worry you felt during your child's weekend at home.

"Well ... our son's G-tube slipped out late last night while I was diapering him, but we didn't want to take him to Emergency because they always find him such an interesting specimen and put him through a battery of invasive tests. So we were brave and managed to thread the tube back into his tummy while the nurse at his group home gave us directions over the telephone." While some members of the group's mouths drop so wide open flies are tempted to take up permanent residence, at least one sensitive soul will say quite sincerely (and this is the best you can expect): "Wow. I don't know how you do it." At worst, they move away from you on the bench and you don't dare to bring up such gory clinical details to the gathering again — if indeed you ever have the guts to go back!

Not everyone understands the rather unusual circumstances our families confront every day. Interestingly, in every interview for this project the mothers and fathers I met uttered a similar heartfelt phrase: "Shannon (or Johnny or Ollie) is a rare and precious gift to our family. We are all so much richer for having her in our lives." I have said these exact words myself about my own son, feeling a deep appreciation for the truth in the statement.

The fact that these parents make such earnest statements — almost uniformly and without prodding — suggests there is more than meets the eye to the intense caregiving relationship they share with their children. From several points across the country and from people of many different backgrounds, a chorus of voices hits the same note: Despite the extraordinary parenting responsibilities they carry, parents of disabled children also reap a great deal from the relationships with their beautiful, high-maintenance children.

I have wondered what lurks behind these pronouncements of enormous love. For adults who find themselves parent to a particularly vulnerable infant, there may be an instinctive response to protect one's flesh and blood. Could they continue such a relentless care schedule without that impetus? No doubt these feelings are conditioned by one's age, ethno-cultural background and other factors. It is likely that a part of this instinct is also spurred by guilt, a useful adaptive mechanism (in some situations) that ensures a mother's sense of obligation.[48]

There are times, of course, when the mother cannot or will not nurture a child. In many circumstances, such an act is considered morally reprehensible. Unfavourable views toward women who do not want children are commonplace. Unlike prevailing wisdom in earlier decades that encouraged families to institutionalize their children with disabilities, when a child has a disability today what are we to think of the mother who decides she cannot handle it? And yet, few fathers who skip the scene (and there is ample empirical and anecdotal proof that there are more than a few) are held to the same standard.

In civil society, it is generally accepted that there is a practical and moral responsibility to afford protection to the disabled and elderly. There is also a popular notion that this kind of work — caring for the infirm, the disabled and the needy — confers a certain goodness upon the carer who is usually, but not always, the mother. It seems that in best-case scenarios, it can bring out the best in us as human beings.

Why? Relations with our vulnerable children are not market driven, but based on ethics quite alien to such exchange values.[49] The parenting work described here is not *better;* it is qualitatively *different* in intensity, and it tends to endure over a much longer term (i.e. diapering a thirty-year-old or bathing an obstreperous, strong teenager).

At the same time, social norms and expectations shape the values mothers express about what they should be doing with and for their disabled child. The usual prescription rarely includes speaking out; naming frankly the truth of each day in all its joys and frustrations. Sharing experiences honestly with others in similar straits is a huge bulwark against isolation.

Without truth-telling, it is impossible to break through the mythology of the good mother and appreciate the unique and complex qualities that define our experience of motherhood. This sharing is a wellspring from which hope may emerge. As in other socio-political situations, it is collective experience (rather than isolation) that creates the political space for making change, to resist the apparent inevitability of living on the margins of society.

FAMILIES IN SOCIETY

While all households tend to be atomized by the structure of North American society, families with disabled children are hard pressed to escape the periphery. For those caring full-time for children with disabilities the isolation is heightened. These particular women find themselves on the edge of ordinary mothering because they experience a disconnect from society, one more heightened than that experienced in the early months by mainstream mothers.

In addition, families raising a child with a disability live with constant uncertainty that the assistance they have secured from governments and agencies will disappear at the dash of a pen. Instead of capturing the opportunity that disability challenges may offer, the situation is posed as a problem that needs to be solved.

Canadian society is not organized at present to assemble the bevy of support services our children need. What we need is social and health care programs that provide a spectrum of supports. Families' ability to make informed choices between adequately resourced, wide-ranging programs ought to be maximized.

Meg Luxton and Heather Jon Maroney, on the politics of parenting, write: "A social reproduction perspective understands children as 'individuals' who have rights to make citizenship claims on the world community and on the particular states, local communities and families in which they live."[50] Seen from this angle, children are both dependents and members of their society. Thinking in these terms would shift our view of society's responsibility toward children and families. Women who raise the children and feed the primary wage earner, do laundry and go to PTA meetings are simultaneously caring for the people they love and reproducing labour power. In addition, women's unpaid work enables the primary wage earner to sell his labour in the market. In this formulation, the woman is meant to hold down the domestic fort while also assisting family members who are particularly vulnerable or infirm. Smack dab in the middle of women's prescribed tasks is meeting their disabled kids' considerable needs. It's the ticket to achieving a spot on the "good mother" merry-go-round.

Neo-liberal ideology and government policy forces each family to be treated as a separate, private entity — like so many ice cubes huddled in a tray. So long as this is the case, inadequate supports to these families will continue. It is when children — and this includes children with disabilities — are embedded in networks of family, community and other social ties and institutions that they will be fully included in our society and benefit from the social and economic goods it offers.

In this book, I have applied this analytical lens in exploring how families with disabled children construct their reality. Families alone should not carry exclusive responsibility for their children. "The more that care of our children is understood to be a social, collective responsibility, the greater are their chances of avoiding poverty and experiencing the benefits of social inclusion."[51] While all youngsters would benefit from a "village" to raise them, the families of children with disabilities have an even greater need for a nurturing network of support.

Vast societal barriers in childcare, in schools, in governmental and agency programs, and in the lack of adequate resources to support our children and families, all currently contribute to bolting these families at the periphery of society. When families attempt to access services for their children, relations of power underlie every contact made with agencies or school boards. As discussed previously, the programs to support families with disabled children in this country are woefully inadequate.[52]

Not surprisingly, in social and political terms these families are well placed to become engaged in their communities, to organize toward improving their children's lives. It is in this sense that the margins of society may become a volatile place; they have the potential to constitute an exciting locus for resistance to injustice.[53] When the breaking point is reached, a flurry of activity may be unleashed to combat unjust conditions. Some of the interviews described in section two bear this out.

As I interviewed the parents in this project and, later, delved into their stories more deeply, I did not hear complaints. Even the difficult moments were galaxies away from "Oh, woe is me." Rather, the message I received was crystal clear: going it alone is simply not a reasonable alternative. Where community exists, however defined, there is a better chance that these young people and their families will flourish. Like most of society, when we belong to a network of friends or family, a school or faith community; when we have somewhere to go during the day and people know us; when our health and shelter needs are met and we have love in our life, we fare better. A sense of belonging is paramount.

Unfortunately, at present, the landscape for vulnerable families today radiates rebuff and rejection; if children with disabilities are shunted to the sidelines with their mothers also relegated to the circle's edge, is it any wonder that winds of despair waft through their lives?

CHAPTER FOUR

Embracing the Social Model of Disability

I MET A MOTHER not long ago who told me a rather disturbing story. After waiting weeks for test results during her infant's second hospitalization in Toronto, a doctor on duty approached her and said, "Your baby suffers from a rare neurological disorder and while it may not be related you should know that his testicles are abnormal." She was shocked. "What was I supposed to do with that information?" she asked me. She told me how numb she felt at that point, still just trying to give her baby sustenance. She and her husband were living day to day she said, even hour to hour in the intensity of neonatal hospital ward life. What concern could anyone possibly have about his genitals? I shook my head in disbelief.

In the course of my research and advocacy work I've heard more than a few such instances of out-of-touch doctors acting more like robots than human beings. It seems many families have an outrageous story or two to tell about their experience with medical professionals. It's these stories that help motivate those of us in the disability movement to fight for treatment that is consistently humane, inclusive, compassionate and supportive. It is difference defined as a medical pathology that underlies much of the discriminatory practice.

Tenets of the Disability Movement

The disability movement emerged in Great Britain, the United States and Canada during the 1970s to voice opposition to discriminatory treatment of disabled persons by medical personnel and the rest of society. Persons with disabilities were viewed as less than fully human, defective and a drain on society. Such attitudes demonstrate a craven disregard for fundamental values of courtesy and respect between human beings. Those with a variety of health and intellectual challenges found their personhood ignored. Frequently people with disabilities were considered less than whole and reduced to their health conditions. Disability was considered a personal tragedy, the disabled referred to by such phrases as "the poor cripple" or "stupid retard." Assistance offered to disabled people was imbued with notions of charity — it was considered a good work rather than a right to which all are entitled. Medical and psychological interventions tended to reinforce the ideology that positioned the person with a disability as "sick." In effect, charitable, health and educational organizations and institutions exerted (and continue to exert) power as a means of social control.[54]

In the more recent past, views that reflect subtle (and sometimes flagrant) patronizing attitudes are coming under attack. The disability rights movement differentiates between an individual's supposed shortcomings and the surrounding society that both misconstrues and detracts from the person's abilities. It is society's attitudes and structures that are disabling. Charity is unacceptable. Respect and dignity for those with disabilities must be pursued vigorously.

PEOPLE FIRST

In my conversations with families that appear in this book, several noted that their child was invisible as a person to many of the medical practitioners with whom they came into contact. I was told that, at least initially, many doctors saw syndromes and deficits rather than a human being. Medical practitioners who note syndromes and deficits first and the child second are numerous. While some physicians are familiar with disability issues beyond simply diagnosing a child's condition, the majority lack in-depth knowledge about disability in society. And medical training rarely imparts humility, a necessary precondition to elevating a patient's humanity above diagnostic hubris.

By missing our children's personhood, the physician (with or without derision, pomposity or malice) contributes to the alienation that a new parent may feel from his or her baby. Watching the tiny little fellow tucked into an incubator with an IV line tacked onto his head is probably not how most new parents imagined the first months of their life with baby. Similarly, every time the staff neurologist refers to a little girl as an "interesting case of x syndrome with multiple deficits" (especially when there are young medical students hanging on to every word) rather than a pretty blonde-haired child who so resembles her dad, the specialist is missing the child's humanity. In the portraits found in the second section of this book, examples of this kind of behaviour are recounted with both sadness and anger. At minimum, a derisive attitude from medical personnel certainly poses another challenge to adults who, in the early days of diagnosis, are trying to make sense of their unusual parenting experience. Such insensitivity — no matter how benign the doctor considers his or her remark — is yet another barrier to the delivery of humane health care.

THE PHYSICIAN/PARENT RELATIONSHIP

In several of the narratives in this book, when parents advised their medical practitioner(s) of concern about their newborns, they were urged not to worry. When Aude Catherine's mother asserted for the second time her disquiet at her infant daughter's lack of startle response, she was told that being a first-time mother likely accounted for her concern.[55] Discounting a mother's opinion is far too common. Parents taking care of their child need a seat at the table; their insights are valuable and need to be heard as part of clinical planning. A best-practices approach would be for medical personnel to respect parents as full members of the team charged with offering competent care.

Breaking down the structural relation of power between physician and family is crucial, but certainly not easy. Doctors determine the treatment of choice and recommend surgical interventions. It is through building a relationship of trust with parents and truly listening to their concerns and knowledge that the child's best interests can be met. A few positive examples are also recounted in the narratives below. The physician who delivered Jeremy, for example, showed a keen understanding when he explained to Mary Ellen gently that her newborn son was "still a full person" in his disability. Similarly, in a conversation last year about the risks presented by scheduled immunization injections, my son's paediatrician used a lovely turn of phrase when he referred to Jake as "a finely balanced fellow." Sadly, such a compassionate demeanour tends to be the exception to the rule.

Parents who accompany their infant or child to the hospital for appointments at specialized clinics or for surgical procedures often have many questions. Some demand information. The gargantuan scope of unpaid caregiving hours parents (usually mothers) deliver ought to confer upon them the right to know, the right to be treated with respect by professionals. In the interviews that follow, only Simon's mother Julien, a nurse, could attest to such treatment. Instead, as one's child grows older and a mother learns more about the baby's health and individual challenges, she may be viewed as hysterical when she insists that her views be considered by the treating medical team.[56] In reality, however, most mothers (and some fathers) are best acquainted with their children's symptoms. Decisions about a child's care must be made in partnership. A child is not a widget in a system; a child has rights. The child and family deserve to be included and treated with consideration and respect.

When a person is expected to be a passive recipient of assistance, the individual becomes disempowered.[57] Acting upon one's freedom to participate fully in society determines the relationship between all people, including those with disabilities. The social model of disability that I propose is intended to meet the standards children with disabilities deserve. This model recognizes that disability is not simply the result of an individual impairment but rather results from interaction between individuals and an environment that is not meant or designed to enable participation. Moreover, it recognizes that social causes, economic, political and social structures contribute to disablement. I apply this model in section two, "Portraits." These families insist that their children be seen first and foremost as human beings, not as some rare syndrome.

The Social Model of Disability and Inclusion

This model underscores the point that it is the attitudes and physical space that surround a child with special needs that is disabling. If the individual differences of all persons in a society are valued and accommodated, then pernicious attitudes regarding disability need not dominate lives and identities. If respect is found for difference, then prejudice might lose its throat-hold on the lives of these children.

Advancing the social model of disability also resonates in terms of pursuing inclusive practices. When persons are excluded from the mainstream of society, enormous shortcomings are set in motion. When there is no sign language interpreter available (and advertised) for the library "moms and tots morning story hour" or no place for kids in wheelchairs to sit with their friends during a birthday party at the local cinema, exclusion is in full-tilt. For individuals and groups to involve themselves in social and political activities — the stuff of citizen participation — they need to be seen and recognized as a constituency. This is true of children with special needs and their families. Parents' desire to effect positive change in their children's lives can be a powerful impetus; their children's circumstances may be the catalyst for greater involvement in their communities.

It is when we reject the medical model and instead appreciate others by respecting their differences that a potent political space is created. This is where children with disabilities and their families can choose to exercise their rights. In essence, this means lifting the veil of silence and speaking the truths of their experience. No longer will they be absent from the public sphere. It is in this way, through political action both personal and collective, that families may give voice to their vision for a better future. With this recognition, and our commitment not to waver, all children may be valued and enjoy the dignity they so deserve — and may no longer have to struggle to simply be included.

THE ETHIC OF CARE

One aspect of a strategy to spark concrete changes in these families' lives would be to apply a humanist (as opposed to market-driven, utilitarian[58]) ethic to social policy. The concept "ethic of care"[59] was developed by social justice theorists, philosophers and feminist bioethics specialists in Britain, the United States and Canada. It is not inconsistent with the social model of disability, especially in terms of the communitarian values it advances. The ethic of care arises from the notion that human interdependency is morally fundamental. We are persons to the extent that we relate to one another.

This differs sharply from the views of liberal and moral theorists who have for centuries defined the human self as independent, rational, self-interested and autonomous. Those who agree with the ethic of care argue that moral reasoning must be rooted in specific contexts and not in the abstract. For children with disabilities, the ethic of care promotes inclusion in that it relies upon case-by-case decisions as to what care modalities will be most beneficial. In a social policy framework that at present offers only fragmented services, the ethic of care is a useful concept to guide political action and policy change.

Families want to exercise informed choice about programs that are properly resourced. Embedded in the ethic of care is social responsibility for the well-being of all children, including special needs kids and their families. If we apply the ethic of care to how services and programs for families with disabled children are organized in Canada, it is obvious that the standard is not nearly met. While society attempts to protect children who are cared for poorly, as in instances of abuse and neglect, little is done to engage families in providing best care for children.

An ethic of care lens assumes that a social and moral good is achieved in providing services and programs from which families may choose. In other words, scarcity is not acceptable as the prime determinant of social policy. Rather a higher moral and social good is recognized, both for individuals and society. This suggests that unless a range of options is made available to parents, within which decisions about appropriate care, schooling and housing may be made, there can be no justice or high-quality care for these children and families.

Lives are built in relation to one another, in community. People come first. With these kernels as the starting point, it should be possible for us to develop best practices that highlight kids' chances to be included. For families with disabled children, all evidence points to the importance of valuing the social, communitarian values that breed success in education and other significant life-building activities. Away from the simplistic and denigrating attitudes (and practices) demonstrated by many physicians and charities in the past, our children will flourish in the cradle of care that only a well-resourced, well-informed and highly participatory community infrastructure can deliver.

COMMUNITY LIVING: STRATEGIC CONCERNS

A dilemma mentioned by more than a few of the parents I interviewed arose in relation to the very strong pro-integration position advanced by the community living movement. Many people benefit from efforts by community living associations to make it possible for people with disabilities to live independently, so long as they obtain appropriate supports. Integral to the ideology of this movement is complete integration of people with disabilities into communities and educational institutions. It's a commendable goal. Nonetheless, as with any solution to complex circumstances, many parents suggested to me that pursuing integration in all situations would be unwise for their child. Ollie's mother Lillian and Jeremy's mother Mary Ellen both expressed this view clearly. For their particular children, experience in an integrated school setting proved second-best. Today their children flourish in situations that encompass both integrated and segregated aspects.

In order to achieve the impressive gains that they have made, including paving the way for many children to participate in public schools and community recreational activities as well as exposing the inhumane medical testing and sterilization of persons with disabilities by so-called experts, community living advocates have had to be tough and uncompromising. Sadly, when a group's position becomes entrenched, particularly that of a marginalized group that feels under constant threat, little room remains for divergent opinions. But dogma rarely opens doors; it tends to reflect a blunt instrument at work rather than the finely honed initiatives these complex situations demand. The irony is staggering. The very spokespersons for community living who are demanding that difference be recognized and accommodated are sometimes intolerant of those who choose to make different decisions on behalf of their own children. As Mary Ellen expresses it, she felt as though she might be letting down some people she had met through finding services for Jeremy when she found a particular integrated setting not to be in her son's best interest.

It strikes me as a grave error for people to engage in movement politics without respecting families' right to make informed choices regarding their children's well-being. To achieve sustainable gains, disability activists and their allies must strive to not reduce the integration/segregation debate to a simple either/or. As Michael Bach correctly points out,[60] it is inclusion families are seeking for their children. As we will see in chapters to come, for Colleen and Johnny, Lillian and Ollie, and Cheryl and Enosh, there are, in fact, several paths to inclusion.

Families and youngsters, in consultation with the professionals involved, must make a case-by-case evaluation vis-à-vis school, housing and extra-curricular activities. It seems obvious that inclusion is a meaningful objective and perhaps, in our minds, the "default" should be integration. Certainly at the level of ideology — if only to insist upon a strict distinction from awful crimes committed against disabled persons in the past — integration is a valid point of departure. But room for the needs of complex human beings must be preserved.

As in other arenas, one must consider the arc of a child's entire school life. There may be some programs and specific learning methods that are best delivered away from an ordinary classroom. Sports offered in a segregated league may (or may not) best suit a child with mobility impairment. Similarly, it may be advantageous for a child with severe developmental disabilities to learn life skills in a group of his peers. Does that in any way preclude setting up opportunities for interaction between disabled and non-disabled children on the same school property? Of course not. At another time in a learner's life — whether that learner be disabled or not — a different pedagogical model might work better.

When a youth experiences a serious clinical depression, for example, and is disabled for a period of time, many educators will support allowing the young person to learn from home. With the assistance of computer technology, a student may function in this fashion for a temporary period before a gradual entry back into mainstream schooling is achievable. Similarly, a chronic or episodic illness might necessitate periods out of school with a bridge back into the school when the learner is ready. This strikes me as a common sense approach and certainly one that is already in practice in many jurisdictions.

I would argue that one can experience more inclusion from home during an episodic illness than on school grounds. Individualized learning that minimizes stress levels makes common sense. At the appropriate time, that is, when a youngster is ready, contributing to a group project with other students might be advantageous for all concerned, especially if part of the objective is to break down barriers of ignorance and discrimination. Non-disabled young people who are encouraged to shift their attitude toward mental illness become more understanding and compassionate adults. At the same time, they may learn useful skills to help identify warning signs regarding their own, or a friend's, mental health, for example. At minimum, the experience of disability broadens their knowledge base and scope of emotional literacy.

In a related vein, the learner based at home will be engaged in other activities to get through a clinical depression, such as therapy and exercise; school rules should be malleable enough to promote both healing and learning. Such accommodation might take some creative thinking on the part of teachers, parents and medical advisors but is hardly the stuff of MENSA meetings. Unusual circumstances demand innovative strategies. Similar opportunities for mixed approaches to learning are explored in the interviews that follow. Young Johnny in Newfoundland attends a school program for medically fragile children like himself. And yet, his school employs a creative approach so that he has no shortage of contact with non-disabled children. In fact, once the either/or polarity is blown off, substantial opportunities for inclusion present themselves.

Further, practising inclusion and building community capacity are inextricably linked. Unless a move toward valuing children with disabilities is made, they will continue to be locked out of civil society. There is, however, much to be gained from their full inclusion in all aspects of community life. Building a cohesive society means valuing on a very concrete level (not just in rhetoric) the strength diversity brings.

Unhampered by exclusionary practices, people are empowered to act toward improving their situation, to take action. In effect, this is the purpose of political action: working toward change that improves conditions of life for individuals and groups. Practising inclusion can help communities develop their ability to both effect and weather change. This would be capacity-building at its best. The possibility of progress is before us; together we must harness our creative energy and move forward.

SOCIAL AND POLITICAL INCLUSION

Recent work by Canadian academics and social policy experts in Europe and Great Britain explores the paradigm known as *social inclusion* to see how it may be applied to the issues facing disadvantaged populations. It developed in response to the growing gap between rich and poor that resulted from "new labour market conditions and the inability of existing social welfare provisions to meet the changing needs of more diverse populations ... Social inclusion calls for more than the removal of barriers or risks." [61] It calls for recognition of diversity as well as social investments and actions to bring about the conditions for inclusion.

Inclusion is at the heart of most challenges facing disabled children and their families. To argue for integration is to recognize and value "difference." It means seeking to accommodate difference. It also entails acknowledging that diversity and difference can be enriching at many levels, personally and more broadly. Learning to accommodate individuals' difference in the workforce, at school and in childcare need not detract from anyone else's rights. In quite concrete terms for example, when ramps and elevators are constructed in a subway station, just as a person in a wheelchair is accommodated, so too is anyone pushing a stroller or bundle buggy. Unfortunately, in a public service landscape devastated by scarcity, the services and programs that children require are often shelved; they are considered too expensive or too difficult to coordinate. It is also, most evidently, a matter of political will. In the absence of significant political pressure, accommodating children with disabilities is way off the radar.

The multi-dimensional concept of social inclusion may be instructive in arriving at a fuller understanding of how systemic discrimination plays out through the intersecting of class, race and disability. Disadvantage is simultaneously economic and social. Long-term unemployment, poverty, access to health and social services, welfare and education are all indicators of inclusion or its opposite. Social inclusion does not focus on equality of outcomes but is linked fundamentally to the freedom to enjoy the rights of citizenship. It is the recognition of diversity among people and their differing ability to seize opportunity that is at issue.

Author Amartya Sen, who won the Nobel Prize in Economics in 1998, argues in his recent book *Development as Freedom*[62] that social inclusion means improving the capabilities of individuals and communities to better participate in the life of the society. The barriers to this participation — such as race and class discrimination — are of key concern. The onus is on society to ensure that it enables participation. Putting the onus on society finds a potent parallel in the disability movement's assertion that it is society's attitudes, not disability itself, that is fundamentally disabling. As such, exploring how inclusion/exclusion operates can be instructive in forming political strategies to effect change.

Freedom to participate, Sen points out, means freedom from deprivations such as hunger, illness and illiteracy. Freedom from "capability deprivation"[63] may also include developing better health practices to avoid risks such as low birth weight in newborns. If parents participate in the life of the community, become engaged in civic concerns as a means of improving their children's lives, they could have a significant impact. Leadership and a keen focus on achievable gains presuppose that parents harness and direct their political energies. The objective may be defined in two ways: facilitating better access to special education and necessary therapies or fostering a comprehensive network of respite care services. It is, at bottom, a question of power. When we struggle to be fully included, it means we refuse to give up our own power. We refuse to be left dejected on the sidelines. Mothers especially may move out of the margins and into the mainstream and win battles to achieve inclusion for their children and families.

To be entitled as a citizen to participate in the mainstream of society is to be a full member, with the same expectations of respect, rights and dignity as anyone else living in the same society. The point is that families of children with disabilities must be at liberty to participate in all institutions in society: cultural, social, economic and political.[64] This speaks to a notion of civil society in which inter-relatedness (i.e. community) is the basis on which social decisions ought to be made and implemented. It speaks to citizenship as consisting of full democratic participation and meaningful inclusion in society's institutions.

One of the exciting aspects of the social model framework is that this inclusion would result in forms of social identity, reciprocity and solidarity that provide a foundation for rights to be realized in relation to others for a life well-lived in community. This is a much broader approach than simple *integration*. Moreover, in political terms, the ability to create a voice of pride in a group is to create and maintain positive images of identity. For the disability movement, so often mired in the personal (literally – one's person) and individual issues, making progress together in creating a unified voice and acting collectively would move the agenda forward considerably. Market forces must not delineate best practices for any child. When economic imperatives rule, genuine inclusion is reduced to a frill. As parents and allies we may claim collective voice and actively oppose any false impression that children with complex needs are just so many widgets. Practising inclusion means removing the insidious filter that defines a child as the sum of her symptoms — something that benefits everyone. It means tearing down the walls of fear and prejudice so that the child, bursting with humanity, emerges whole.

CHAPTER FIVE

FAMILY RELATIONSHIPS, FAITH AND COMMUNITY

A CENTRAL CHALLENGE IN my own parenting has been how to weave bonds between my daughter and her brother who, because he needed 24-hour complex care, was unable to live with us. In approaching other parents I wanted to know what kinds of challenges they faced in raising both non-disabled and disabled children. How did they build community around their child with special needs? Did they rely on members of their extended families? Where might neighbours, other families at their child's school or their faith community fit in?

In mothering Jake, I realized that while the publicly funded care he received was both absolutely necessary for him to live well and the bottom line without which our family would fall apart, relationships of another sort helped keep me on track. I needed to keep my emotional balance, care for my daughter, stay in the workforce and somehow remain whole. While I sometimes faltered (and became exhausted to the point that my doctor insisted I take sick leave from work), throughout Jake's life there were people who helped me. That support somehow redoubled my determination to fight for the quality care Jake and other medically fragile children require. In my conversations with other parents I wanted to learn what kinds of informal or community supports they found helpful.

I was also curious as to how other parents balance the emotional and physical needs of their children. I wondered if parents found their non-disabled children taking on uncommon caregiving responsibilities or if they were resentful of the attention their sister or brother needed. When the child's disability is cognitive or involves limited verbal expression do sisters and brothers, nonetheless, engage one another in relationship? I wondered how parents handle their worry about a child's future conditions of life once family care is no longer feasible.

SIBLINGS

How parents explain to their children the challenges a disabled sibling faces varies greatly but is most complex when a child's condition goes beyond a relatively obvious physical impairment. There is a qualitative difference between blindness and a mobility impairment, for example, and developmental or psychological disabilities that can affect a person's capacity for decision-making. In essence, a limit to a person's ability to exercise his or her agency is a more substantial impediment to the goal of reaching autonomy. In addition, many of the latter disabilities tend to present over time, the development of an infant's or young child's capacities being so reliant on a variety of opportunities at home and therapeutic interventions.

Of course, one always must find age-appropriate explanations for children. Young people experience their sister's or brother's impairments in a number of ways and at different levels. The relationship alters over time and across various stages in their lives. Not unlike parents who initially grieve the loss of the child they expected and then, hopefully, learn to embrace their child as the person she is, kids too experience a sense of loss that ebbs and flows.

Many non-disabled children, whether younger or older, tend to take on an elder sibling role. They may help with the child's physical care or, as does one young boy in the narratives that follow, commit to memory the exact medication doses and schedule that his brother needs so that he can inform an auntie or babysitter when his mom can't be present. Our kids seem to learn early to defend their siblings. I doubt this varies a great deal from other sibling relationships, but the need may arise more often if a child with special needs is made fun of or otherwise castigated in public. In best-case scenarios, I have seen young children emulate their parents' level of comfort with their disabled child.

Again, I do not presume that these family relationships are necessarily substantially different from those in so-called ordinary families. But I do believe there are some qualitative differences that engender additional layers of complexity and which require parents' attention. It may take conscious effort by parents to foster the complex attachment between these siblings. When a brother does not speak and only communicates with his eyes and sounds, everyone in the family must learn to interpret what is wanted. If we imagine an English-speaking family where (for some reason) one child speaks only Cantonese, perhaps we can grasp how extra attention and effort toward communicating effectively must occur.

I also believe the knowledge that a non-disabled child is likely to accrue in the family is, on balance, enriching, notwithstanding that there may be times that she wishes for a "real" brother, as my daughter expressed at age five when we were enjoying a weekend visit with a family bursting with vocal, active kids. In short, perhaps our kids learn early that life isn't always fair and/or there are not fully scientific, rational explanations for everything that occurs. I am convinced that the way in which parents frame their explanations of disability to their children profoundly affects the nature of family relationships.

Research indicates that some non-disabled children feel a need to compensate for their sibling's limits in order to please their parents.[65] Some mothers told me they were conscious, in celebrating their non-disabled kids' activities at school or sports, of not wanting to put extra pressure on them to achieve. Others were aware that their non-disabled child occasionally experienced guilt because he was fine while his sister had certain challenges. Some non-disabled children feel jealous that less time (and likely less energy and/or financial resources) is available for a visit to the zoo or to go to a hockey game.

My daughter missed her brother because he lived far from our home. I think, moreover, that especially when she was between ages five and ten, she would have liked a companion to play with in our home, without having to wait for a play date on the weekend. On occasion, I even wondered if she was picking a fight with me because, in the absence of a sibling nearby, she would bounce her scrappiness off me. Her friendships became increasingly important as she became older — as for many children — and she found intimacy with certain youngsters that gave her the sort of closeness one might enjoy with a sister or brother. It is quite possible that these traits are simply indicative of how only children mature.

Many of these dynamics are illustrated in the portraits presented later in the book. I was struck (and profoundly moved) by the expectations that these parents held for their non-disabled children.[66] The similarities were remarkable. Mothers expressed again and again that they would not allow their non-disabled children to take responsibility for providing primary care to their brother or sister in future. Encouraging a sense of obligation in their non-disabled children was strictly out of bounds. Parents went to great lengths to give their non-disabled children as ordinary an upbringing as possible.

In one case, for example, an older child is sent to a different school simply to give her a break from a stressful home scene where unabated seizures and raspy coughing dominate. Her mother insists that she develop her own sense of self quite apart from her younger brother's weighty medical needs. Another parent makes a point of spending some quality time with his young non-disabled daughter right after school, so she can tell him about her day and they can play together. Afterwards they include her sister in the ménage and all make dinner together.

A CHALLENGE TO AGING PARENTS

Notwithstanding parents' reluctance to press their non-disabled children into service as primary caregiver, every family I have come into contact with has expressed concern over their vulnerable child's future. What care will be available when the parent is no longer able to carry the responsibility? What happens when mothers and fathers can no longer lift their growing child or endure the long hours and sleepless nights? As parents age and encounter their own infirmities, their ability to provide care is diminished. Even with the best intentions of reliable, loving parents, young adults with severe behavioural issues may be too hard for them to handle and even dangerous in physical terms. Making meals, dressing the young person, offering recreational opportunities and attending to health appointments may require energy that has long since departed.

The parents I have spoken to (not only in these interviews but during campaigns to keep open facilities and programs threatened with closure) had mulled over what the future would hold for their child. In the narratives that follow, we will see that different solutions are contemplated depending, in part, on the young person's abilities. For a blind or deaf child, a full education program adapted to her needs will most likely lead to a relatively independent adulthood. A thalidomide victim is far less likely to manage his own personal care without the assistance of a full-time attendant. A child who is medically fragile often dies before her parents; still, the concern that care be provided on a reliable basis is frequently a source of worry in a time rife with spending cutbacks.

As mentioned previously, most of the parents made clear that they did not want their non-disabled child(ren) to have to take responsibility for their sibling's care — at least not as a long-term proposition. Although there seemed little doubt that some of these sisters and brothers would advocate on their disabled sibling's behalf and continue to include them in their lives, most parents were adamant that the full load of care not fall upon the shoulders of their other children. Interestingly, the more complex the care required, the more firm the parents' resolve.

It strikes me that this perspective reveals a considerable generosity of spirit. These are not families who would ever say their special needs child is a burden. Still, the parents acknowledge that the special circumstances in their families' experience mean siblings share the spotlight constantly with someone whose needs will always be more urgent, more intense. In compensation, or even to assuage the guilt that seems to accompany so much of our parenting, young adults are encouraged to launch into their lives.

Even so, in the stories that follow several beautiful moments of sibling care are shared. After finishing high school, for example, a young man decides of his own volition to take a year off school to be one of his very ill brother's primary caregivers during (what turned out to be) the last year of his life. A devoted older sister is urged emphatically by her mother to go off to university out of town in order to pursue her studies and chosen career. A young boy who is blind knows that the sky is his limit as he gets older and that his elder siblings will always be there to watch out for him.

Many parents' fear for the future is more acute when a child has been cared for in a residential facility. As I write, the Ontario government has announced its plan to close the last three remaining Ontario facilities for people with developmental challenges. During the 1960s there were sixteen residential institutions for six thousand people with a developmental disability. Very few community-based supports were present at that time to assist these individuals to live more independently. But as the community living movement burgeoned across North America (and elsewhere) many people with developmental disabilities began to integrate more fully into community settings. Governments shifted resources away from residential institutions. Five provincially operated residential facilities were closed and the funding to several others reduced during the late seventies and early eighties, at the same time that the government's funding of community-based programs increased from $10 million to $181 million.[67]

The trend has continued over the last twenty years and the three final closures mark the complete transition to the new era. Despite funding promises, some have questioned the extent to which the government will be held accountable for the delivery of necessary services in the community. In a 2004 article, Helen Henderson, an insightful columnist at *The Toronto Star*, both lauded the government's direction and sounded a cautionary note.

> The aim of giving all people with disabilities the option of having their needs met in the community is commendable, but it will work only if community resources are significantly increased. In the past, too many people moved out of institutions have found themselves stranded. Cash-strapped communities lack the wherewithal to meet their needs and the province short-changes them ... Will we see even more families stretched to the breaking point trying to make up for Queen's Park's abandoned promises?[68]

I am even less hopeful. Henderson mentions "giving people with disabilities the option of having their needs met in the community." As facilities close their doors, is a genuine choice truly offered? When vulnerable individuals leave a group living situation that supplies structure to each day and a certain degree of supervision, a new series of challenges is posed.

Greater isolation is definitely not the answer. Medical, nursing, dietary, dental, psychiatric, therapeutic and recreational services offered in the constellation of a large facility are significant resources that could be applied to a broader population in the community. Sadly, closures most often constitute the dispersion and net loss of core services.[69]

Why not continue to provide care to high-needs individuals and open the doors to provide community access to crucial, specialized programs? Rather than applying cookie-cutter solutions to complex situations, policy-makers must make respect and responsibility the cornerstones of any decision to reconfigure services. Typically these values are absent when governments hurl wrecking balls informed more by ideology than accountability. How is an aging parent meant to manage when a family member seems to be falling through the cracks? Worst of all, as parents' own health fails, they cannot know with any certainty that their child — of any age — will receive consistent, quality care.

FAITH AND COMMUNITY

As I met with the families in this book, I was interested to know if faith or spirituality played a part in their lives. Did it contribute to the sense of community they imparted to their children? Did they find meaning or comfort in certain practices or rituals? I wondered if faith helped them to deal effectively with their life situation. Often families with disabled children find themselves on the outside looking in; the response they receive from the rest of society frequently serves to isolate both children and their parents. In exploring how personal belief systems play out in experience, I found a wide spectrum of views.

In the "Portraits" section that follows, parents use different words to express the power of the connection they feel to their children. Spirituality is evident for some but not others. Clearly, the complex ways in which faith, ritual and community inform people's lives bear consideration. It is the texture of these attachments that fascinates me and, especially, the palpable affection these families demonstrate that often reaches beyond the confines of a typical family unit. Community that surrounds our children, like the sturdy bond of chain-link steel, stands guard against harm.

For Colleen, her faith has always played a key role. Her belief in God gives her both strength and solace in mothering Johnny, the most vulnerable of the (live) children described in this book. Not surprisingly, when it came to explaining Johnny's condition to her then three-year-old daughter, Colleen spoke of God's will in a manner that fit her view of the world. She finds community both in her church and with the other families involved in Johnny's developmental delay unit at the school. Not only do the children share certain similarities, but the intensive organizing project they embarked upon to keep the unit open created greater solidarity. Such deep bonds are often formed through struggle.

Colleen's faith helps her to endure the demanding circumstances she faces every day. She told me that Johnny "… is an individual and a person. He is a social being ... I look at Johnny and I say, 'When God takes Johnny back, he's going back as wholesome and as pure as the day he came to me ... Probably even more so because of what he's given to the world ... My hope is that Johnny will continue to touch people's lives ...'"

Her words convey a powerful snapshot. Johnny's frailty has given unexpected purpose to Colleen's life. "Johnny can't physically [advocate for] himself but he inspires me and motivates me to do what needs to be done ... [on behalf of] so many people living with disabilities."

Cheryl Gaster sought the involvement of her family and friends as a way to surround and support Enosh. Cheryl's mother went door to door in apartment buildings near her home to find volunteers to help with Enosh's early treatment program. A brave band later gathered to fight for his right to attend an integrated classroom. I am struck by Cheryl and her husband's ingenuity and the strength they drew from people around them. Together they took very deliberate steps to ensure the family did not become isolated. And at key moments, it was that support group that acted with alacrity to forestall crises in the family.

When Enosh reached his thirteenth birthday, a time Cheryl refers to as her son's "fabulous middle years" when he was well and relatively healthy, they celebrated Enosh's coming of age. His bar mitzvah, she told me, was also a way to thank the many people who had participated in various phases of her son's life. They developed an original and alternative ceremony, and this remarkable young man and his family were able to observe the traditional Jewish rite, celebrating his transition into manhood.

Of course a spiritual commitment is not necessary to practising inclusion. But it may help. If one understands the world to be created by a higher power, it may be easier to accept that forces beyond our control govern what happens to us. Perhaps when a child's challenges are thought to be part of some greater plan, it assuages the urge to know more, to want to conquer rather than accept. The faith that one feels — that opening up of generous spirit — is certainly akin to the process of acceptance that the disability community demands from the rest of us.

One can live a secular life and still take the steps needed to broaden understanding and perspective. The hegemony of so-called normalcy rules, but when we question its supremacy, barriers can shatter like window panes under pressure. Spiritual values and ritual may contribute to developing a more open-minded attitude, but not necessarily. And there are other paths.

A few of the mothers I interviewed expressed concern that their husbands have never fully accepted their child's challenges, at least not as a deeply integral part of the child's very being. There may be something in caring for a person intimately that stimulates mothers (usually) to embrace the entirety of their child's character. Learning to accept one's offspring, not unlike learning to value difference and the essential humanity of all our children, is the first move toward achieving just treatment. I do not believe that the move toward inclusion happens automatically. It is learned in contact with the very people we tend to fear.

The role that other people play is significant; it is in community that we find understanding and strength. As Jean Vanier writes,

> To be human is to accept who we are, this mixture of strength and weakness. To be human is to accept and love others just as they are. To be human is to be bonded together, each with our weaknesses and strengths, because we need each other. Weakness, recognized, accepted, and offered, is at the heart of belonging ... [70]

It is my sincere hope that we find a way to recognize the intrinsic value that each and every child brings to the world. From there, anything and everything is possible. To participate in the mainstream of society is to be a full member and to hold the same expectation of respect, rights and dignity as anyone else. We are not alone, but live among others. The point is for families of children with disabilities to demand space as part of all institutions in society: cultural, social, economic or political. This speaks to a notion of civil society in which inter-relatedness is at the core. It speaks to citizenship composed in full democratic participation and inclusion in society's institutions. For these children and their families, acting together is the best way to propel the agenda forward.

I have always considered myself an atheist. When I am enveloped by nature, breathing in the moist, mossy air of a north woods trail or paddling on a pristine lake where only the loon's lament breaks silent reverie, I am conscious that a creative force far greater than humankind inhabits all places. Living with my son as he struggled for breath, I never felt — as some do in their own situations — that he and I were living out God's will. Rather, as I sat with him I often felt moved by the incredible and primitive, powerful grip that Nature sustains on us. Just as Cheryl's family observed their son's coming of age, with the help of some very close friends, I wrote an alternative bar mitzvah ceremony for my son Jake. A compassionate and learned man led the service. Gathered with my family and a broad group of friends and colleagues, young Jake touched the sacred Torah and then his sister wheeled him around the synagogue. I hoped that she would always remember the day as a respectful act we created to honour her brother. Music and readings emphasized our relatedness as a community and the strength these bonds brought to such a vulnerable life. Jake's voice could be heard cooing above the music; he was in his element.

Making a bar mitzvah for Jake was not an expression of religion. I wanted to celebrate with our wider community the fact that against all odds and expectations he had made it to thirteen years old. During the years since his birth, many people had contributed to his well-being, and to my daughter's and my own. They affirmed his humanity at all stages of his life: with intimate personal care and song, birthday parties, hope and love — as well as supporting our activist struggles on his behalf and for other children like him, in print, radio and television documentaries.

Touching the Torah for the first time at a religious bar mitzvah ceremony is something Jewish boys have done throughout the ages (and more recently, girls). This ritual allowed us to embrace Jake's humanity and to draw a historical line from his roots through into his own life. Close friends and family, plus some politically engaged people who had helped us along the way, took part in the service. While our observance and celebration reflected a particular set of values, families of diverse backgrounds may derive particular meaning from their community rituals.

In the interview with Sharon Daniels, she told me how she draws upon elements of native tradition as well as her Christian upbringing when she grapples with her daughter's frail health. Shannon experienced repeated health crises, the most acute of which was a cardiac arrest. Sharon explained how traditional healing practices, including prayer and song, help her both to engage in pitched battle against illness and to contend with the wrenching alarm that takes hold whenever her daughter suffers.

Sharon's extended family and community unleash a joint, powerful appeal to assist Shannon in her times of crisis. The telephone is a living link in real time back to their community. In Peguis, the medicine men and elders chant for Shannon's healing and supervise several age-old rituals to enhance her well-being. In the same heartbeat, Sharon's niece sets in motion a Christian prayer vigil in the hospital chapel with forty or fifty members of the extended family and friends.

Sharon believes that both of these interventions help her daughter to survive. When the family gathers around Shannon in hospital, they are able to bring their cultural practices with them, unhindered by hospital staff or regulations. Certainly in both traditions that Sharon described to me, the common thread was the central role of her extended family and community in gathering together to express their love and support for a young woman and her family.

Listening to Sharon's words, I wondered how our respective belief systems function to help us cope. It seems evident that one's faith or spirituality sits amongst a complex array of values, not hived off from daily routine like a hatbox hidden in the attic. As I had an opportunity to converse with these families, it became clear to me that how they situate spirituality in their lives does not flow from giving life to a particularly vulnerable child. Faith is linked to upbringing and a value system that usually long predates the child's birth. How they explain their child's challenges and the demands made upon themselves as parents, however, is very much filtered through their spiritual gaze.

Despite differences among the families interviewed for this project, as well as other families I have encountered in my work, they all seemed to cast a much wider net in defining quality of life and what constitutes being human. I join them in bumping up against preconceived notions about human-ness as I raise my own family. Given our families' challenges, what choice do we have but to open our hearts and minds?

Toward Transformation

There may be individuals who do not have preconceived ideas of what a human being looks like or how one behaves. If they exist, I have not met them. I suspect that for most of us there is a learning curve. How open we are to it determines how we view our children and the extent to which this experience is transformative. As I develop friendships with colleagues who are deaf or blind, for example, it is their humanity, their individuality that becomes real for me. This would not have been the case several years ago. I connect (or do not) with people I meet as fellow persons — not objectified (I hope) by the cane or signing they use to communicate.

I also realize increasingly at an emotional — not just intellectual — level that *normal* is not a terribly useful category. Our world includes a wide variety of individual potential and capacity. It is my ability to open my consciousness to those who are different from me that transforms my perspective and behaviour.

Cheryl Gaster illustrates this process for us when she describes how she recognized with great consternation that the powerful love she felt for her son did not transfer automatically to other children. At least not at first. A profound experience at a special needs nursery school made her realize that she needed to broaden both brain and heart to accept children other than her own son; in essence she deepened her understanding of how human-ness tends to be defined. Other parents I met also seemed to experience similar growth while parenting their own disabled child.

I suspect that as we gradually make sense of our children's challenges, we also expand our views about who needs care. Our own experience teaches us that need is manifest in many different ways — and that our child's needs are as worthy as any other child's. In a way, the advocacy we undertake reinforces this point of departure. Not only must we broaden our own conceptions as to what constitutes human, but we engage in processes that we hope will lead to others changing their views. Community tends to be found among those who, like ourselves, make this empathic journey.

Like Cheryl, while I bonded very deeply with my baby, I could not immediately offer that generosity or acceptance to all other children with disabilities. It took time and a deliberate effort at first to open my heart to the medically fragile little ones at Jake's group home. One takes a step into a different and somehow frightening world. A warm-hearted and wise friend, when about to visit Jake at his group home, expressed to me that she hoped she would not feel horrified by any of the little ones she met. I understand this apprehension; these kids, with all their developmental and physical difference, are not part of our daily experience. Although Jake was tremendously beautiful to me, I continue to work at opening my heart to others. It is clearly not a one-time lesson, but an orientation that one can purposefully foster.

Building lines of mutual support that endure through adversity takes an appreciation of our own fragility. It means acknowledging our own intense need for intimacy among strangers, for a sense of belonging. It seems that this need underlies many diverse rituals and spiritual practices. Appreciating the involvement of other like-minded individuals in our lives is part of experiencing community — whether that experience is spiritual or activity-based. Something brings us together.

For those of us with severely disabled children, we often seek community to meet multiple practical needs in the absence of adequate public supports. Many families experience ties based on more than simply mutual assistance. We often wish to find a safe place for our kids and our own feelings; a place where the different quality of our lives is appreciated and accepted without question. For some, this safety may be found in religious or spiritual endeavour, but not for everyone. It is more likely that acceptance, like the warmth of a familiar cozy blanket, cultivates an enduring strength that keeps us snug through the chilly times we inevitably encounter.

RESPITE CARE AND CITIZEN ENGAGEMENT

A BROAD-BASED RENEWAL and reconfiguration of service delivery to disabled children and their families is long overdue. Improved respite care is one element in a comprehensive set of options that social policy experts underscore. One aim of respite, also known as caregiver relief, is to enable families to live so-called ordinary lives in the community. Experience shows that adequate respite care can also allow parents to participate in training opportunities or the paid workforce. In addition to providing parents a needed break, the aim of developing quality respite opportunities is to enable these individuals to participate more fully as engaged citizens in the social and political life of their communities.

Certainly overhauling service models and instituting a broad range of reliable supports for these children and their families is a critical social need. But I believe the abysmal state of respite care also provides a strategic opportunity. If one identifies the lack of adequate respite as fertile ground for community organizing, the prism casts its light differently.

More specifically, we humans tend to become engaged politically when we believe there is something to be gained that can directly improve our own lives. As became obvious with the individuals I interviewed, a broader commitment to social justice may or may not be present amongst families raising children with special needs. And yet, even people with no experience in political engagement are moved to act with respect to concrete matters.

The gap in care families experience could, properly harnessed, lead to resistance against governments' shrinking commitment to publicly funded, not-for-profit social programs. In the remainder of this chapter, I will explore this opportunity and argue that not only parents, but the paid caregivers who support their children, have a role in garnering high quality, affordable respite care services from the public sector. A community organizing perspective holds promise for improving this one piece in the system of supports families of disabled children require. It may serve as a unifying force between clients and service providers.

Very practical issues emerge in the absence of adequate respite care opportunities. Every activity — from grocery shopping to making a prom dress — is more complicated, especially in a lone-parent led family. It can be extremely tough to get a breather away from the routines of caregiving. In my research, parents' ability to balance family members' needs was linked fundamentally to how much relief they obtained. The presence of other adults in a family's daily life — not just to help with caregiving but to take youngsters to a ball game or help them with homework — makes an enormous difference. More elastic family boundaries allow for this kind of helpful interplay with neighbours or friends.

CHOOSING RESPITE

Gaps in services at the individual family level could act as a significant catalyst for people to break out of the isolation inherent in the privatized family mould. Why? When we acknowledge a need for improved caregiver relief, it means believing that the state must share social responsibility for the well-being of its populace. Ironically, the very people who most require such relief are least likely to have the time or energy to achieve improvements. Instead each family tends to do battle on its own with program eligibility criteria and shrinking global budgets.

However, the structure of respite offered in the home, in particular, means that workers interface directly with families (clients). Home support workers know about cuts occurring in their agencies — even if precise details of their roll-out are kept under wraps by management. In carrying out their day-to-day duties, support workers encounter gaps in service directly and experience crushing caseloads that make constructive client relations difficult. Staff members in a particular agency are also mindful of inefficiencies and/or waste. Would it be unprofessional to point out shortcomings in client care? I don't think so. Rather, I posit that home support workers and the parents concerned must combine energy to create the political space in which positive change may be fostered. It will take resourceful, systematic lobbying of politicians, public officials and the media. This approach was successful in the case of the Thistletown Regional Centre for Children and Adolescents near Toronto, where the partnership parents and their children's caregivers cultivated proved effective in thwarting government plans to shut the facility down.

In a research paper prepared by Fraser Valentine for the Canadian Policy Research Networks (CPRN) 2001, he proposes a paradigm shift from patchwork initiatives to a systemic comprehensive change approach to social policy and its implementation. Respite care is part of a best policy mix, he says, that enables parents to exercise choice about how they rear their children and contribute to the economy.[71]

What does respite care or caregiver relief include? First, it is useful to regard respite care as an outcome rather than just a series of programs or stopgap measures; an outcome that opens up the range and scope of assistance from which parents/caregivers might most benefit. Respite care may be delivered in the family home when, for example, a trained individual spends four hours a week caring for Shannon so that her mother may do errands necessary to running the household, including seeing to details regarding her other children and family members. Of course, four is a woefully inadequate number of hours.

Not all families find having another person in their home a genuine break, however. As is often the case with medically fragile children, care is complex and unrelenting. Colleen's arrangement with a woman nearby that allows Johnny to spend part of alternate weekends at her home has allowed Colleen to seek paid employment and to preserve her own health; her son awakens repeatedly at night with unsettling convulsions. Other modes of caregiver relief helpful to families would include support during unexpected needs (emergencies or other health crises) or someone to help with housekeeping and outdoor home maintenance. At present, a family must apply for publicly funded care and the little they receive is reviewed at regular intervals.

Families should be able to easily access a range of supports. Yet as Sherri Torjman, a policy analyst with the Caledon Institute of Social Research in Ottawa states, "Choice is real only if it embodies the notion of voice."[72] Professionals may make recommendations but it is the caregivers themselves (and this includes parents) who are best able to define what is needed. Parents need a break and, in addition, their capacity to participate actively as full citizens may be enhanced when respite is available. A best policy mix would build such capacity in communities and, at the level of the family, provide a more solid foundation for the "... future citizenship of all Canada's children."[73]

Social policy experts emphasize the need to balance a family's functioning and to prevent marital breakdown, which has an incidence as high as 80 percent among families with severely disabled children. A truckload of recent research indicates several different models for provision of respite care: in-home, out-of-home, with evaluation of short- and long-term needs and so on. These are largely only potential — not actual — options because they do not exist in any standard or systematic way across the country.

Sharon Daniels had her respite care services removed when it was deemed by an agency official that she was managing to provide Shannon adequate care. At the time of our interview in December 2003, Sharon had just had the four hours per week relief reinstated. As she told me, it was very difficult to get all the household errands completed in that time, let alone have a quiet cup of tea. During our discussion I thought my line of questioning might elicit a response of frustration or anger at government-initiated cuts. Instead, she expressed appreciation for what she does receive and mentioned other families she knows who receive less. In the existing climate of scarcity, we are encouraged to feel grateful and discouraged from demanding change.

CONTINUITY OF CARE AND THE HOME CARE BUSINESS

I found a common thread in the concerns parents tend to raise. One is that when they do receive respite care in the home, they cannot count on the same person to arrive at the door on a consistent basis. It is not easy to leave one's fragile child in such circumstances, especially if she requires technological assistance such as an oxygen tank or feeding pump.

Parents want their child (or young person) to receive consistent care. In an out-of-home setting, it is helpful when the same group of workers is available on a regular basis. A child enjoys benefits when staff turnover is minimized. The comfort derived from routines that can be established when a child has his own room and toys and is supervised by staff members who know which bedtime songs are soothing cannot be underestimated. Similar to the acknowledgement of parents' comfort level with respect to in-home workers, the knowledge that their child is safe and content goes a long way in assisting families to carry on with their lives confidently when they *do* get a break.

To illustrate, one mother I spoke with (prior to undertaking this book) was allotted two afternoons respite over six weeks; the family's doctor had requested this help for the mother after her three-month-old daughter was diagnosed with a seizure disorder. The infant was not yet stabilized on an effective medication regime. The mother had been much relieved since there was no kin nearby to help out. Respite was needed and, certainly, helpful — the family doctor had correctly recognized signs of exhaustion and knew the mother would benefit from a regular break during which she was to establish an exercise routine outside the home. They recognized together that an ounce of prevention would help stave off the kind of depression that sometimes afflicts women isolated in this kind of situation.

She was perturbed, however, when a different person arrived for every shift. Each new caregiver was shown the baby's feeding and sleeping routines before the mom stole away for a few hours. The care seemed competent and the baby did not suffer unduly. Yet, it was far from ideal. As for any new mother leaving an infant — even for a short period of time — her sense of security was tied to a level of comfort with the caregiver.

The caregivers who came in during that short period, she told me, didn't receive their shift schedule until a day or two before; they worked on an on-call basis for the agency that employed them. Most of the women that came in were new Canadians; many had training that was not fully recognized here. Further, the caregivers were not well paid, did not receive any benefits and, since their assignments changed so frequently, there was less job satisfaction than that possible when a caregiver is able to develop a relationship with a particular child and family. All of these factors contributed to a high rate of turnover.[74]

Not surprisingly, corporations and private agencies have moved into the Canadian home care field with alacrity. Managed competition is the common delivery model. Not-for-profit home care providers are driven away by the Ontario government (as well as several other provincial governments) in favour of low wage for-profit care peddlers.

Interestingly, the Manitoba government has moved away from its previous home care delivery model since recent research indicated that turning the system over to private operators did not lead to significant cost savings. In fact, private sector delivery is characterized by low wages, low status and increased staff turnover — the last of which, in particular, affects the quality of care received.[75]

When Sharon Daniels (in Winnipeg) and I talked about the respite she received, she commented that the support workers coming in December 2003 did not have the same level of training as previous in-home workers dispatched. For her daughter Shannon, who then breathed through a tracheotomy tube, it was vital that the person have nursing skills in order provide appropriate care. For obvious reasons, Sharon was disturbed by this change.

RESTRUCTURING AND ACCOUNTABILITY

The restructuring of health care in many provinces has meant once-distinct jobs are now amalgamated. The homemaker who assists with housework, groceries and meal preparation also becomes responsible for procedures once carried out by nurses or physiotherapists. There is little distinction made in staff training for the diverse supports delivered by caregivers in the home.

> The services currently in place are not adequate in terms of persons who are medically fragile. When special needs arise, such as bladder infection or pneumonia, the required supports usually are not available. This lack opens the door to serious medical errors and clearly causes stress for families.[76]

As informal caregivers are frequently trained by accredited professionals to carry out so-called routine procedures, the degree of skill applied in each case is understandably diluted. The expertise developed in a formal nursing education cannot be transmitted in an afternoon. Accessing professional know-how on the spot becomes less feasible, a fact that may mitigate against the consistent delivery of high-quality home care.[77]

Changes in how agencies determine the skill sets required to perform necessary duties also have a negative impact on client care. Moving toward the "generic worker" corresponds to a flattening of salary levels. As one home support worker in Toronto recently told her union representative, "We do everything from bowel procedures to giving home hair permanents."[78] De-professionalizing supports offered in the home is problematic. One advantage of larger facilities is that they provide a nexus of trained staff. In most instances, such facilities pay higher wages and benefits in a unionized environment. Increasingly the relatively small agency employers rely on part-time workers, limiting opportunities for full-time work and a corresponding compensation package. Not surprisingly, conditions of employment like these lead to high turnover.

When employers offer lower salaries to so-called generic home support workers, the turnover causes a corresponding negative effect upon the continuity of care. A for-profit agency may deem the skill set offered entirely acceptable. In private business, the guiding principle is profit, not patient care. In the absence of a public watchdog and regulated standards, what redress mechanism does a family have?

This lack of accountability is troubling. It is not just skill levels that are blurred. Overall responsibility and reporting may not be fully regulated by the government licensing that is meant to protect consumers. Without appropriate hiring principles and reporting mechanisms, especially given that this work is carried out in dispersed households, a young man such as Cheryl's son Enosh is left more vulnerable to intrusive, unsafe or abusive treatment. There is a correlation between government policies that encourage market competition and the ratcheting down of care. Standards of care for the delivery of human services by for-profit agencies are subject to less scrutiny precisely when clients need greater protection. In addition to all these problems, families also have to foot part of the bill. As the 2002 Romanow Report on the Future of Health Care recognized, when care is provided at home, the family must pay part or all of the costs. These are services that were previously available in hospital and therefore covered under Medicare.

RESPITE CARE: THE MANY ADVANTAGES

While the crucial role respite care plays in the wellness of families is documented extensively, adequate funding for a coordinated system of quality, flexible and portable programs just isn't there. A recent Roeher Institute study suggests that there is a gap in services for children with speech or mental health disabilities, which affects a high proportion of families needing care. Mothers indicated in the same study that children with autism or brain injury, many of whom also present mental health difficulties, did not receive adequate respite care.[79]

The impact on full-time caregivers' mental and physical health may affect the long-term ability of mothers and families to provide care in the home. In Colleen's situation with young Johnny, his schooling at the developmental delay unit provides a few hours break for her each day. As mentioned previously, Colleen also employs a woman she knows and trusts to care for Johnny every second weekend. When a child has such high medical needs and requires twenty-four hour supervision, it cannot be expected that a typical nuclear family, let alone a lone-parent led family, can manage it without assistance.

When adequate respite care is available, primary caregivers are able to maintain their status in the workforce or go to school and counter the isolation that often accompanies providing care in the home. Simply put, it reduces the level of burnout and can, in the long-term, reduce the likelihood of descent into poverty. Furthermore, a lack of adequate support services (of all kinds) can contribute to parents' uncertainty in planning support for their children's lives, especially when the children reach adulthood and require non-familial based long-term care. No doubt if a publicly supported assisted living situation were available to Mary Ellen's son Jeremy, as part of the spectrum of services available to persons with disabilities and their families, she could feel more assured in planning for his future.

WHAT IS NEEDED

There are several principles and practices that would ensure families receive more comprehensive and coordinated respite. First, a range of options must be available; not every child or every family needs the same type of caregiver relief. Some social policy experts refer to a "menu" of supports from which each client would create a "unique plate" of preferences according to her/his particular needs.[80] Everything from housekeeping, peer support, food preparation, outdoor home maintenance to time to allow the unpaid caregiver to buy groceries, seek and/or maintain paid employment, study or train for paid work, dance the tango or take a kick-boxing class, volunteer somewhere — all of these interventions, and many more, would help families balance their overall well-being.

Second, the family needs to be fully involved in determining its needs and desired outcomes. Earlier in the book, I refer to this as the need for resourced services, meaning that the assistance is funded adequately to provide concrete, practical supports. While there is little doubt that talk therapy with a personal counsellor or support group is useful, this is not my focus here. It is the structure of the situation and continuous demands that mean no one person can do it all.

As suggested above, a list of options needs to be available. Optimally, the family, in cooperation with a professional who is familiar with their child, determines what options are most appropriate. In some instances the child/young person must also be involved. Ideally, the parties adopt a partnership approach. The family is the key player; the professional advises and advocates on their behalf. Further, a shared recognition that the child and family's needs may change over time is important. Flexibility, accountability and continuity of care are required.[81]

Respite services ought to be portable between communities and provinces. A full-fledged system of respite would provide for unexpected needs, similarly to a home daycare setting where a parent can drop off his child when, for example, the regular childcare centre cannot accommodate his daughter if her chickenpox is still contagious.

Out-of-home respite, in particular, needs to be part of the roster of services available in the community. An integrated childcare setting for a pre-schooler with disabilities may work for some families. Other families (or communities) might find a setting, such as the developmental delay unit that Johnny attends in St. John's, Newfoundland, more appropriate.

Moreover, out-of-home respite must be made available to children with multiple disabilities and/or those who are technologically dependent or medically fragile. A delightful child like Ollie, for example, requires 24-hour supervision. Assistance is costly and it is doubtful that most Canadian families would have the means to purchase an adequate level of care in the home. No family should be refused a respite opportunity because their child's needs are too complex or the eligibility criteria prohibitive. If, for example, in hospital a nurse is required to delve into a person's throat to change a trach tube, a nurse (certainly a person with the proper training and credentials) should be handling this responsibility in the home. It is unacceptable for parents or paid caregivers without qualifications to be assigned these complex tasks. Once an adequate listing of services available is developed, they must not be unreasonably withheld. As Romanow documented, affordability must not constitute a barrier.

These programs or facilities should be funded from the public purse. Respite services are not frills. This is not about tummy tucks. It is about offering supports that allow a family to define itself in the best way it can. Parents are to be encouraged to make informed choices between resourced options. Not only do individual families benefit, but providing human services also builds community capacity. Jobs are created and opportunities for sustainable growth increased since such programs must procure a myriad of goods such as equipment, linens and food.

Moreover, given that the numbers of severely disabled children is on the rise as technological advances keep a greater proportion of particularly vulnerable infants from dying soon after birth, it is highly unlikely that the demand for respite will wane. In addition, as the population ages, a larger proportion of families will require assistance for their young adult children with special needs.

Dispensing adequate caregiver relief to assist families is a worthy objective. But romanticizing any private family grouping would be unwise. It must be recognized that children and adults with disabilities are not always safe in their families. Not only must policy and practice recognize this, checks and balances are required to ensure that abuse of any kind does not occur. When it does, as for any child or elderly individual, immediate steps must be taken to protect the vulnerable person from further harm.

DIVERSE POPULATIONS

Needs for assistance in rural areas may manifest differently than in urban settings. For Jeremy, in Toronto, learning to navigate public transit safely is a huge part of his path toward independence. A young person in a rural area will require different skill sets. Nonetheless, in each situation, creative solutions that bring people together for the purpose of respite must be found, perhaps along the same lines that schooling is organized and funded. Why should the arena of special needs children's services be considered any less central to society's well-being than mainstream services?

Supports must be available in the language of the persons receiving them. At minimum, language interpreters must be provided at the point of intake. As noted earlier, knocking on an agency's door for help always involves a hierarchical relationship — especially if you are poor, a lesbian or person of colour. One's sense of entitlement is always in play. Services in one's own language help to empower the family to make its needs known. As suggested in at least one of the interviews, language can be a powerful barrier to achieving best practices. It can also contribute to an uneven playing field for immigrants or new Canadians by complicating a family's access to the (often elusive) point of entry.

Fighting for Respite: Alliances and Possibilities

The improvements outlined above require political will to become reality. Until enough noise is made by parents and the workers who support them, governments will not be held accountable for their lackadaisical approach to funding the broad range of services people with disabilities require. By coming together to challenge governments' lack of action, we can put civic authorities at all levels on notice that they must come to the table ready to deal. First, we must look at the structure of current parent/support worker relationships and their differing perspectives as this shapes our ability to come together.

Workers providing respite care also need to be included. Ongoing training opportunities, reporting to a central staff location for in-service programs, decent wages and working conditions including health and safety and workers' compensation protection are vital to the mix. Employers should not be permitted to take advantage of home support workers by unilaterally reducing their hours to part-time or split shifts. Optimally, these workers would organize themselves into an association or union that is able to negotiate on their behalf.

I believe it is completely understandable and valid for disabled individuals and their families to want to select their own support persons. To deal with this desire for autonomy, one that stems primarily from the historic wrongs that have been done to people with disabilities, several provinces are adopting a model known as *individualized funding*. This is similar to a voucher system — the person or family receives a funding envelope and then proceeds to purchase help as they see fit. In most instances, wages are set at whatever level the market will bear. Unfortunately, this model triggers several difficulties at both a micro and macro level.

Families who take on the role of employer are subject to administrative controls such as tax reporting and bookkeeping. They do not automatically possess the skill sets necessary to carry out these tasks. Moreover, knowledge of — and a commitment to — fair employment practices is not a prerequisite for receiving public dollars. I believe this funding model creates and deepens potential conflicts between clients and workers while providing precious few tools to resolve them.

Persons with disabilities need to exercise greater control, but not to succumb to supporting unsavoury employment practices. In the absence of definite controls and protections on both sides, this approach is very dangerous. At minimum, neither worker nor client is protected from mistreatment. In broader societal terms, this funding model encourages further privatization of care rather than a collective response to ensuring both persons with disabilities and the people who work to support them are treated justly.

The challenge is to arrive at fair and respectful practices for each of two distinct sets of interests. These workers recognize that the care they provide is personal and often intimate; persons with disabilities do not want to be unduly touched or managed by strangers or control freaks. Since the parties to such an employment relationship are complex human beings and not automatons, any gig is bound to blow up in certain circumstances. Is there any way to defuse a bad situation before it blasts?

I submit that one essential element to assist in this highly combustible relationship is to develop a dispute resolution mechanism for clients and workers. It would require expedited access to mediation, under the auspices of a (lean) public tribunal designed for this purpose. Mediating a solution between the parties would be the objective; only persons with proven mediation skills would be granted such responsibility. Where a mediated settlement is not possible, that employer-employee relationship would be brought to a close. An association or union that negotiates workers' overarching terms and conditions of employment (including wages and benefits) would maintain a roster of qualified, trained support workers. The aim would be to institute a measure of fairness on both sides, as well as to minimize interruptions in care or employment.

I anticipate no lack of detractors to this proposal. Some will call this approach naive. "Unions protect their members no matter what ... What about clients' rights to achieve their self-defined interests?" they might respond. I can already hear the voices, dripping with cynicism, "How can people with disabilities, so steeped in individual rights-based ideology, possibly see the value of a collective bargaining approach?"

The answer, I would argue, is twofold. Labour legislation that does not hamper part-time, contingent workers in the informal sector from organizing would be one precondition. The counterbalance would be strong, enforceable disability rights legislation to advance and protect individual rights. (At a more immediate level, the players need to look beyond the most obvious sources of conflict to see what accommodations can be made on either side.)

An innovative project would be to join forces and insist upon higher standards of care. There is an opportunity both for people who work in the system and those who are recipients of services to come together. Recipients are not without power. By trying to work in concert, model standards of care can be defined. Workers and consumer organizations need to insist these are negotiated with funding bodies. Backing off the rhetoric (on both sides) would be a good point of departure. It only fuels governments' propensity to play one set of citizens off against another.

Each side has expertise and a part of the story; neither has enough clout on its own to force governments to deal. Why not negotiate standards of care — through the related pillars of workload, working conditions and wages? Boost wages to the levels earned in unionized facilities. As noted previously, the value of this human service work goes well beyond what any funding body is willing to shell out. As the campaign in this country during the last twenty-five years to increase childcare workers' wages tries to show, there is an alternative to low pay. Make no mistake — when parents accept that paying low wages to caregivers is okay, they are complicit in underestimating our children's worth and our own.

Alliances between staff and clients around very specific objectives can be developed. Community organizing means taking small steps, one project at a time. Working with not-for-profit agencies to lobby all levels of governments against the rising tide of privatization is a laudable goal. A community organizing model would include citizen action groups speaking to municipal councils, school boards and children's services community boards. It can also involve unions negotiating standards of care by developing central wage grids, equitable methods to evaluate performance and staffing levels appropriate to sustain a high quality service.

In a climate of scarcity, when we are constantly told that the list of options is ever-so-limited and encouraged to believe that working for change is futile, it is even more vital that staff and families make every effort to embrace partnership. Blowing the whistle on inadequate or unsafe procedures is something workers can be counted on to do when they have a measure of employment protection, but not otherwise.

We know our children benefit from regular routines in which they are cared for competently with respect and love. Enhancing our children's lives involves improving continuity of care by maintaining a consistent caregiver cohort and insisting upon safe working conditions and fair wages — that is, a system funded by the public sector in which these needed programs and services are obtainable and sustained; a system that offers respect and dignity to both the client/consumer and the paid care provider.

There is a simple lesson to be captured here: It is the people with specialized skills who are most successful in their work with our children and who encourage them to become as independent as they can be. That work ethic — also known as devotion — persists because the worker can imagine the child making leaps forward. It is having that positive vision and sharing it between support workers and families that makes it possible to fight for change in local communities, one project at a time, building trust as we go.

Today, we are witnessing a society in flux — a dynamic situation that can be influenced by deliberate social and political action. Debates about health and childcare sit squarely on the public agenda. These debates are not going away. So it's a question of what vision will carry the day. A political space is rapidly emerging where barriers and misunderstandings between families, the disability movement, unions and childcare advocates could be broken down.

Genuine differences of opinion exist. Significant power differentials are also present. Making change means moving beyond past disagreements and gracefully throwing rhetoric out the window. The political space that we need to grab is already drenched with accusations, laments, territorial battles and outright untruths — usually conveyed by the controllers of the purse strings or those who stand most to gain financially from new initiatives. Not one stakeholder is without some culpability; nor can any one group claim to have all the answers.

Why not start with families' dire need for respite? Policy specialists' notion of developing a much broader network of support by implementing far-reaching networks of services makes enormous sense. Until these families have a voice, however, and a powerful set of allies, not a lot will change. We must be strategic. Change is achieved in measured increments. If improved access to appropriate and high-quality respite care were to become a rallying cry for families with disabled children, hope could emerge triumphant and parents' energy would be freed up to wage the rest of the battle.

We can choose to seize this opportunity. Citizen engagement is an admirable, even lofty, goal, one that entails skilled husbandry. It is built from the ground up, based on the genuine hardships people face. Adopting respite care as a central focus would be a means toward achieving best practices for the children, their families and the people that work to support them. It would lay much of the groundwork needed to face the remaining challenges. Besides, joining forces is one hefty counterpoint to isolation. And these children and their families, perched on the margins of society, have the potential to move into the political arena, shake things up and make their voices heard.

II

PORTRAITS

The Power of Narrative

A PERSONAL NARRATIVE, OR STORY, provides us with a window on how someone lives. The person we encounter in such a narrative may move outside our daily sphere of concerns. Getting to know an individual whose life is different from our own leads us to a more complete understanding not only of that person's challenges and dreams but of the world around us — the society we live in. My hope is that in sharing these stories, certain stereotypes about parenting children with a range of disabilities will be laid bare. Shattering myths and uncovering greater truths with respect to how these families conduct their daily lives is a first step in attempting to foster change.

In this section, I draw upon personal narratives in order to paint a series of portraits. The interviews revealed certain details of daily routines as well as the individuals' understanding of how their lives unfold. The young people in these families live with a variety of disabilities. I spoke with parents at some length and gently probed about past events, current situations and, occasionally, intimate moments.

Each interview captures a particular moment in time. The "painting" I have made from the colours, light and shading they provided me reflects a truth of their own lives, as recounted on a particular afternoon or evening. I believe it is important to recall that these conversations took place outside of each interviewee's daily routine, allowing a number of reflections and perspectives to emerge.

In most of these portraits my interlocutor is female. The conversation is relatively relaxed. We take time to pause, to recall incidents that stand out, to change topics midstream and return to stories that beg to be told. We may look together at photos or a child's drawing. Occasionally, there are tears. During most of the interviews we also kibitz a certain amount. But the *moment* of the interview is just that — the speaker's recollections, at that particular point in time, about her life. The moment is valuable to me precisely because it is both her understanding of what took place and how she reassembles it. From an ocean of memories — often discrete as Post-it notes lined up on corkboard — the material I pursue exists in how she has organized her sense of the past and present, that perception giving a frame to how she continues to make her way in the world.

In these portraits it is the parents' voices, their reflections and truths we discover. The power of storytelling is that it helps us to make sense of our own experience. We witness others sharing their stories and may discover a wellspring of empathy that leads to greater bonds. Some writers suggest that the sharing of personal narratives has an inherently moral-transformative nature. It is in that sharing, it is argued, that we create the potential to transform our world.

To begin, imagine a series of snapshots. The first depicts two women sitting down with mugs of hot, foaming coffee. We see them take off their winter coats in a lively café. In this first photo, details of the surroundings share the spotlight equally with the individuals' outlines. This first contact appears warm, but tentative. It seems anticipation is sizzling just below the surface.

The researcher is asking her subject to dredge deep into memory, to share the joys and challenges of her experience as a parent. In the next snapshot, the lens is focused on the two people leaning in, engaged and listening to one another more intently. They are apparently unaware of their surroundings. For the person being interviewed, some memories are vivid, crystal clear. Others are less so. She tries her best to recall and describe incidents accurately, telling about her feelings at the time and now, in retrospect.

In the next snapshot, the two women are laughing, sharing a story that resonates with both of them, such lightheartedness made easier because the researcher is also mother of a child with a profound disability. In the final photo, the women are disengaging from the conversation, lipstick is applied, a parka snuggled into before they each venture out into the night. The look on their faces is calm now, more serene than in the first photograph.

Two relative strangers or casual acquaintances have shared a great deal, in the comfort of knowing they walk similar life paths. In their time together, the woman interviewed has spoken her truth as she understands it.

In response to the researcher's gentle prodding, she has revisited her memories and put them in order. Intimate stories, hopes and fears — rarely spoken aloud — have now been named. They dangle in space between the two women. It is in this exchange, this series of snapshots, that a portrait of the person's life as a parent emerges.

I must acknowledge an important distinction between the perspectives of the interviewee and myself. The joys and difficulties she faces in raising her children do not end with our conversation. There is no pretty bow to tie on the package. She goes back to her home and continues to provide care to her family in the best way she knows. Our time together is but a brief departure from an ordinary day; our contact an opportunity to look beyond the daily rush of activity and scratch beneath the surface of her experience. Like the subject in a portrait, she has her own point of view. It is distinct, perhaps not the same as the painter's. I hope my rendering of our conversation is as accurate as the precise shading she has so generously given me.

MARY ELLEN WITH KATIE, AGE 6, AND JEREMY, AGE 3,
IN THE GARDEN AT HOME IN TORONTO, ONTARIO

CHAPTER SEVEN

Mary Ellen and Jeremy

Mary Ellen Jones is the mother of a blond-haired, sixteen-year-old young man named Jeremy. He was born with Down Syndrome. Mary Ellen and I spoke in April 2003. Her youthful appearance belies her years and depth of experience as an early childhood educator. She came to Toronto from Midland, Ontario, at age eighteen to attend York University. In addition to Jeremy, she has a daughter, Katie, who is nineteen years old. At the time of our interview, Mary Ellen is supporting the entire family, including her husband and her daughter's boyfriend. Mary Ellen makes ends meet on a childcare worker's salary.[82]

"Jeremy can be a really pleasant, social person. He relates well to other people, and I think he likes himself. Sometimes I think he likes himself more than his sister Katie likes herself," says Mary Ellen. "He likes himself because we love him."

Jeremy is truly becoming a teenager. He has told his mother that he'd like to have a girlfriend. Friday nights he frequents a social group for teens with developmental delays where facilitators organize discussions and dances. Some of the young people have begun to pair off. Jeremy likes that idea.

As she speaks, it becomes clear to me that the series of challenges Mary Ellen faces in raising her son are both the same and quite different from those encountered by many parents.

We first met at the school my daughter attends. I would see Mary Ellen bring Jeremy to the daycare when he was quite young. My daughter, Emma, participated in the same program. Although each of us was always on the run, we developed one of those urban "Hello, how are you?" acquaintanceships around our children that I've come to like. I told her about my son Jake at some point; she filled me in about her daughter's escapades at high school. All of this while we zipped our kids in and out of winter coats and sent them on their way.

Often when I arrived at the daycare to pick up my then kindergarten-aged daughter, I would wait (and wait ...) while she refused to disentangle herself from the activity she happened to be immersed in. She would greet me and then keep playing with her friends, so I sometimes went over to say hello to Jeremy. He was often playing with a toy on his own, off to one side of the other kids' action. I'd ask him about his day, and when Emma was ready, we'd all wave our goodbyes.

Some years later, as Emma had graduated into the "big kids" after-school program, Mary Ellen became assistant supervisor at our daycare. Surrounded by energetic school-age children completing art projects she had cooked up for them, she remained neatly turned out and cheerful. She always filled me in on Emma's adventures and, on occasion, we spoke a bit about our lives. I would ask about Jeremy since by then he had moved on to another school and after-school program. When I asked if she would allow me to interview her for this book, Mary Ellen was reticent.

Eventually, we agree to meet at the café across from the school and day-care. It is a damp evening. The sidewalk is adrift with baby strollers sporting colourful umbrellas, dogs tugging on leashes, their owners taking in the moist spring air. Once inside, I am immediately struck by Mary Ellen's ability to focus. Coffee is grinding in industrial proportions to our left and noisy preteens at the table across from us have discovered the pleasure of carousing in public, but Mary Ellen is poised to tell me her story.

Jeremy's Birth

Learning that their son had Down Syndrome wasn't easy for Mary Ellen or her husband. When Jeremy was born, they knew immediately. He had the characteristic facial features of a baby with Down Syndrome.[83] "All our prenatal expectations fell away in the first hour," she said.

Down Syndrome is the most common cause of human birth "defects" and occurs in 1 out of every 660 births. The vast majority of newborns diagnosed with Down Syndrome have an extra copy of the 21st chromosome.[84] Medical texts suggest that Down "usually, although not always, results in 'mental retardation and other conditions.'"[85]

Mary Ellen speaks with admiration of the physician who delivered her baby. He urged her and her husband to accept that Jeremy "was still a complete person in his disability." She found meaning in those words, discovering some solace and light in the moment. She believes that this is what her doctor was trying to impart. She is less certain that this notion was as helpful to her husband.

Mary Ellen explains that because Down is a relatively known disability, they left the hospital already linked with certain community services. They knew, for example, that a publicly funded infant stimulation worker would visit their home very soon after they were discharged. It was 1987.

Talking with her husband about Jeremy, something all the professionals around them were encouraging keenly, was not very effective, Mary Ellen told me. At a certain point, "... all the pushing to communicate became more annoying than helpful."

"He and I talked about it in different ways. I would be talking about my fears and my worries and he just wanted to talk about practicalities."

"Actually, he wanted everything to be 'business as usual,' but the fact was that while there were things about Jeremy that *were* business as usual, there were things that were exceptional too."

LIFE WITH JEREMY

"At sixteen, Jeremy is an active boy with good manners — when he chooses," says Mary Ellen. Jeremy attends high school during the day and participates in several after-school and evening activities at Variety Village Sports Training and Fitness Centre, a community resource for special needs children. The centre offers a wide range of programming, including aquatics. Jeremy practises with a swim team there during the week. On Friday nights he attends a teen social evening, which is offered by Neighbourhood Link, a local social service agency. Mary Ellen is pleased that her son is able to take advantage of these programs.

"It is important for him to belong," she says. "The more places he feels like he belongs, the more confident he's going to be." She describes Jeremy as a boy who is inquisitive, but shy. He loves to play games and to go to movies, as long as they're not too raucous; he is terrified of loud noises. He has an amazing memory for people's names and certain details. "He'll remember a child's bedroom (and the toys) we visited years ago, but not a simple math equation he did minutes before," she says.

She has always tried to accept him for who he is. "He is Jeremy and every cell in his body is affected by Down Syndrome. I don't think I've ever done that 'what would he be like if he didn't have Down Syndrome?' because this is who he is ... and I think that's helped me be really positive about it."

Jeremy still loves to play, she tells me. "He has that great love for dressing up ... like when he was little at the daycare and he used to wear a cape ... or a funny hat ... It's something he still truly enjoys. Now they have drama groups in the city for kids who are developmentally delayed. I might check it out."

SERVICES AND EDUCATION

Mary Ellen's approach, she says, was to learn as much as she could about Down Syndrome. As an early childhood educator, at that time running a family daycare from her home that included then three-year-old Katie, she was very familiar with the milestones children usually reach. She felt the more she could learn about Jeremy's situation, the more help she could offer him.

Every two weeks, an infant stimulation worker would come into the house to work with Jeremy. Mary Ellen comments that only now, in retrospect, does she realize that helping him with body positioning, trying to speed up his development, could not change the overall outcome.

Jeremy has always found speech challenging, and he received some speech therapy through the school system which did help. Unfortunately, as he became older, the number of hours allotted diminished. From Grade 9 on, speech therapy was cancelled entirely. Mary Ellen is quite troubled by this service gap, and she says private speech therapy was "out of the question" for financial reasons.

Consequently, certain speech issues plague Jeremy to this day. He can be difficult to understand because of these issues. For example, Jeremy cannot pronounce certain consonants. Not everyone has the patience to ask Jeremy to repeat himself, and this affects his communication with the world. As Mary Ellen explains, "It's hard because you want everybody to like your child ... and you can't make people like your child, nor can you make your child behave so that people will be more inclined to like them."

The fact that further speech therapy could help Jeremy overcome his communication challenges but is unaffordable is a source of great frustration to Mary Ellen. I can see how irritating she finds this shortfall in services. It is fundamentally unjust. Especially since the long-term impact on her son's ability to communicate and therefore his independence will be affected profoundly.

Jeremy's big challenge as his mother and I speak is to learn to navigate on the public transit system. Specifically, he needs to travel to and from school safely by himself on the bus. He will begin a supervised a process in which each task involved is broken down — getting to the bus stop, paying his fare, ringing the bell and getting off. An educational assistant will work with Jeremy to understand each task, and then accompany him. Next, Jeremy will ride on public transit, shadowed by the educational assistant. Then he will travel by himself. Mary Ellen is both excited and nervous for her son, as one would expect.

During our conversation, Mary Ellen questions herself, reflecting upon how successful she's been at urging Jeremy to become independent. She tells me that at one time he showed an interest in running errands to the IGA grocery near their home. Of late, he is less motivated to do so.

"Maybe I didn't do enough to encourage him," she says, "and now he expects me to take care of it." She describes this as her laziness, suggesting that Jeremy could be doing more everyday jobs in the nearby community. I suspect she's judging herself too harshly. Of course there is always more any one of us could do in raising our children. One fewer pizza dinner, one fewer television show per night and so on.

I refuse to judge any action Mary Ellen may consider less than ideal. She is a mother who has had to construct a safe learning environment out of every single interaction and step her son has taken. After I pose a few questions in this light, she does allow that Jeremy is probably at about an average stage of independence for someone with his level of developmental delay.

"All along," she says, "it helped that as an early childhood educator I knew what was considered normal childhood development. But more important, in dealing with agencies and professionals, I was able to 'talk the talk.'"

FAMILY RELATIONSHIPS

At the time of my interview with their mother, Jeremy's sister Katie is unemployed and living with her boyfriend at the family home.

Mary Ellen describes the relationship between her two young people.

"Katie loves Jeremy a lot but is frustrated by what she sees as the inequality in the household. She's always getting nagged at to do things, and he gets away with murder."

"I talk the talk, but I don't walk it, according to Katie. Why isn't he doing dishes? Why is he not doing his own laundry? He's capable of doing these things and does them at school; why isn't he doing them at home?"

"And now, because she is unemployed, she says it's not fair that I'm always spending money on him. He's going to programs that I'm paying for. It's hard for me to tell her: 'He can't just go out, he can't just hang out in the neighbourhood, and it has to be structured and probably always will have to be.'"

COMMUNITY

Even for an extremely devoted mother like Mary Ellen, the sheer weight of the demands on her can be overwhelming. I asked how she handles these pressures. She had two answers. One, she says, she learned from her grandmother who died some time ago. "As long as you're here, you do it," she says. "I just hope I can keep going."

Her second answer has to do with finding a renewed sense of purpose through her faith. Mary Ellen's mother was a French-Canadian raised as a Catholic, and her father was a Methodist. In Midland, where she was raised, they attended the United Church. In recent years becoming involved in the United Church has become an important part of her life. She participates in an English handbell choir and says with her typical wit:

"It's mine, and I've only got one life. If I want to be an English handbell ringer, then why not?"

She bakes cookies for the church's Out of the Cold program in aid of homeless people and volunteers her time and energy in the community. She finds that these activities help bring balance to her life.

Mary Ellen explains that she has always made sure to have something of her own — whether it was guitar lessons or night courses in daycare management. I understand her need to hold onto her sense of self as an independent person, especially when working outside the home and also balancing a complicated family situation. It sounds like a marvellous strategy for anyone's life. She adds that she has also "... always sought out a therapist when I felt like I just couldn't cope anymore, just to try and put things into perspective."

ADVOCACY

"You know," says Mary Ellen with the hint of a smile, "After sixteen years, I know how to fill out forms in the way that is most likely to get you what you want."

I had asked what advice she might give parents trying to access services for their children with disabilities. She says she thinks about how she wants Jeremy to be perceived by the funding body ... does he need to be portrayed as more or less capable, according to the particular program's criteria?

Since children with Down Syndrome are generally not as needy as some children, says Mary Ellen, she has sometimes felt guilty. "The money might go better to another family — overall, the amount is always so limited." I am struck both by this woman's thoughtful determination to advocate for her son and her generous awareness of others. "Since Jeremy was small," says Mary Ellen, "I've wondered how immigrants, whose first language isn't English, navigate the system. Centennial Infant and Child Centre staff will go with people and help them to fill out forms, but if they're not even connected to that, what do they do? How do they deal with the Toronto District School Board, Community and Social Services, doctors and hospitals? How do they know when they're getting enough information to make good decisions?"

Mary Ellen gives some very sound advice to anyone needing to learn to advocate for his or her child. She says to find a really good mentor. She means someone you can watch in action. Listen to how they deal with their own concerns (shadow their meetings with various officials, if possible) and then take the traits you admire and try to incorporate them into your own way of dealing with issues.

"I've pulled ideas from all kinds of people along the way. You have to know what your energy level is. When to fight a big fight — and when you cannot. Some people are so aggressive. Emulate or run from them. Not that one is the same all the time. You have to trust your gut instinct."

I am beginning to understand more plainly that Mary Ellen has consciously developed different approaches to attain the best care she can for Jeremy. Not unlike her initial response to my request for an interview, she has learned to gauge her own energy level and, after having done so, budget her time accordingly. This seems to me an extremely practical accomplishment for any person and crucial for individuals who advocate for others as a way of life.

"Having Jeremy has meant I've met so many incredible people — compassionate, bright people have come into my life only because I gave birth to him. I never would have met any of those people without him ... And, I suppose, if I hadn't gone seeking them out too."

Mary Ellen tells me about a topic that has proven quite sticky between her, some other parents and the Down Syndrome Association. The Association takes a very pro-integration position. In her experience Mary Ellen has learned that there are high-functioning children and high-functioning parents ... "But what about us regular parents who fought what we thought was the good fight and then we've [decided to take] our children to a segregated setting? We feel like we've let people down. We're trying to figure out who we let down. Did we let our child down? Ourselves? Other parents? Did we let the Association down?" Her view today is multi-layered, reflecting her experience: a landscape painted in brilliant hues, intertwining colours of joy and determination and yes, the occasional battle scar in partial view.

"This has to be about personal choices," she affirms. "Like for any parent ... the question is when do you decide to push? Swimming lessons or school choices? You know your child best."

Planning for Jeremy's Future

Mary Ellen was very clear that she does not want her other child to have responsibility for Jeremy later in life. But she has not yet spoken about this with her daughter. "I don't like going too much into the future with her because I don't want her to feel like somewhere down the road she's going to end up being responsible for him. We don't talk about that too much although I'm sure we both think it. And she's probably quite afraid of being totally responsible for him."

Mary Ellen has not yet prepared a will or established a future guardian for Jeremy. She is thinking about who might fill this role, but feels it would be a great deal of responsibility to pass on. She thinks it would be too much to burden someone else with. As we speak, she quickly runs through the options; it's too much to ask of a friend, there's her sister in California, but they would have to investigate cross-border legal issues. She doesn't think her husband's siblings would be up to the challenge. "It's touchy because it's not just facing my own mortality," she says. "It's determining my son's future. It's more than just letting it happen, because it is more complex.

"Whoever ends up with that responsibility will have a lot of really tricky decisions to make," she says. The financial part of it is complicated because once he starts having some income (as Mary Ellen hopes he will as an adult) it affects his disability pension. And any kind of inheritance impacts upon it too.

"I've learned how fragile and miraculous life is ... having a special needs child causes you to look at your own life and values differently. It is also accepting his limitations ... there are things that are easy to face and those that only come to you in the dark hours of the night when you're awake. But I'll get to it, I'm kind of plodding along, and I'll sit down with a lawyer soon."

I find Mary Ellen's calm during this part of our conversation quite remarkable. These are huge issues. She doesn't minimize her concerns but she knows that one way or another, she will ensure that Jeremy gets the special care that he will need for the rest of his life.

When I asked Mary Ellen what dreams she has for her son, she replied without hesitation. "They're way out of line still, and I'm just going to leave them there for now. I see him living in some kind of partially supervised housing, going out everyday to do something, having those routines. My dreams are getting knocked around now," she adds, "as we see so many social service cuts."

"It might take him until he's twenty-eight or thirty to live independently, and there's an awful lot of work that has got to go into developing him between now and then. And we have to find money somewhere because all of this costs big time. That was the other rude awakening. Once he finishes high school, if he's not working — I think it helps if you have a nice family business that you can just slide your kid into which isn't the case — then almost everything he's going to do has to be paid for in some way."

Mary Ellen explains that parents try to piece together a week of activities for their young adult children. The week might have a volunteer component and participation in a day program at different venues. But it is very difficult because there tend to be wait lists at most agencies and the costs are prohibitive, although some government funding is available.

"Cuts made to social services quite a while back have not been made up for in any way. Now there is a rising up of private sector day programs, at thirty-five to forty dollars per day, that one can apply for through the province's social service ministry," she explains. "This is a considerable expense.

"When I see Jeremy's future, I see that the brunt of the responsibility is going to be mine, just because it has been all along. I've been the organizer, the go-getter, the one who thinks ahead." Mary Ellen reaffirms her point that if one has financial resources, it is possible to purchase more services, to have more respite and, perhaps, less worry about long-term care options.

We're coming to the end of our conversation and her unwavering love for her son shines through brightly. "Jeremy truly likes himself, and we like and love him," she says again. As we move past shelves fragrant with coffee beans and luscious desserts, we can see that the drizzle outside has turned to rain. The sidewalks are empty, even the rowdy teens now tucked into their dry homes. As I get my keys out, ready to race between raindrops to my car parked across the street, we stop for a hug. In that moment, I am transported by Mary Ellen's buoyant optimism. She will do everything humanly possible to ensure that Jeremy's future does indeed include the brightness he deserves.

*

About six months later, I am stopping by the school to drop something off to my daughter's classroom. Just before I open the heavy doors and climb up to the third floor, I see Mary Ellen waving to me from outside the toddlers' room down the hall.

"Wait," she says in almost a stage whisper. "I have a codicil."

I'm sure I look quite puzzled.

"A 'codicil' — isn't that the word?"

I finally twig that she has something important to tell me as she swings up beside me and says very quietly,

"Nobody but Jane [the daycare supervisor] knows, but I've filed for divorce."

Giving her a hug, I say, "I kind of felt you might be working up to it. How are you doing?"

"Well, it's hard right now because we're still in the house and, of course, he's hoping I'll change my mind," she says. "But I'm sure. This weekend I'm taking Jeremy out to my parents' so we can relax and get away from all the stress."

It was Thanksgiving. Mary Ellen looked tired but very relieved.

"Hey", she says. "Now you can help me make my way through the tunnel you've come out of!"

I smile, and we hug again, promising to get together soon. Watching her gather like goslings a few toddlers who are straying out the door of their playroom, I am struck again by how the links of sisterhood are forged in so many ways; and how often it is by sharing the love we carry for our children.

SHANNON ADDRESSES A FIRST NATIONS MEETING ON
DISABILITY RIGHTS IN WINNIPEG, MANITOBA

CHAPTER EIGHT

SHARON AND SHANNON

THE BEST THING ABOUT DONUT SHOPS is that they feel familiar no matter where you happen to be. On this particular December 2003 afternoon in Winnipeg, Manitoba, I plunked myself down in a corner booth, hoping its dividers might dull the clunking of boots on unforgiving linoleum. Crullers and coffee were making fleet trade on this cold, bright day. Watching customers coming in, stomping the snow off their boots and flicking their toques clean, I waited for Sharon Daniels, a woman whose daughter has cerebral palsy.[86] Today would be our first meeting.

Finding a mother with a disabled child in a First Nations community in or near to Winnipeg had seemed a daunting prospect at the outset. I made some inquiries through union officials who represented social service workers, some of whom were Aboriginal, to little result. Then I realized, even if I located such a mother, she might not agree to meet with me.

To my great delight, when I contacted the First Nation Disabilities Association of Manitoba in Winnipeg, I received a warm welcome and interest in the project. With not a hint of hesitation, the program coordinator promised she would find an appropriate mother for me to meet. It took us about a week to make the necessary contacts and then I was able to speak with Sharon. She and I spent some time on the telephone feeling one another out, and it seemed that she was interested in telling her story. We agreed to meet a few weeks later, when I would travel to Winnipeg.

Not long after I had arrived at Robin's Donuts, a woman came in and stomped her feet vigorously to warm up. She slowly removed her coat, first unwrapping the thick woollen scarf from her hood. Only then could I see her long black hair pulled back out of her face, which she'd told me to watch for to recognize her. She had walked the twenty blocks from her home to the donut shop in weather cold enough to bite your fingertips — minus eighteen degrees Celsius.

What struck me most in those first few minutes was the commanding grace with which Sharon carried herself. Upright, with a sturdy build, she kept what at first seemed a cautious distance as we began speaking. Fortunately we were able to dispense with safe talk about the bristling cold weather fairly quickly. She asked me about the project I was interviewing her for and whether I would be speaking with any other First Nations mothers. I said no but that I was meeting with a cross-section of parents in different parts of the country.

I told her a little bit about my kids and that I too was raising a child with a life-threatening disability. I showed her a photo of Jake I carry in my wallet, and in a short time we engaged in comfortable, relaxed conversation. I suspect that our common experience as mothers of vulnerable children allowed us to move a step away from the dreaded sociologist-at-work dynamic I desperately wanted to avoid. This struck me as especially vital in this interview; I was concerned that our cultural differences might keep us from entering personal topics with the level of intimacy I desired. As we continued talking, drinking coffee together, much of my initial trepidation waned and, more importantly, what I had perceived as her reserved demeanour melted away. During the couple of hours we spent together Sharon became quite animated at times. She had a delicious sense of humour. We laughed a lot during our exchange, kibitzing in a way that allowed us greater camaraderie.

I wondered, given the challenges she and her family faced daily, where laughter figured in her survival kit. To be frank, the humour felt very familiar — gently self-deprecating on the surface, a frame of steel below. Most of all, her sense of humour became a bridge to some difficult subjects and, with her incisive wit, we were able to broach deeper concerns.

Sharon is trained as a social worker. She has worked in different agencies and has experience as a residential youth care worker. She first met her husband the summer she turned fourteen, she tells me. "My friend and I went from school to a track and field meet, and I saw him there. I told my friend I was going to marry him. She said, 'No you can't. He's older than you'. Clarence was in a residential school in Portage at that time. I didn't meet up with him again until I was sixteen ... closer to seventeen." During their thirty-two years of marriage, they have raised three young people: Shannon, age thirty; Sherri, age twenty-eight, and Shawn age twenty-one.

Sharon and Clarence are Ojibwa and have lived in Winnipeg for the last many years, a choice Sharon describes as bittersweet for them as a family. While the older children are quite conscious of their First Nations heritage, the youngest has not had the opportunity to live among his people. "I feel like he has missed out a lot," says Sharon.

Shannon's Birth

Shannon was born in May, 1973. Sharon was nineteen at the time of her daughter's birth. "I knew the first day that something was wrong because of her inability to take food in ... The nurses told me they were having a hard time giving her the bottle, and she didn't have that sucking motion — the reflex — the muscles around her mouth needed for swallowing."[87] Sharon stayed in hospital the four or five days then standard for new moms, but she had to leave Shannon a little longer because the infant still needed intensive hospital care. After a few harrowing days, they were referred to the Children's Hospital. "I felt anxious and kept wondering 'what's going on, what's happening?' Shannon couldn't cry. There was no sound from her. The doctors used to prick the bottom of her feet to see what reaction there was." Sharon had many more questions than answers in those early days.

"I was worried right away," she says. "But there was nothing unusual during the pregnancy. I didn't drink; I probably smoked a little. I followed a nutrition plan. I had lived in the city while I was carrying Shannon ..." Sharon explains she didn't lack health information or resources — milk, food, shelter and so on — during her pregnancy. The days following Shannon's birth were a scary time for the young mother and father.

Life with Shannon

Shannon required a great deal of special care from her mom and dad during her early days. The baby was often ill with bronchitis or pneumonia and Sharon found she was frequently spending time in hospital with her tiny daughter. Sharon's worries increased as she realized that Shannon was falling far behind other children. She was not reaching the expected developmental milestones, a source of concern both to her parents and professionals.

Sharon never felt she was getting a genuine picture of the parameters of her daughter's condition. Sometimes, nurses would give her bits of information, but these barely quaffed Sharon's thirst for knowledge. She was aware that doctors don't always know exactly what a child's health challenges will be, especially when they are newborns or toddlers. Often it takes time and the child's own growth to give the necessary diagnostic clues. Still, Sharon's frustration and feelings of stress escalated. She told me it was the powerlessness one feels in such a waiting game that was really vexing.

Shannon had trouble chewing, swallowing and digesting food. She did not have the muscle tone to handle these functions. For many years, she was diagnosed with a variety of eating disorders and, at times, hospitalized to follow intensive treatment. "Her body was literally starving. Since she couldn't get anything into her stomach, the nutrients her body required couldn't get into her system," says Sharon.

Then in January 2000, at age twenty-seven, Shannon's electrolyte balance went out of whack and she suffered a cardiac arrest.[88] Sharon's voice changes markedly as she recounts the details of this gruelling saga. The trauma she feels is still palpable; if it were any more real, we'd have to sidle over to make room for it in the restaurant booth.

Just after the cardiac arrest, the nurse most involved at the time told Sharon her daughter's lungs had collapsed. She should prepare for the worst, the nurse counselled. Shannon would likely not make it.

In the aftermath of Shannon's heart attack, intensive round-the-clock care was imperative. For Sharon and her family, the watch continued. Shannon did not die, but her suffering seemed to go from bad to worse. She continued to hover in that grey area between life and death. "Shannon had the worst type of pneumonia," says Sharon. "In the last three years, I've dedicated my life to Shannon. I've had to continually reassure her, tell her that everything will be all right."

It wasn't until Shannon became gravely ill that a specialist with the necessary savvy came onto the scene. He carried out a series of tests and spoke at length with both Shannon and her mother. After a comprehensive medical investigation, this physician delivered his scientific verdict. In his opinion, Shannon's food-related difficulties had been misdiagnosed. He had pinpointed a much more specific cause. He said her so-called eating disorders were actually an indication of the specific palsy[89] from which she suffers. Sharon told me they now understand that although food goes down Shannon's oesophagus, it gets stuck where the passage narrows. As a result, food is repeatedly regurgitated. "I have lots of bitterness and anger about all of this," says Sharon about the years of misdiagnosis.

"Her mind has always been sound," emphasizes Sharon. "It's her body that doesn't work. When you look at her, you see the physical. But when you sit down and talk with her, there's nothing wrong with her mentally or intellectually. She speaks well and is a very smart person."

In fact, Sharon tells me with pride, Shannon was accepted recently to the University of Winnipeg. Now that funds are available for higher education, the Band from which Clarence hails and with whom the family lived for a time in Peguis has approved her funding. Shannon is hesitant to throw herself into a university program at this point, but her mother hopes she will eventually take the plunge. Sharon will certainly do everything in her power to encourage her.

Services and Education

When Shannon was nearly three years old, the family moved to Brandon, Manitoba. Fortunately, a psychologist from the Child Guidance Clinic in Winnipeg happened to meet the little girl and asked to test her periodically. This led to her participation in a special nursery school program next door to the Brandon General Hospital. At ages three and four Shannon attended publicly supported nursery school full days and took part in intensive physiotherapy and speech therapies. She also enjoyed guided water play to strengthen her limbs and promote greater flexibility. Meanwhile, the original professional contact person from Winnipeg travelled every six months to Brandon to carry out tests and map Shannon's progress.

Sharon explains that this program was marvellous for her young daughter and their family. Not only did she make significant progress in all skill sets, the program encouraged mothers to bring in siblings as guests. Consequently, Shannon's younger sister Sherri was able to participate from time to time along with other youngsters. Shannon was exposed to more non-disabled children and vice versa, in a safe therapeutic setting. Later, Brandon University asked to have Shannon attend their Kindergarten school so that they could observe her at play and offer their expertise in child development. The environment was similar: the group was composed mainly of children with disabilities but also included some non-disabled children.

Again, Sharon was pleased that Shannon was receiving special attention as it helped her to develop her mobility and communication skills. In addition, the setting was at least partially integrated — a definite bonus for her daughter. "If we hadn't had these special schools helping her, I don't know where Shannon would be today," Sharon says. "She learned so much just from being there, especially as a very young child."

In Ojibwa culture, it is traditional for the wife to join her husband's band and to raise their family among his people. Peguis is the community to which Sharon's husband belongs. When Shannon was six years old, the family left for Peguis, about two and a half hours north of Winnipeg. Clarence had a job there. He and Sharon felt there would be benefits to raising their children in a First Nations community.

Sharon speaks about this time in a very positive tone. She explains to me that until Shannon's health took a significant turn for the worse, her daughter experienced several definite advantages. "Shannon is Native — she could identify. These were her dad's people. There was family, and she felt accepted."

"Moreover, in the school system, the teacher had begun to know her. She's a bright, intelligent girl, and they really worked hard with her," says Sharon. "They moved her up a grade. They were able to help her. There was help from special education for a few things, but they weren't mean about it."

Sharon indicates that they might very well have stayed in Peguis had Shannon been more healthy. But as it became clear that she needed various specialized services to flourish, the family's choices were limited. At that time, the Band didn't have funds to finance the various medical and physical therapies Shannon required.

Sharon would take her daughter from a young age to Selkirk, Manitoba, for speech therapy. The drive took two and a half hours in good weather.

Suffice to say that in northern Manitoba, long snow-filled winter months abound. The chill of frosty picture-postcard beauty, however, rarely translates to stellar road conditions, and these winter treks were wearing.

Shannon's need for special care increased. Her serious stomach and digestive problems meant she required more and more trips to Winnipeg. By age nine, Shannon had developed a hiatus hernia and was compelled to seek ongoing medical treatment and monitoring. Sharon explains how she tackled the drive from Peguis with two other small children in tow. I'm struck by the absolute determination and single-minded focus she must have needed just to get to these appointments.[90]

"It was hard on us. For me, having baby Shawn in diapers and Sherri with me as well, it meant taking the three of them when I came to Winnipeg for Shannon's appointments. Lots of times I took Sherri out school ... and we'd come the night before for an all-day appointment and return that night."[91]

The family stayed in Peguis for three and a half years, at which point Sharon and her husband decided to separate for a time. She took the three children and moved to Brandon. It was not an easy period for any of them. In our conversation, it is her deep concern for Shannon that resonates as she describes this challenging stage in their lives. "Shannon lost a lot of ground as a result of this move. She lost all her friends," says Sharon. "She had a lot of losses, and I think it broke her heart ... she lost her home and her dad. It had a profound effect on her, and she became sad then."

I sense from Sharon's description that the move to Brandon presaged a significant turning point. In mentioning Shannon's sadness, I understand that Sharon regrets what her daughter went through then. It may be the kind of guilt we tend to feel as adults when decisions we've made seem to throw our children for a loop, even temporarily. There's not much more disturbing for a mom than to watch her child hurting.

About a year and a half later, Sharon and her husband reconciled and bought a house in Winnipeg. Things improved, services were more easily accessible. When it came time for Shannon to attend the regular public high school, however, an unwelcome surprise awaited. She had fully expected to join the other students as they rotated between classrooms. But the school insisted that she join the special education classes for Grades 10, 11 and 12. It was a traumatic soul-crunching experience for Shannon.

As we speak, Sharon's calm demeanour belies the fire in her belly. The high school's unilateral edict still spikes her anger. While Shannon's academic ability was fine, her mother tells me, her physical needs posed some challenges — but they certainly weren't insurmountable. Due to her digestive troubles, Shannon would sometimes vomit and need help cleaning herself up. She was also frequently ill with pneumonia and missed school entirely.

Sharon relates to me the sadness that her daughter felt, but it is her ire that shines through; indignation that the school would not accommodate Shannon's needs. I am cognizant that both mother and daughter experienced this wound deeply. It remains open, and the subject arises a few times in the course of our conversation.

"I think Shannon shies away from the classroom setting now because of what happened in Grades 10, 11 and 12," say Sharon. "She had a really difficult time; she felt alone and rejected. In 1994 she graduated from high school, but I don't think she has ever worked through that awful treatment. I think she's now afraid to pursue her education further because she thinks she'll fail."

As we continue our conversation and I learn more about her family, it is evident that Sharon is devoted to each of her kids. Not surprisingly, however, the sheer intensity of her overall caregiving responsibilities can be exhausting. In this kind of situation, there is no doubt that respite care is essential. At one time, a registered nurse came into the home two days a week to care for Shannon, allowing Sharon time to do errands and also have a bit of time to herself. Knowing that a skilled professional was with her daughter also gave her some peace of mind.

That respite care was cut out some time ago when the person who makes assessments for home care figured Sharon was doing a fine job on her own and didn't require assistance. Later, after a change in personnel at the agency level, Sharon obtained twelve hours per week. That has now been cut. The worst of it, however, is that "... the new person is not a nurse but a health care aide and her skills aren't the same.

"It's not a real break if you jam-pack everything into those six hours. By the time you get home, you're just so tired." She also has the entirely reasonable concern that Shannon be cared for properly, especially now that she has a trach (pronounced 'trake') as well as other critical medical needs. The one other form of respite available through social services comes via Shannon's caseworker. With the funding allotted, she arranges for an agency registered nurse to come into the home four weekends per year.

FAMILY RELATIONSHIPS

"My Mom raised us in Portage la Prairie ... from when I was age fifteen," Sharon tells me. When her parents separated she left the Reserve (Long Plain, Ojibwa Nation).

Sharon hadn't much choice but to grow up fast. In addition to the usual adolescent trials, she and her seven sisters and brothers witnessed their father, well-lubricated with alcohol, abuse their mother repeatedly. It was a trying, confusing time.

"I was brought up very traditionally by my mom, even though she's Catholic. She still planted the seeds of our Native traditional belief system. My father was an alcoholic, and it was a very abusive background. Mom stayed in the marriage for twenty-six years. Whenever she wanted to leave, Dad threatened that if she took the kids away, he would get them back and she would never have them again. She tried to get home to her parents but she was married, and the Catholic way was to stay in the marriage.

"She lived a hellish life. My mom raised eight kids. She had ten, two died. Sometimes I try to see the connections between our lives. Maybe because my mom stayed in her marriage so long and continued to raise us, to take care of us, to teach us; maybe that's why I continue to push and push and push for all the right things for Shannon ... maybe that's the link between my life and my mom's.

"When Shannon is having lots of difficulties, I spend most of my time with her," says Sharon. "I've been in the hospital with her almost every time. A few times when we came to Winnipeg I might have taken a break and gone visiting for a couple of hours. Just to find some kind of balance. But for the most part, I have been with her. Sometimes I have help, but she's been my total responsibility. Because she came out of my body, I feel responsible."

I can empathize with Sharon's feelings. Guilt is a powerful force that provokes us into action as well as into painful territory. Of course

Shannon's disabilities are not Sharon's fault. But I know that emotional place; as a mother I too felt compelled to be with my son whenever his health deteriorated. It never felt onerous, just part of what I expected of myself.

"There were a lot of family problems ... my husband would get tired of Shannon binging and going to the bathroom, throwing up. He was scared she would die and he would get angry. And when somebody is angry at your child, it just hurts so badly. I would come to her defence, and the other two children would come to her defence. There's four of us against one, and we went round and round in circles ... We went to family therapy, the kids hated it ... My husband was really trying to protect her from dying...that was the whole issue ... He wanted so badly for her to eat proper foods, to eat more fruits and vegetables. It was very hard on us as a couple.

"There are times I just wanted to be alone with Shannon, to comfort her. I think it was harder for Clarence to understand. He wanted her to be tough, to be strong and not let anything eat away at her or knock her down. He tried to really build that in her ... and he succeeded, because she can be anything and do anything she wants in this world. But at the time it felt like he was always on her case."

Shannon's needs have often overshadowed those of the other children. As a result, she gets more attention. Shannon and her sister Sherri are just sixteen months apart, and they're very close. Their brother Shawn is nine years younger. Sharon tells me, not surprisingly, that the difference in age affects their relationship. Like most of us, Sharon tried (and still tries) to balance things out between the three children. "But it's difficult to do," she says. "You can't avoid it, you know, but of course as a mom, you try.

"I would never give up on my child. There's times where I've said — just out of despair — 'I give up,' and walked off into the bedroom to sit for a while ... I think we say it, but we never really mean it. It's just not something that a mom does."

Sharon pauses, pulling herself into the present. She describes her husband as a good provider; the family never wanted for anything. I can feel her appreciation for Clarence and the life they have built together. "Shannon's disability is not a hindrance. I am now able to see that. It's the opposite," Sharon explains. "It has taught my husband, me and my other two children a whole lot more than we ever would have known. I fully believe Shannon was a gift to us. Through all of the dreadful experiences, all of the pain, all of the triumphs and setbacks, she's bounced back. She's taught us so much, given us a wealth of knowledge about life. She shows us patience and endurance and is so forgiving, even when other people don't treat her right."

COMMUNITY

"My mom has been my anchor in times of need," says Sharon. "I've gone to her when Shannon's sick, and she's said, 'what do you want me to do?' and we talk about it. Then she makes contact with the medicine men and arranges for a time when we can bring Shannon."

"You take your tobacco," she explains. "Mom will tell me what to get: a blanket, towels or a shirt; something to offer in exchange for help, for traditional healing for Shannon ..."

During the health crises Shannon has experienced, her mother, aunts and extended family have always been close at hand. Shannon is a much cherished young woman. When she was in the Intensive Care Unit after her heart attack, Sharon tells me, "... my niece organized a prayer vigil with about forty-five to fifty people. My sisters and their families were with us.

"When you are told three or four times that your child is not going to make it ..." Sharon sighs. "I have often wondered to myself how I survived those days ...They stand out so much ..." We nod to one another; this is territory I too have walked, and Sharon knows this. After pausing a moment, as if to gather her strength for what is still unfolding, she continues.

"I also remember going to the chapel at the hospital so many times and the whole family coming forward, really reaching out to God to play a hand in this. And I sincerely believe that God gave us a second chance for Shannon. I believe that was His way of telling us to pay attention to Shannon, that she's suffered a lot, to get the right help for her and do what's right for her finally."At this point, we are both moved by the emotion that is brewing like a summer rainstorm. I need a break from the intensity, a chance to digest what she's told me so far. I ask Sharon if she would like another coffee. She declines, prepared to continue.

"Since Shannon was two or three years old and she could not walk, we would take her to the elders. She was still in the walker and her sister had bypassed her. My mom said we needed to take her, and so we went to Sandy Bay. The medicine man doctored her and told us that in a few days she was going to sit up on her own. And that she would be able to walk, in time.

"You know how you're always lugging one kid under your arm and the other one's walking? A few days later my husband was outside with his friends, and he had Shannon with him. He popped Shannon onto the hood of his car, and without realizing — and to this day, he still doesn't know why he did it — he put her there sitting up, and lo and behold, she was sitting up, you know. He yelled for me, 'Come come! She's sitting up on her own!'

"And even with her walking … the medicine man told me that she would learn to walk, but at a later date. He said her legs weren't strong enough yet to hold her up, but that they would be. Her hands and feet were still clenched. She was three when she started walking. My husband couldn't get over it."

Now, Sharon explains to me, the family calls upon traditional healing practices including prayers and song when Shannon's health catapults into crisis. As a mother, Sharon finds this very helpful. For the most part, when the family gathers around Shannon in hospital, they are able to bring their traditions with them, not hindered by hospital staff or regulations. The telephone provides an important link back to their community and to the medicine men and elders. Sharon believes that these interventions, as well as Christian prayer, have helped her daughter to heal. Certainly in both traditions that Sharon described to me, the common piece was the central role of family — extended family and community — gathering together in love and caring to express their support.

ADVOCACY

Sharon has always thought through what Shannon and, I suspect, what each of her children needs to flourish. "It just takes a lot of extra work and will to make Shannon's life as comfortable as possible, while still urging her to take on new challenges," she says. When I asked Sharon how she finds dealing with social services and health care generally and whether she experiences discrimination, she didn't hesitate one bit. She believes she is treated the same in the medical/hospital system as anyone else. "You have to remember, I have a big mouth," she says, with a faint chuckle.

"If there's someone else who has gone through something similar, or even a piece of what we've gone through, if I can be of help to them, I would want to." She suggests to someone just starting out: "Look for all the resources. Shop around. Don't believe every doctor that tells you something. Get two or three different opinions. Get the right services for your child. Don't let anyone tell you who your child is — only you know who your child is. Question someone who tells you after one hour what your child is. Ask how much research they could have done about your child in that time. Be noisy! If you're practically being shoved out of a doctor's office and you've got your foot in the door, saying 'just a minute!' ... you know you're on the right track!"

Planning for Shannon's Future

"I want Shannon to live as normally as possible. My other children point it out to me, 'Mom, let her do it herself, she's not an invalid. Don't dish out her food for her ...' And they encourage her. The challenge is to try to live as normally as possible, in times of stress. I think a person can crack under all the pressure.

"Sometimes I hinder Shannon, as she's dependent on me for everything. I'm trying to tell her that at some point I'll die, and she has to learn to be independent. I'm now reaching out to different agencies and talking with her about eventually living in another setting." Sharon hopes that one day when Shannon is ready she will join an independent living community that offers the practical and physical supports to which she is entitled.

"This is what we want for her, so she can take care of herself and be able to function and carry on with her activities. My other two children and some of my sisters really get on my case about doing everything for Shannon. But since the (cardiac arrest) trauma a few years ago ..." she sighs, "... it's been different." She describes the drill the family has devised for when they have to call 911. Each family member has a specific job to do. Sharon realized they needed this, and they've practised it. "I can't be holding Shannon, trying to suction her, if one of the kids needs me to go and find some other piece of equipment in the closet. Everyone has to help. We're better prepared than we were.

"I've shared a bedroom with Shannon for the last two and a half years. I have to be able to hear her breathe — especially now that she has the trach," she says. "Now she's eating solid table food and she's weaned herself off the inhaler."

Sharon looks at me and shrugs. Helping Shannon to be independent, while also protecting her from harm's way, is an issue Sharon is grappling with sincerely. She must still provide intimate care to her daughter. Each of us struggles to separate from our kids, to let them go; the crises this mother and daughter have endured together, coupled with the sheer extent of physical care involved, makes for a very deep bond.

Shannon is now a young woman with her own activities and a definite point of view. Today, Sharon is thinking about how she will encourage Shannon to make her own way, once she is well enough to take further steps in that direction. Sharon says she is now reaching out to various agencies and also speaking with her daughter about residing in an assisted living situation that offers twenty-four hour care.

"This is what we want for her," Sharon says, "so she can take care of herself, be able to function and carry out her days." It strikes me as very likely that between Shannon's track record for scaling adversity and the unwavering support her extended family furnishes, she will achieve this objective in the not-too-distant future.[92]

LILLIAN AND MICHAEL WITH OLIVER, AGE 12, ELIOT, AGE 15 AT HOME

CHAPTER NINE

LILLIAN AND OLIVER

LILIAN BAYNE AND HER FAMILY LIVE IN Victoria, British Columbia. She and her spouse Michael have two sons, Eliot, age fifteen, and Oliver, age twelve. I first met Lillian and Michael in the mid-1970s when we all attended McMaster University in Hamilton, Ontario. Our paths crossed because of our involvement in the student union. We were part of a loosely knit group of passionate student activists but we'd lost touch after graduation. To my great delight, I heard from Lillian again in 2002 when the Romanow Commission on the Future of Health Care held a stakeholders consultation session in Toronto. She was working for the Commission as Associate Executive Director. I was invited as a stakeholder; I had continued to work in the labour movement and advocated publicly on behalf of medically fragile children and their families. In speaking with Lillian, I became aware that our experience as mothers was not altogether different; in fact, our sons seemed to inhabit very similar universes. I was eager to reconnect with Lillian and learn more about the challenges she and her family face. Our interview was conducted via email.

OLIVER'S BIRTH

Oliver came into the world after only twenty minutes of labour; he immediately experienced difficulties breathing. "He was very quiet — what they call 'flaccid' — at birth," Lillian explains. "We all sensed something was deeply wrong. His older brother, Eliot, made a special visit to the delivery room with his Babar puppet but even that wasn't enough to perk Ollie up. His blood sugar was low, and the doctor wanted to keep him in observation overnight to be sure everything was okay. I parked myself in a room and tried to get some sleep."

"At three a.m. I was awakened by a nurse who told me Oliver had been admitted to the neonatal intensive care unit (NICU). He was having uncontrolled seizures.

"By the time I was taken down to see him he was in an incubator," says Lillian, "with tubes and leads connected to his chest and abdomen, and with an IV to his shaven head administering anticonvulsants. He was about to be hooked up to a respirator.

"For a fleeting moment, he looked like a wizened old man, like the veteran without a face I'd encountered as a child, his eyes scrunched closed and his mouth a wide, open O. It was very hard to watch. I wanted to reach out and tuck Ollie back into the gaping, aching void in my belly, to make him safe again.

"I recall the moment very clearly. The nurse said I seemed so centred. I wasn't certain what she meant but I did know that I wasn't feeling unbalanced by the news. I'd known something was wrong as soon as Ollie was born."

As I read Lillian's description of her son's harrowing birth I was reminded of Jake's birth and his sputtering attempts to breathe. Like Lillian, I was awakened in the middle of that first night by a nurse who told me Jake would be quickly admitted to the neonatal intensive care unit at the adjacent children's hospital. I was luckier, I suppose, in that she had brought Jake into my room so I could see him snuggled into a soft flannel blanket wearing a knit light blue cap. He looked so tiny and helpless, and because he needed a completely sterile environment, I was not allowed to touch him. I remember feeling utterly bereft.

Lillian's experience during the first days of Ollie's life was very similar to my own ride with Jake. "We were in despair," she told me. "Upon return from a day at the hospital, I often retreated to our room and wailed out loud. At one point when the prospect of Ollie's survival was particularly dim we were advised to bring Eliot, then three years old, in to see his brother. He was given a Polaroid snap of Ollie in his incubator before arriving, so he could recognize his baby brother when he saw him. But this failed to prepare Eliot for the real-life version: seeing his tiny, brand new brother with wires coming out of every part of his body was absolutely terrifying.

"It was days before Oliver opened his eyes again and weeks before he made a sound," says Lillian. "When he came home he was on an N-G tube (nasogastric) — being fed through the tube that went up through his nose and into his stomach. We had to learn how to insert the tube and to feed the milk into it from a little bottle. He got nothing but the best — rich breast milk that I produced in abundance with the aid of a bedside electric pump."

Ollie was born with profound brain damage. His oxygen supply was cut off while he was in utero, possibly because the umbilical cord got tangled or caught between him and his mother's pelvis. The brain damage led to a seizure disorder, cerebral palsy and cortical visual impairment (also known as cortical blindness). As Lillian explained, "Physiologically his eyes are fine, but the messaging to his brain is confused so that he doesn't see the way most people do." He has symptoms of autism spectrum disorder[93] though no formal diagnosis has been made.

"Several days after his birth, Oliver declared himself," Lillian says. "He overrode the respirator and began to breathe on his own. The seizure activity subsided and his vital signs stabilized. He was moved to an intensive care nursery, called growers, and three weeks later he was home."

Again, Lillian and Michael's experience in those early days mirrored the horror my spouse and I had felt in trying to protect our son Jake from invasive procedures. Lillian is adamant. "We were clear that we did not want the miracles of modern medicine to keep our son alive against the indications that his body wanted out," she says. "Keeping Ollie alive against his will, just so that he would survive the first weeks of life, seemed an outrage. It served the heroic interests of the neonatologist, but it left the rest of us — Ollie's family and society at large — with the responsibility of a lifetime of care. And every day Ollie spent in the NICU was money not spent on children very much alive and living in poverty just outside the walls of the hospital.

"For some reason we were not permitted to participate in the case reviews held behind closed doors at the hospital. The paediatric neurologists, neonatologists, paediatricians, radiologists, clinical nurse specialists and social workers were all there — but the parents weren't." This was precisely the type of exclusion that my spouse and I had endured at the Hospital for Sick Children in Toronto in 1990. It was encouraging to hear that Michael and Lillian's complaints were eventually heeded. The hospital's policy on admitting parents to case discussions has since been changed.

"Once Oliver had decided he wanted to live, we worked to make his life full," says Lillian. "We had a sense of what the demands on us would be since I'd grown up with disabilities in my family and seen the impact of the care demands on all of us — parents, siblings and trusted friends."

LIFE WITH OLIVER

Now at age twelve, Ollie is a lovely handful and a half. He does not speak but communicates quite effectively. "Mostly he communicates broad brush feelings like 'This is annoying,' 'I'm happy,' 'I'm excited' as indicated by bashing his head with his hand — or anything that comes to hand, laughing until he vomits, or squealing with glee while 'noodling' his body like a funky go-go dancer," says Lillian. "But sometimes it's really specific like: 'I want a bath' which is a happy and unmistakable trill 'ah ah ah ahha'. Hungry and thirsty are also pretty clear; he smacks his lips and makes little sipping sounds."

Ollie feeds himself although, as his mother explains, he's never taken to using utensils. Mealtime is a sensual experience, he likes to feel the food, squish it between his fingers and rub it into his hair.

Lillian describes Oliver lovingly as a "master of disaster." "He's put his head through windows, smashed and drooled his way through three electric keyboards, four second-hand computers from school and innumerable V-tech battery-operated toys."

As he gets older, caring for him presents different challenges. As his mother explains, "He's very strong and his strength is going to prove a problem as he ages. Already he could deck me with a swipe. He only needs to shift his weight when I'm supporting him to throw us both off kilter."

I am reminded of how Jake's growth into a young man made his care more of a challenge. Although he couldn't take a swing at me, his size and absence of muscle tone meant one needed some strength to haul him around, change his diaper and get him settled into his wheelchair and bed.

"Ollie doesn't like to be confined by hugs, but he loves to snuggle up in bed. If you settle in beside him he slips his hand under your body and nuzzles his head into your neck. In the course of the night he manages to propel himself around the bed, eventually ending up horizontally with his head plunked down firmly on your belly!

"He loves to splash in standing water — say the dishes soaking in the sink — and he's a toilet diver so we have learned to keep all the lids shut," Lillian tells me. "He doesn't yet know how to open them. He does enjoy flushing the toilet and is content to listen to that sudden rush of water time and again. This got us into trouble once when he combined it with another of his favourites — plastic bags. Normally he just likes to chew on them but this time he somehow managed to stuff a plastic bag into the toilet (I guess we'd neglected to shut the lid!) and then merrily flushed away. We discovered the impact of his activity when water started to pour down through the living room ceiling. He was found, sitting in an inch of water, happily flushing away still as the toilet, blocked by the bag, overflowed again and again."

Lillian describes how freeing it is for Ollie to be in a swimming pool. "Suddenly all those trappings and appendages — like those awkward feet that just stick out and get caught on furniture legs or doorways — are no longer an encumbrance. Ollie's swimming technique is somewhat unorthodox but it keeps him afloat and even moves him around the pool. New lifeguards are always taken aback," says Lillian. "Seeing Ollie face down in his deadman float or flapping along in his trademark stroke, they think he's on the verge of drowning. But, eventually, after what seems longer than anyone can possibly hold their breath, Ollie will surface, take a great gulp of air, spin himself around like a top once or twice and then settle back into his float or stroke."

Oliver learned to walk when he was about seven or eight years old and is becoming more accomplished every day. "Still, he remains a cautious walker," Lillian explains. "He can negotiate stairs now — better going up than down — but he needs the security of a handrail, he takes his time and often simply waits for a helping hand." He's had corrective surgery for his legs and wears articulated full leg orthotics to keep his legs and feet in line. "These can't be comfortable — form-fitted plastic with honking metal supports that jangle when he walks," says Lillian.

"For those of us who take for granted that we will stand, and walk, and run and — if we're talented — even dance, it comes as quite a surprise that there are so many subtleties to mobility. Though Oliver can walk, he cannot stand up without a support to pull himself upright.

"It was only last year that he learned how to turn around, walking in a little circle to reverse direction. Previously, changes in direction could only be accomplished by reaching a destination, gripping on a support and pushing off again along the return trajectory. This year he is learning how to sidle," she says. For the first time, Ollie is able to shuffle his feet sideways so that he can slide into his seat on the school bus.

"We often wonder what Oliver is thinking. It's clear when he's happy or sad, but his mood can shift, suddenly and sharply. For example, he loves to play at 'hiding hiding'—— a game where he covers his head with the bed sheets and then, suddenly, whips them down to reveal himself. The shocked and surprised 'Oh, there you are!' that this generates sends him into hysterics. But, after three or four games, he'll start to cry, as though the excitement of it all is suddenly just too much. Who knows?"

This sounds remarkably like Jake on his good days when we could play with him. He would smile and giggle to see a light flashing, but at a certain point it was just too much. He would have a seizure and then become far less responsive and tired. All he seemed to want then was a snooze.

"We wonder what he fears," says Lillian. "He certainly fears falling down the stairs, which is undoubtedly born from experience. We know this because he is a very cautious navigator when it comes to descent and because, on more than one occasion, we've found him in a crumpled heap at the bottom with one leg on either side of the banister pole. But in most activities he's quite closely protected. He has never touched a hot stove, been caught before the squealing brakes of a car, fallen off a bike, or been hit in the head by a baseball. So we cannot think what makes him cry out at night. He obviously has nightmares, and these are enough to cause him some distress. But what are they about?"

Lillian tells me that people who are unfamiliar with Ollie's idiosyncrasies would think his behaviour is utterly unpredictable and, sometimes, frightening. "Why did that lad suddenly start to pound on the window of the car? Roar like a lion? Screech and throw his head back? We've become quite accustomed to all of this. Most of Oliver's behaviour is quite predictable. Oliver will begin to slap the window of the car when he recognizes the surroundings — the route to the pool, school, or home again. He roars like a lion when he's leaving the house in the morning, it may even be his way of saying goodbye. He screeches when he is returning, a joyful greeting for Terry, his caregiver. He hits himself in the head with his hands when he's frustrated. Admittedly, we can't always tell what's frustrating him but there's no doubt he's angry."

Oliver awakens quite early in the morning, often well before 7:00 a.m. Lillian tells me they are usually only vaguely aware of him until he starts to play his electric keyboard, cranked to full volume. "Oliver likes to lie with his head pressed up against the speaker, as close as he can get to the *thud thud* of the beat.

"Once he's upended his toy box and had enough of the keyboard, Oliver will make his way upstairs. His unmistakable *thump thump* is a dead giveaway," she says. When he reaches the top of the stairs he either goes into his parents' bedroom or into the bathroom where he loves to pound on the edge of the bathtub, making a deep resonant bong. Ollie will turn on the taps, flush the toilet once or twice, whack the shutters and shake up the shampoo containers before joining Lillian and Michael in their room.

"Here," she says, "he will slam open the door, being sure it makes a loud bang as it hits the bed, just in case we hadn't heard him coming! Then he'll give us a few whacks, nice loud smacking sound of bare hand on bare belly, until we give in and drag him into the bed. If it's still really early, he can often be persuaded to go back to sleep, wedged in the coziest spot he can find between us."

Lillian and Michael get the household moving by about 7:00 a.m. Giving Ollie his breakfast is first on the agenda. "We'll be lucky if we don't have to change the bed sheets," she says. "Usually he'll have soaked the bed. Sometimes, if he's stayed downstairs, he'll have pooped as well. We've had countless episodes of … well, I won't go into the details but suffice to say that we keep lots of carpet cleaner at hand."

I am struck by Lillian's matter-of-fact tone in describing what must be an exhausting morning routine. Of course, she must also get her elder son off to school. I am not at all sure I would have the stamina to sustain such a schedule. She tells me that Ollie is a creature of habit and he needs to follow his daily routines. He has a bowl of cereal for breakfast, along with his morning dose of meds (he takes Vigabatrin twice a day to control his seizure activity) and this is always followed by his first bath of the day. "He gets very upset if you try to bath him before his cereal," she says. "Even if he eats nothing from his bowl, the routine of sitting at the kitchen table and then proceeding to the bathroom is an important one to follow.

"I dress Ollie in the bathroom: diaper, deodorant, socks, orthotics, pants, shoes, bandana (for the drool). It's often a struggle. There's an art to getting the long pressure socks and hip-to-toe orthotics on. Any resistance from Ollie can make it a trial. I pack his lunch, a change of clothing and juice while he's bathing so he can be ready to go as soon as he's dressed. Oliver despises waiting."

SERVICES AND EDUCATION

"Ollie's bus comes for him at 8:00 a.m.," says Lillian. "This is always a thrill. Oliver can see the bus coming up the street and begins to 'noodle' with glee. He's greeted the same way every day by Gary, the bus driver. Now another rider to school, Jackie, loves to help. Gary is careful to seat Ollie where he won't get side-swiped by another kid, and Jackie is there to seatbelt him in and to protect him," she tells me in the understanding tone of someone familiar with each of the children and their unique personalities.

Oliver attends Victor School, a special public school for challenged children. The school has only twenty-two students, divided into senior and junior classes. There is one teacher per class, plus a teacher's aide assigned to every two students. Oliver has had the same teacher's aide since he started at Victor six years ago.

Terry, Ollie's caregiver, has been with the family for just over a year. He has a diploma in recreation and sport management and all the energy and enthusiasm needed to keep up with his young charge. When the school bus brings Ollie home at about 2:30 p.m., Terry is there to meet him.

In addition to the core staff at the school there are weekly visits from music therapists, physiotherapists, occupational therapists and regular access to vision therapists, speech therapists, mobility and seating specialists and others. According to *The Globe and Mail* science and health columnist André Picard, the tiny Victor School is one of only a few such educational institutions in the country.[94]

At the start of every school year the core staff and therapists sit down with the parents or caregivers of each student and jointly work out an Individualized Educational Plan. This IEP sets out mutually agreed upon goals for fine and gross motor skills, communication, toileting, mobility and behaviour. It records parents' sense of where their child is now and then becomes a reference point over the year to ensure efforts are coordinated between school and home.

"This is a school full of joy for life and learning," says Lillian. "The children who attend are all low incidence kids, meaning they have relatively rare conditions. Several have cerebral palsy, autism spectrum disorder, and epilepsy. Most have limited mobility. Some are deaf, few can speak. Not one is toilet trained.

"It sounds odd to say it in an age of civil rights," says Lillian, "but Victor is a segregated school — it serves only children with special needs. Many of the kids here have tried integration and found it didn't work — not for them or for the school they went to." She explains that the children present a very challenging set of behaviours and needs. "One family I know attempted integration for their child several times, moving house and home in search of a location and a school that would meet their needs. The principals they met were welcoming, the teachers were sympa-thetic and caring, but no one could handle the self-mutilation, the violent rages, the sudden, unpredictable mood swings, and the physical attacks on other students and teachers that were routine behaviours for their child.

"For Oliver, the experience was different," she says. "Short and sweet. His first taste of integration was at the local junior school five years ago. He loved it! As soon as we wheeled him into the brand new building with its high vaulted ceilings he began to scream. Loudly. The effect was mag-nificent! His eardrums buzzed as the high-pitched peals bounced off the walls and ceilings. He was ecstatic.

"All around him, hands went to ears, and heads appeared at doorways as the children from each classroom leapt from their seats to find the source of the commotion. The visit lasted twenty minutes. Happily, Oliver was in-vited back, but only 'in thirty minute blocks please and once a week is fine.'"

FAMILY RELATIONSHIPS

Although the children at Victor learn in a segregated setting, they have opportunities to interact with non-disabled children. "We were interested in Ollie getting to know some of the kids in his local neighbourhood," says Lillian, "and looked for the opportunity for him to be integrated once a week at the local primary school. Until last year, this was the same school that Eliot attended."

The integration experience was harder than Lillian and Michael had expected it would be on Eliot. Whenever Oliver arrived at the local school — Eliot's school — all the children would run to the doors of their class-rooms to see what could be making all this noise. All of them except Eliot who would sit mortified, with his head on his desk. Why, he asked, were we letting Oliver ruin HIS school experience?

"We talked to the counsellors at Eliot's school and the folks at Ollie's school and they agreed to put on a disability awareness day. Victor's school therapists and teachers worked on an educational day that would expose the kids at Eliot's school to the life experiences of disabled children. The kids got to wear blindfolds, ride in wheelchairs, try out some of the com-munication and mobility aids available at Victor, and talk about what it was like to live as and care for someone with a disability. It was a roaring success," says Lillian.

"And, best of all, Eliot was a hero — someone who knew all about it from personal experience. It really changed his and the other children's attitudes about the disabled kids who were among them or visited once a week.

"Some people are strictly against segregation of special needs children. I can tell you that Oliver would likely not be walking today if he had not had the special attention he receives at Victor School," says Lillian. "Integration is great for some children, but ask any of the families at Victor and you'll hear the same thing: integration did not work for their children *or* for the children with whom they were being integrated. We are so incredibly fortunate to have this public resource available to us and to have the opportunity to choose what works best for Oliver. I only wish that everyone had the option."

COMMUNITY

Lillian says she's found a sense of community at Victor School. "These children fill our lives, mine and all the other parents', and all the other teachers', the therapists', the caregivers', with laughter, love and hope. We learn so much from them," she says. "How to provide specialized care and attention, to be patient, to be observant, to communicate, to trust and, most of all, to love unconditionally."

Parents of the children at Victor School measure progress in terms of unique benchmarks that rarely hit the radar for most of us. Our kids move "... ever so slowly towards the goals we set out at the start of each school year: to improve balance, to recognize cues, to grasp an object, to sit patiently, to communicate needs," adds Lillian.

Lillian's words echo those of several parents I interviewed. The intricacies of each child's disabling condition and personality are like snowflakes — each child is unique, their needs diverse. It makes sense that charting a course to genuine inclusion be guided by principles of elasticity over rigidity.

In addition to the regular school activities, Ollie has favourite classes including art, music, computer, gym, social studies, baking and swimming. Ollie goes horseback riding once a week through an arrangement with the Victoria Riding for the Disabled Society. The kids take frequent class trips to the llama farm, the corn maze, the bug zoo, the mall — they are out and about in the community. The specialized school actually allows the children more community involvement than they'd get if they were in other educational settings. This support not only allows both Lillian and Michael to work outside the home, but also for them to be involved in the community.

Advocacy

Victoria is relatively rich in public resources, at least as compared to other parts of the country. British Columbia's provincial government offers assistance to families of disabled children through the At Home Program. Based on the assumption that children like Oliver would be cared for in an institution if they were not supported at home, the program covers the costs of all medications, orthotics and a wheelchair every three years.[95] As well, the program includes a contribution for respite care. These are non-trivial expenses. "The first wheelchair we acquired for Oliver would have cost $3,500," says Lillian. "That's more than we spend on our second-hand cars!" Nonetheless, the family pays more than $40,000 a year in after-tax dollars to cover the wage costs for the childcare and respite workers Oliver requires. There's no way around it: this happy, energetic young fellow needs a lot of supervision.

While she and Michael have always paid for some respite care during the week, they only recently began to pay for overnight care some weekends. A woman named Rebekah has known and cared for Ollie since he was an infant. He absolutely adores her. She picks him up on a Friday evening and takes him to her home, some thirty kilometres northwest of Victoria. She drops him off on the Sunday evening. "Oliver is besotted of his darling Bekki, so it works out really well," says Lillian.

For the first time in many years she and Michael are able to spend more one-on-one time with Eliot, take him out to a restaurant, ferry him around to his activities and friends more easily, as well as do the necessary weekend errands. She and Michael find they can also now invite friends to dinner or even get the occasional evening out together. "It's incredible to now have this freedom.

"But," says Lillian, "there are simply not enough services to meet the needs out there, and it is always a fight to keep those special needs services we have." Victor School, for example, is perennially threatened. The provincial funding system is based on a square-footage-to-student ratio which, of course, disadvantages schools like Ollie's that have to accommodate wheelchairs and special seating arrangements. Parents at the school write letters and raise funds to support its continuation and further strengthen the program. They've even had some success capturing national media attention with respect to the integration/segregation issue. As mentioned earlier, André Picard, science and health columnist with *The Globe and Mail*, wrote an article about Victor School in February 2000. Several parents at the school were interviewed and described in vivid terms the benefits their children and entire families derive.

They also raise funds. "One particularly active parent worked hard to secure donations for a new van to transport the kids on their school outings," Lillian told me. "We all turned out ... to celebrate and thank the donors." She has a few tips for families (and groups that come together) to try and raise funds to improve their kids' facilities. "We are committed thank-you letter writers. I think this helps," she says. "People love to do the right thing. Helping them to do so and pointing out the impact of their support shares the rewards all around." The group even managed to get a small reduction in city taxes, just by writing letters and seeking relief. It seems to me we can all take a page out of Lillian's advocacy book!

PLANNING FOR OLIVER'S FUTURE

Oliver is a very healthy and resilient young man, but as he explores almost everything with his mouth, he tends to get a fair number of colds and flu bugs. It's expected that he'll continue to develop his capacity for mobility. Yet the window for walking may be rather narrow; that is, while Oliver is still small. As he gains bulk and height it's unlikely his muscles will be able to bear the full weight of his body. "So, we are making the most of this time while Oliver can move himself around, expecting that he may be once again reliant on a wheelchair in later years.

"I would like Oliver to live a happy and fulfilled life. It would be great if he could be toilet trained. I hope we will be able to find a group home that he can move into when he is ready. Toilet training, and any other independence he can gain, will help. He is so proud to accomplish things, like walking down the stairs unaided," says Lillian. She worries how Ollie would manage if she and Michael were not there to look after him, at least to visit on a regular basis. "I think he would miss us terribly, though, provided some of his other caregivers remain on the scene, the loss could be mitigated. Eliot is attached to and protective of Oliver now, and I expect that attachment will continue and hopefully become richer as the years go by."

I find Lillian and Ollie's story truly inspiring. I am convinced that she will do everything possible to continue to surround both her sons with love and safety. I also suspect that she and Michael will continue to work, each in their own way, toward harnessing the political will we need in this country to ensure that high-quality, accessible health and social services are in place for young ones like Ollie and his buddies at Victor School.

AUDE CATHERINE, AGE 11, AND VINCENT, AGE 8 DURING A VISIT TO THE
AFRICAN LION SAFARI NEAR CAMBRIDGE, ONTARIO.

CHAPTER TEN

MATHIEU, AUDE CATHERINE AND VINCENT

MATHIEU JOLY IS EAGER TO TELL ME about his children's experience
growing up. On an early summer's evening, we've met up at his sister
Dominique's modest home in Vanier, a predominantly francophone community in Ottawa's east end. I've driven up from Toronto to interview
Mathieu for this project. After an informal supper of Chinese take-away,
we settle in on the comfortable sofa in the living room. The room is neatly
appointed and has a lovely open feel, hardwood floors setting off furniture

in tones of light coppery beige. The walls are decorated with prints evocative of a faraway desert. From where we sit I can see out back where Dominique has been carting soil and manure to create a new garden. She joins us, adding occasional details and reminiscences to the conversation. We converse in French.

Mathieu works as a computer analyst for the federal government and enjoys music and movies in his spare time. His daughter Aude Catherine is eighteen years old at the time of our conversation. She is an engaging, attractive young woman and wears her dark, wavy hair long. Eager to be independent, she lives in Montreal where she attends a secondary school and boards with a family. At one time she stayed there with her maternal grandparents. She hopes to study medicine or veterinary science.

Vincent is fifteen, attends high school in Ottawa and alternates residence between his parents' houses, since Mathieu and his wife, Suzanne, separated a couple of years ago. A bright, auburn-haired boy, he has an appealing (if somewhat mischievous!) nature. At this moment, Vincent has his eye on becoming a race-car driver, but I'm told he is a very talented computer wiz and may be lured away from the drama of speedy pit stops. Both young people were born profoundly hearing-impaired.

I have a vivid recollection of the night Aude Catherine was born. Mathieu called me late that night, as I was among the wide circle of friends waiting to hear his and Suzanne's news about the birth of their first child. I lived in Ottawa and had recently begun my first real job as a union organizer, still living in student digs not far from the house Mathieu and I had shared as roommates a few years before. They were first in our circle to leap into the responsibilities of parenthood; we were a cluster of older students, translators and young people passionate about our first jobs. A handful of friends, including Mathieu, had worked overseas with non-governmental organizations before returning to finish university or graduate school.

In 1981, I had moved to Ottawa from Quebec City and searched for a francophone cooperative house to join. Mathieu, Dominique and a group of friends occupied the house I happened upon. It turned out to be a good fit, and as I began my graduate studies at Carleton, I was able to keep a foot in the francophone world I so enjoyed.

Although we lost touch after I moved to Toronto and became embroiled in a busy career and parenthood, our friendship rekindled some years later. Dominique is a translator in high demand. She and I met up again professionally and, during the opportunities we worked together, became close friends.

When my son Jake was born and the seriousness of his condition became known, Dominique and Mathieu reached out to me. In time, my marriage ended and in May 2003, the occasion of our interview, Mathieu and Suzanne were also separated, giving us something else in common: the challenges of sharing custody and co-parenting our children.

AUDE CATHERINE'S BIRTH

Shortly after Aude Catherine was born, her mother Suzanne became quite concerned about her infant daughter's ability to hear. She took the baby to a specialist who suggested she ought not to worry, although it was understandable since she was a first-time mother. Not satisfied by this response, Mathieu and Suzanne forged on to explore tiny Aude Catherine's health. Fortunately, Mathieu told me, their paediatrician was top notch. He referred them immediately to the Children's Hospital of Eastern Ontario (CHEO) where precise tests could be done. At eight weeks of age, it was determined that Aude Catherine hears virtually nothing without amplification, such as a hearing aide.

Suzanne and Mathieu were quite surprised and, initially, distressed by this news. There was no family history of hearing impairment on either side. They wondered about the jaundice Aude Catherine had experienced at birth. Could it have caused hearing loss? The doctors explained that jaundice would also have affected her balance, not a concern noted. Rather, the reason for her condition was unknown.

"Frankly, we felt a bit lost," says Mathieu. "Fortunately, we knew some friends of friends who had a three-year-old who was hearing-impaired. They helped us a lot." Suzanne and Mathieu arranged to see these acquaintances soon after Aude Catherine's diagnosis was made. The other couple oriented them toward programs offered at CHEO. They learned that the hospital's Audiology Unit had a very good reputation. It advocates an approach known as auditory-verbal education/training to assist hearing-impaired children.

Mathieu explains, "The approach is based on the notion that most hearing-impaired children have at least some hearing capacity and that through amplification and training, the child can learn to hear and speak." Less than 10 percent of these children live without any hearing capacity at all. The auditory-verbal approach, the new parents learned, is not based on learning sign language. For some individuals and families, learning ASL[96] (American Sign Language) is a strong matter of preference, of opting to participate as full members of the deaf community and culture. For French-speaking Canadians, the equivalent language would be La Langue des Signs Québécoise (LSQ), and Mathieu and Suzanne understood that community to be much more accessible in Montreal than the Ottawa area.

"They leave the choice to embrace this program up to the parents," says Mathieu. "Our decision was perhaps not the most enlightened, but we considered several issues. It's true that we didn't know a lot about the deaf community, and our friends were already using this approach with some success.

"But I think more important was the calculation we made regarding the double minority status Aude Catherine would find herself in. That is, the deaf community is a minority within society and, in Ontario, we French speakers are a minority. It didn't seem fair to narrow down our daughter's world to that extent.

"In addition, no-one in our families knew sign language or was particularly familiar with the deaf community. Our greatest wish was to raise her in a hearing world so that she would be able to integrate into society rather than be part of a small minority."

As a result, Aude Catherine received a hearing aid at ten weeks of age and immediately began an intensive education program, delivered primarily by her mother Suzanne, who worked with her at home diligently during the next five years.

"It is a very labour intensive program," explains Mathieu. "Suzanne had to go to the hospital at least once a week to learn how to work with Aude Catherine." Parents, particularly the primary parent at home with the child, must embrace the challenging method fully for it to reap the desired results.

"Whereas a hearing child learns naturally that a certain sound means 'x object or concept,' for a non-hearing child, in addition to learning how to use a hearing aid, the primary parent must repeat the sound over and over until the child gets it," he says. In essence, the parent is teaching their child to associate a particular sound with a given object. The learning curve can be quite steep when a child is profoundly deaf.

"For Aude Catherine and for Suzanne, it took a lot of concentration and a great deal of repetition. For our daughter, even with the hearing aid, her sensory perception is like hearing a whisper behind a door."

Vincent's Birth

Vincent was born in 1988. Once again Suzanne and Mathieu experienced doubts during the first month of their infant's life about his ability to hear. When he was four or five weeks old, Suzanne took Vincent to CHEO for tests. Their fears were confirmed.

"We were quite surprised. Never did we think there was a genetic possibility of hearing impairment," says Mathieu. "Suzanne, who had already put in three years of concentrated work with Aude Catherine, could now foresee a similar challenging stretch with our son. It was very discouraging. To make matters worse, I wasn't there when she got the news, something I truly regret."

A few weeks later Mathieu took Vincent back to CHEO for further testing. He received his hearing aids at about two months of age. Mathieu says it was obvious from Vincent's behaviour that his hearing was somewhat more acute than Aude Catherine's.

Life with Aude Catherine and Vincent

The auditory-verbal method emphasizes the child's auditory capacity. "Both our children began to read lips, but we were advised against encouraging this." Parents and other family members are told to hide their faces when they speak with their children. Suzanne and Mathieu found this rather awkward, as it felt unnatural.

"When you're a parent, communication is the key," says Mathieu. "There's a practical aspect to it. At the supper table, I might tell my kids 'eat your soup' or 'no dessert if you don't finish your vegetables.' What counts in that moment is that there is meaningful communication between us."

Another difficulty that arose, primarily for Suzanne as she had the lion's share of interaction with the CHEO specialists, was the feeling of pressure if the child's progress did not meet the professionals' expectations.

"Of course there were plateaus in Aude Catherine's and, later, Vincent's development, but Suzanne sometimes felt that she was being judged unfairly if one of the kids didn't measure up," says Mathieu. "The fact I was at work full-time didn't help. She had to bear the greater responsibility. Of course I contributed once I got home."

Further in our conversation, Mathieu made an interesting observation. He ventured that in a family where both parents work outside the home, this model would be untenable. It requires one parent to devote her or himself full-time to assisting the child's development. Both parents must engage in rigorous, constant follow-up with their child. In their case, they were able to carefully juggle their family income so that Suzanne stayed out of the paid workforce for five years, something she would not have done under other circumstances.

I remember how much Suzanne enjoyed her work outside the home in various educational museum programs before the children were born. I think I would have found it difficult to sustain such an intensive training at home over five years as she had. It strikes me as a very selfless way to parent.

SERVICES AND EDUCATION

Aude Catherine continued with the auditory-verbal approach until the age of four. Mathieu feels that the program was successful, although her language development proceeded slowly. In order to spur her on before entering Grade 1 at a community school, Mathieu and Suzanne enrolled Aude Catherine in a Montessori program. Their hope was that since a prized virtue of the Montessori Method is the emphasis it places on language, their daughter would get a boost in catching up.

"We knew it was a rather elitist program," says Mathieu, "but it seemed to be the right solution. Although it was very expensive, we felt that she needed to develop language skills in order to move ahead." Their objective was clear: that Aude Catherine become ready to function on her own in a regular classroom in an ordinary public school.

As it turned out, Aude Catherine spent two years at the Montessori school before entering a French public school in the neighbourhood. In between schools, she needed assistance from one of the highly trained Montessori staff as well as a skilled private teacher. Her parents engaged this privately paid guidance to help their bright young daughter complete Grade 1 successfully. To their great delight, since the cost was truly prohibitive, Aude Catherine's maternal grandmother was able to secure a one-time charitable donation from her employer to cover much of the cost of this crucial specialized education.

Extra attention to speech training, in particular, has helped Aude Catherine and Vincent improve their communication skills. Both children have benefited a great deal from contact with an itinerant teacher for hearing-impaired children employed by the French School Board. Mathieu says that her extra work with the youngsters over the years has proved a terrific help in speech development and other specialized learning.

"We are extremely fortunate," says Mathieu. "This teacher is extraordinary, and it just happens that we have her services in Ottawa. Outside the city, even in communities only thirty or forty minutes away, there are no teachers to provide services to French-speaking hearing-impaired children."

As I listen to Mathieu, I empathize keenly with his assertion at the beginning of our conversation. The relatively sparse availability of services in French, the family's native language, constituted a driving force in their inclination to teach their children to function well in a hearing world.

When Aude Catherine turned twelve or thirteen, specialists at CHEO suggested that she would be a good candidate for a cochlear implant. At the time, the procedure was still fairly recent. Usually it was performed on children younger than Aude Catherine was.

A cochlear implant is an electronic device designed to help severely to profoundly deaf individuals. It consists of two main parts: an internal implant and an external part known as the speech processor. Sounds are picked up by the processor's microphone and turned into an electrical signal. This signal is coded (turned into a special pattern of electrical pulses) and these pulses are then transmitted (by radio waves) to the implant in the person's ear. The implant sends a pattern of electrical pulses to the electrodes in the cochlea, a snail-shaped structure in the inner ear which is sometimes referred to as the body's microphone. The auditory nerve picks up these tiny electrical pulses and sends them to the brain. The brain recognizes these signals as sound. The sound is then sent to the speech processor, a box about the size of a pager that is worn on the body.

"Aude Catherine was alerted that the process would involve at least a year or two of re-education," says Mathieu. "She would need to learn to distinguish between the varied sounds she would hear for the first time. Apparently, sound(s) would register very differently than they do with her hearing aids."

Aude Catherine had only one implant. She continued to place her hearing aid in the other ear. Mathieu explains that her brain was confused by the conflicting input it was receiving. After two or three years, Aude Catherine was fed up. "It wasn't the miracle she was hoping for," says her father. Mathieu also wonders if there might not be an aesthetic concern, since having the cochlear implant means one must wear a little box and wire all the time — something he wagers an adolescent might find awkward.

"The same teacher helped Aude Catherine with her training while she was trying to adapt to the cochlear implant. She even accompanied her to therapeutic meetings at the hospital," says Mathieu. "Now she assists Vincent primarily with his pronunciation of certain sounds that are difficult for him in French and in English. She also reviews parts of his homework with him. She says that Vincent's vocabulary is at the level of a twenty-year-old."

Aude Catherine continues now with the use of a hearing aid in one ear and uses other techniques such as lip reading. Although the implant remains, she does not make use of it. By all reports, she manages to communicate effectively, if not perfectly, in a hearing world. According to Mathieu, it was Suzanne's work with the children during their early years that made all the difference.

FAMILY RELATIONSHIPS

Both parents found it more difficult to devote as much time and energy to the auditory-verbal program with their second child. The sheer volume of laundry, diapers and meal preparation for two young ones is onerous enough, before adding the necessary rigour of such a program. As I spoke to Mathieu, it occurred to me that most of us experience something similar with the addition of a second or third child to our families, except the stakes involved in shaping the infant's early development are not nearly so high.

As we speak, I am reminded of the sense of urgency that captured me when Jake was an infant. He needed intensive physiotherapy during his very early months, and the public home care waiting list was overflowing. I suspect that Suzanne and Mathieu must have felt a great deal of pressure to do the right thing for the kids.

Vincent progressed well as Suzanne continued to devote her time to the children's development. He learned to speak at a somewhat slower pace than his sister. As both children matured, however, their parents discovered an interesting and unexpected dynamic.

"The kids communicate without words. They read each others' lips," says Mathieu, explaining that they mouth words but do not make any sound. "No-one around them can follow. They have a private understanding." Each of the young people has also had significant relationships with members of their extended families. They share some activities and interests with their aunts and grandparents, including games, sports and hobbies.

Community

Interestingly, Vincent learned English mainly from watching movies with subtitles in English. He improved his ability to lip-read by watching film characters' mouths and anticipating what they would say before seeing the subtitles.

In terms of sign language, Mathieu notes that at one point, Vincent showed some interest in learning to sign. Mathieu enrolled in a few courses as a "fallback," he says, in case one of the children decided sign language was truly their preferred means of communication. Ultimately, however, neither Vincent nor Aude Catherine has opted to sign. More recently, Vincent is considering the advantages and disadvantages of obtaining a cochlear implant.

I asked Mathieu if he felt the kids were meeting the objective he and Suzanne had set early on — to function independently in an ordinary school — and whether this has provided the community engagement they'd hoped for.

"Most definitely," says Mathieu. "If you say they are 'handicapped,' they feel insulted. They are so-called normal children who happen to have hearing loss." He mentions that, in general, Aude Catherine is somewhat easier to understand than Vincent, but that adapting one's ear to their speech is possible with some effort.

I note that in a family — and a city — where many people speak at least two languages, a more fluid attitude toward verbal communication might mean that people make a greater attempt to understand language that, at first, sounds unfamiliar.

I asked Mathieu about the young people's social circles. "Making and keeping friends is an area that has been more difficult for them," Mathieu tells me. "Aude Catherine finds that the girls at school (big surprise!) tend to cluster in groups. If there are more than two or three together in a gang, she has trouble following the conversation."

"Vincent is more at ease, but he doesn't bring friends home after school anymore. When he was in primary grades he had friends in the neighbourhood, but now everyone is so spread out. So it may be harder."

Advocacy

Mathieu has made a point of becoming active in various associations that lobby to enhance services for hearing-impaired children and young people. "The provincial association, Voice for Hearing Impaired Children, helped us quite a lot, especially at the beginning," he says. "This organization holds conferences and meetings, offers help to individual families as a support group and also lobbies the school boards and government."

It now has a mandatory representative on Special Education Advisory Committees (SEAC) in each school district. Mathieu sits on this committee as the Voice representative. His involvement over several years increased, including more than one term as president of the entire SEAC.

As an individual, Mathieu has always expressed his social conscience by volunteering in community organizations. He had a natural inclination to play an active role in his children's education. Involving himself in the political aspect of lobbying for better special education services, particularly during a period in which these were being slashed by the government of the day, was time-consuming, but also satisfying. He has, as a result, developed a certain expertise regarding services available (and lacking) for children with special needs, particularly in Eastern Ontario.

Adults in Mathieu's close-knit family also speak excellent English, although French is their mother tongue and language of choice. While Ottawa is one of the best-served areas of the province in terms of language services to French-speaking hearing-impaired children, these programs are extremely precarious. As Suzanne and Mathieu learned through their experience as parents, they were obliged along the way to cover necessary costs to fully prepare their children for regular public school education. As Mathieu described, extra financial pressures arose at very critical points in each child's development. The family was aware that missing these very specific developmental junctures would have had lasting, damaging effects. Clearly, he says, coming up with extra cash is not an option for every family.[97]

PLANNING FOR AUDE CATHERINE'S AND VINCENT'S FUTURE

When I asked Mathieu about his hopes and dreams for his children he hesitated momentarily. It was rather touching to hear a father's hopes and, not too far below the surface, just a soupçon of worry.

First, he told me, he hopes that each of them is able to proceed on their chosen career paths without encountering too many barriers.

"They've been raised to pursue their dreams. That's the approach we took," he says. "Becoming a doctor, as Aude Catherine hopes, is a huge challenge. I hope they can each continue to make their mark, without limits. And I hope they find loving companions with whom to share their lives."

*

Mathieu and I had occasion to touch base again in February 2005. He was thrilled to describe an important breakthrough in his relationship with his daughter, only made possible by technological advances in long-distance communication. Aude Catherine is working at Chateau Lake Louise in Alberta and they correspond via instant messaging in real-time chats. He notes that the chat medium puts them on the same footing.

"We both have to type and read our exchanges, sometimes waiting for the other to respond," he says. "Now we can have free-flowing conversations."

Using this tool means their communication is boosted light years ahead, Mathieu explains. This is in sharp contrast to spoken conversations with hearing persons, where he recognizes Aude Catherine and Vincent are often at a disadvantage.

"When they miss something or do not fully understand what is said to them, they have to either go on with incomplete information — which may lead to later misunderstandings — or stop the flow of the conversation," he says. "Asking the other party to repeat or restate his or her previous words can cause a great deal of frustration for both people.

"We have rediscovered each other somewhat," says Mathieu. "Our chats often last more than an hour, and it's helped me to know Aude Catherine as a young adult, sometimes showing a maturity beyond her years." I can hear the profound joy and pride in her father's voice.

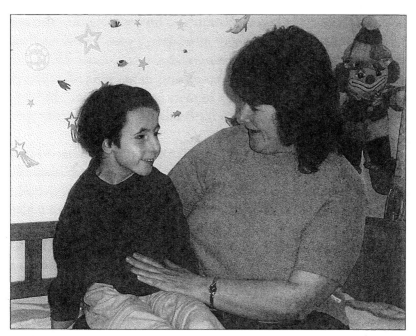

JOHNNY, AGE 13, WITH HIS MOTHER COLLEEN

CHAPTER ELEVEN

COLLEEN AND JOHNNY

ON THE MORNING I WAS TO MEET Colleen Fitzpatrick and her family for the first time, I left my motel room to get a breath of fresh air. It was a damp Newfoundland day; the cool springtime mist licked my cheeks as I walked. The streets of St. John's were quiet at this early hour. Before long the moist air began to creep down the back of my neck and the stiffness setting in my spine made me yearn for sunshine. The harbour was still clear of icebergs, the April Easter weekend too raw to marshal their appearance. We were socked in, the fog pierced only by headlight beams and the occasional flicker of an uncertain sun.

I needed to get my bearings before our first meeting that afternoon. One of my colleagues in the labour movement, a proud Newfoundlander and activist in the disability community, knew of Colleen. He had seen press reports about her fight to fend off cuts in her son's education program and suggested we find a way to meet up. At the time, I had only a vague sense of the extent to which the familial and political landscapes of our lives coincided.

Some months earlier, Colleen had sent me an email message. Our mutual friend had by then told her about the book I had published about my son and other children with disabilities.[98] She wrote that she could see herself in the pages of my family's story. As it turned out, the resemblance between how our lives as mothers had unfurled was rather striking.

I had included in the book a detailed account of the lively and ultimately successful community organizing effort in 1996 to keep open the Thistletown Regional Centre for Children and Adolescents. For me, recounting that tale virtually blow by blow was a deliberate means to convey to other families that they could protest effectively to defend their children's rights. I felt (and still believe) that as governments make ill-advised policy and funding decisions about our children's care and education, we have much to learn by sharing our stories about fighting back.

To my delight, Colleen told me in her note that a well-thumbed copy of my book was making the rounds of parents at St. Matthew's, the school her son Johnny attended. She was drawing upon the Thistletown experience to motivate friends and neighbours to fight to preserve the programs their special needs children required. She had contacted me in the hope that we could talk through the advocacy strategy the parents were employing. They were making a bid to stave off the closing of the developmental delay unit at St. Matthew's, a specialized classroom where a dozen children, including Johnny, spent their school days. I readily agreed to act as a long-distance sounding board.

Since that initial contact, Colleen and I had kept in touch, sending letters by email to discuss her presentations at public meetings in St. John's. Not surprisingly, as in so many informal networking experiences, we slipped quite naturally into relating news of our respective children, inquiring about their health and achievements.

During that early spring morning, however, as I anticipated our first face-to-face contact I felt a bit on edge. How could I simply arrive at a relative stranger's doorstep and expect her to divulge the bittersweet details of her life? Would the cyber-camaraderie we had found help Colleen to feel comfortable opening her heart to me?

The moment I arrived at her modest home, my nervousness evaporated. Colleen was as warm in person as she had been in our correspondence. We embraced immediately, stirred perhaps by the knowledge that we were fellow travellers in a peculiar mothers' club. Our sons were not just disabled; they were very vulnerable. Both were known to be medically fragile. According to doctors, neither of our boys would reach manhood.

At the door, I also had the pleasure of meeting Colleen's intelligent, red-haired daughter, Krystal, Johnny's sixteen-year-old sister. Together they ushered me into the living room. Colleen and I sat on the sofa facing one another. Johnny, thirteen, was on Colleen's lap. Apart from the faint whir of the tape recorder, we could have been any two forty-something women having a cup of tea, chatting casually about our families. Krystal joined us, listening intently from an easy chair by the window. The family puppy scampered about playfully, insisting on snatching the limelight from time to time.

When I turned on the tape recorder, Colleen warned me that her nature was to talk and talk and that I should rein her in if necessary. I didn't. Stories of Johnny's birth, the ending of her marriage, Krystal's academic achievements and more came spilling out. During the five or six hours, we spent together over two days Colleen filled me in on the constant challenges of caring for little Johnny, her "earth angel."

Johnny's Birth

"The morning after Johnny's birth, a nurse wheeled my son into my room in an incubator. He was wrapped in bubbled plastic to protect his body temperature. The nurse said that she was bringing him in to say goodbye to Mommy, before he left for the Children's Hospital. She suggested I put my hands inside the small opening of the incubator so I could touch him. Oh God, I found it so painful."

John David Penney was born February 12, 1989 to Colleen Fitzpatrick and John Penney of St. John's, Newfoundland. As she and I visit, Colleen is recalling her son's distressing delivery and its aftermath.

"I remember standing in the hospital window and watching a team of medical doctors and nurses taking my baby to a waiting ambulance to transport him to the Children's Hospital. I just froze at the window. I couldn't even cry. I guess shock does that to a person."

Colleen and her husband already had a healthy, inquisitive three-year-old daughter, Krystal. Their life was busy; before starting a family, they had worked hard to build a photography business with studios across the island. Johnny's birth rocked their world.

In the space of days, Johnny's birth catapulted Colleen onto an unfamiliar, frightening path. Early in her pregnancy, she had felt intuitively that something was wrong with her baby. Specialists treated her high blood pressure routinely but none of the tests performed revealed anything unusual. The baby she carried seemed fine.

In fact, Colleen's intuition was right on the money. Giving birth to her son bore little resemblance to the arduous moments in which she had pushed Krystal out into the world. From the time Colleen went into labour, "Johnny's heartbeat dropped really low and, for the first time, the medical staff suspected something was wrong. He was born with the umbilical cord wrapped around his head, choking him …"

Soon after Johnny's birth, a passel of paediatricians whooshed in to examine the baby. "I was still on the table and they were sewing me up. The specialists were saying: 'Your son has several holes in his heart and one is quite large. We are either dealing with a normal child that has deformed hands and a bad heart or we are dealing with some kind of a syndrome.'" Exhausted by her labour and distressed by diagnoses tossed about among the medical men, Colleen felt an eerie shadow descend.

"I don't know why, but I didn't want to look at his hands," she says. "He had a big head of dark hair and weighed four pounds and three ounces." Johnny was born with his fingers flexed, spread like an eagle's talon. His diminutive size and difficulty breathing meant an incubator and neonatal intensive care would be *de rigueur* for some time to come.

Colleen visited Johnny every day during the weeks he was confined to hospital. Life was hectic. She had a household to run and a young daughter who needed her care. By then, Colleen's husband had returned to work. He had always travelled a great deal for business and, at that time, his work was located in northern Newfoundland. He was five hours away by car.

Colleen's blood pressure was, by then, blasting out of control. When Johnny was one week old, she received a telephone call from a specialist at the Intensive Care Unit. He was curt. "John David has Trisomy 18," said the doctor. "We give him two weeks to live."

"I just fell to the floor ... we knew the prognosis was awful," says Colleen. "90 percent of these babies die before they reach one year old. If they do survive, they are severely disabled, both mentally and physically."

Trisomy 18 is a condition due to a person's anomalous genetic makeup. Johnny has an extra 18th chromosome in every cell of his body. He is a medically fragile child, a term reserved for infants and youngsters who teeter precariously on the knife-edge between life and death.

But today Johnny is very much alive. In fact, he's responsive and engaging. He sits in his mother's lap, glancing around, smiling, as if to take stock of his surroundings. When I speak, he looks me right in the eye. Colleen strokes his brown hair and, at that moment, Johnny seems comfortable and content. There is absolutely no doubt that this fidgety fellow is one cherished little boy.

Trisomy 18 occurs in approximately one in five thousand live births and affects girls more than three times as often as boys. The range of difficulties such infants and children face is extensive. Some of the most common symptoms are congenital heart disease, microcephaly (small head) and clenched fists. The hands, with flexed fingers and often the third and fourth fingers overlapping, is a frequent diagnostic indication of Trisomy 18.[99]

Many such babies have feeding problems that involve breathing, sucking and swallowing difficulties. Sight and hearing deficits, as well as profound developmental delays, are also associated with this condition. Kidney malformations, as well as structural heart-lung defects at birth contribute to the children's enormous vulnerability.

The vast majority of Trisomy 18 infants fail to thrive. Their lifespans are short. Johnny and his counterparts can die from natural causes at any given time.[100]

LIFE WITH JOHNNY

"After two months, it was finally time for Johnny to come home. The doctor who had given me the diagnosis chased me out as I was leaving the hospital. He said, 'Colleen, now I want to tell you something honey. These last two months we've flown nothing but negativity at you ... I want to tell you that 98 percent of this child's progress will depend on how he's treated at home.'"

I find this physician's comment to Colleen quite irksome. Certainly there must be another way to send off a mother facing such a huge challenge. I bide my time, not wanting to interrupt the telling of her story.

"Johnny came home and for the first year of his life, we waited for him to die. We were just waiting because that is what the doctors told us," says Colleen. In Newfoundland, public health nurses carry out assessments of young children with physical and/or developmental challenges. Referrals may be made to various agencies although programs vary between regions. In-home supports depend very much on the resources available to a particular regional health body. Some financial support is provided toward the purchase of specialized equipment. At the time of our interview there was no publicly funded program to deliver in-home or out-of-home respite care to families with medically fragile children.[101]

As Colleen describes this first roller-coaster episode of her life with young Johnny, I am riveted by her devotion to the handsome little fellow sitting on her lap. He is a small active bundle. I watch her manoeuvre to arrange him comfortably in her arms, Johnny straining like a toddler intent on leaping from his mother's grasp.

Of course, he cannot. Johnny's limbs move about involuntarily. A mischievous grin belies his inability to wreak havoc in the ways one usually expects of a boy his size. Johnny is thirteen years old. He is very thin, able to keep down only a minimal amount of nourishment. Acid reflux from his stomach is a constant source of discomfort. And yet the boy who locks his eyes with mine is smiling, evidently a very good-humoured chap.

To this day, Johnny keeps his mother up half the night. His stomach pain and seizures make peaceful sleep for either of them only a dream. Colleen sleeps on a cot in Johnny's room to make sure she can hear any distressing changes in his breathing or to soothe him when he is jolted awake by a seizure. I am reminded from incidents with my own son that solace seldom accompanies the isolation felt in the darkness of night.

SERVICES, EDUCATION AND ADVOCACY

"When I put Johnny on that bus every morning, my first concern is not who he is playing with, who he's integrating with," Colleen explains. "My first concern when I hand him over is 'please God, let him come back today still alive.' My son doesn't belong in the mainstream school system on a full-time basis ..."

Colleen's voice has risen. I can tell from her expression and the strength of her words that she is utterly determined to protect Johnny. She is a mother propelled by devotion to her son to ensure that his days are spent in a safe setting where he can receive competent care and love. It's easy to see that Johnny and other such youngsters have a powerful advocate on their side.

Much is at stake. Colleen is locking horns with the school board and province to preserve the developmental delay unit housed at St. Matthews. Johnny's program, designed specifically for medically fragile children, is slated for closure.

"Johnny's been in the same class with the same teacher and same program assistants for seven years. His personal needs are taken care of ... he will not get that in the mainstream." It seemed Colleen had limitless energy. She roused the other parents to work together. Rescuing the developmental delay unit from the axe is the focus of their campaign.

As main spokesperson for the ad hoc committee, Colleen explored all avenues. She argued vociferously to the school board and province to preserve the program. No stone was left unturned; public meetings were called. Interest in the issue kindled quickly in the St. John's community as the hastily formed parents' group captured newspaper headlines. The parents became single-minded in putting a compelling case before various levels of government.

Colleen explains to me, with some regret, that her group's position resulted in a full-scale dispute with the Newfoundland Association for Community Living (NLACL). Like Community Living associations in most provinces, the NLACL was committed to a different model of care for children with disabilities. Integration in education and independent living are the rallying cry of disability movements internationally. St. John's, Newfoundland, was no exception.

Colleen and her group did not disagree with these fundamental aims. That many people with disabilities, their agencies and advocacy groups embrace this goal was most definitely not at issue. But for Johnny and other medically fragile children and infants, this ideology could not meet their families' concrete needs.

Colleen and the other St. Matthews' parents remained the best judges of their children's sheer vulnerability on this earth. Any school situation was fragile for these kids, let alone an integrated classroom. Integration, proposed as a standard solution, offered no panacea for these families. Seeking cookie-cutter conformity in every situation just wouldn't do. The parents firmly rejected a definition of integration that ignored the unique conditions each of their children faced.

Today, integration — the unifying tenet for many people with disabilities — is by no means a neutral concept. It has become an ideological as well as practical issue. The families clustered around the St. Matthew's developmental delay unit feared their children would lose the precious individualized care they received.

"The NLACL has to re-evaluate their system for categorizing our children," says Colleen. During the peak of frenzy, "We heard someone from the NLACL on television comparing herself to us. This mother was saying that all kids should be in the mainstream. Her daughter sat at the table talking, feeding herself and having a conversation. This is a young woman who works at one of the local supermarkets stocking shelves!"

Colleen pointed out that many of the authorities, including the NLACL, mistakenly referred to children with disabilities as if there were some homogeneity; that is, without taking into account the broad spectrum of children's level of functioning or disablement. Medically fragile kids were nowhere in sight.

Colleen was astounded that social policy — and the ideology on which it is based — made no distinction, for example, between her child and a girl living with Down Syndrome. For Johnny's mom, the campaign was not a bit theoretical. She knew that in an ordinary elementary classroom, her son's ability to survive the bacteria count alone was doubtful. Protecting Johnny's future meant charging into pitched battle.

As spokespersons for the NLACL failed to distinguish the qualitative differences between the developmental delay unit and other children they represented, the tenor of the battle ratcheted up. As in many such conflicts, dramatic differences between parents' views were heightened by the media attention they received.

"What upset me about this association more than anything," says Colleen, "and I made sure I told them this, was that they made all of their statements and formed opinions about our children and our environment, and they had never seen it. They had never come to visit or seen any of our children."

Although the NLACL told her over the telephone that its purpose was "to help parents achieve what they want for their children," Colleen says that for her this statement rang hollow. In her experience, at least, respecting families' wishes was not even on the map.

In truth, says Colleen, the developmental delay unit classroom at St. Matthews was treated as a full part of the school in which it was housed. The school had developed a creative initiative to enhance contact between non-disabled children and the kids in Johnny's unit. Known as the Friendship Club, it encourages children from many different classrooms to spend time in the special needs unit.

"Children in the school are gradually introduced to the unit from Kindergarten up to Grade 4. By the time they reach Grades 5 and 6," Colleen explains, "they take on more responsibility and do more activities with our children ... they have been raised with our kids."

Non-disabled youngsters read stories aloud, engage the special needs children in music and rhythm activities and also learn some of the special care techniques the unit's children require. These opportunities provide integration in action that is, according to Colleen and her group, appropriate for extremely vulnerable children that need twenty-four-hour complex nursing care. In short, the Friendship Club is an effective means to demystify developmental disabilities and serious health conditions for the non-disabled children.

What a marvellous model for inclusion! If only schools and childcare centres across the country could incorporate this kind of integrated program, our children might all experience the degree of acceptance that Johnny enjoys in his community. The creative impetus behind this school and its club reminds me that rejigging Canadian social policy and practice for our children need not be considered rocket science. Interestingly, the Friendship Club's impact at the primary school has also been felt in the community. Especially since she and the other parents went public to defend their kids' unique classroom, Colleen has received very positive feedback. She told me that, "in the local mall parents of all these Friendship Club children are coming at me from every angle. 'Way to go Colleen,' they say or 'Don't stop Colleen.'" Some have gone so far as to express to her frankly that, "my child could never give to Johnny what Johnny has given to my child."

"… Before my children entered the Friendship Club," one parent told her, "I didn't know what it was like for them to come over and say 'can I have a hug?' They just didn't do it."

"And now in the Friendship Club where the whole purpose revolves around love and commitment and dedication, these young people now feel so special because they're taking care of these special little children. They know they're helping these kids … and it means so much to them," Colleen tells me. "They're talking about it at home."

"If the government takes away this unit … they're robbing all of the future children that would be exposed to these kinds of morals and ethics, ones that can't be taught in a book. They're robbing them of that."

Until the public campaign, government and policy-makers were relatively ignorant about the specific needs of this distinct set of constituents. As in other provinces, medically fragile kids like Johnny were not even a minute bleep on the radar — not just for the authorities, but sadly, for more mainstream advocacy groups. No doubt, a climate of cost cutting makes fertile ground for controversy and, typically, governments sow conflict between families who clamour for (insufficient!) pots of funding.

FAMILY RELATIONSHIPS

At sixteen, Krystal is a mature young woman. She has a close relationship with both her mother and brother. Colleen says that she spent a lot of time and energy after Johnny's birth ensuring that little Krystal did not feel that "… his disability had a constant negative impact on her life … that she not be ashamed or embarrassed to invite her friends home because her brother had deformed hands."

"We have to battle every day to try and give our other children as normal a life as we can," she says. "Part of that is to protect Krystal from the constant level of stress that there is at home." Colleen purposely sent her daughter to a different school so that she could focus on her studies and not see her brother during the day. "Krystal knows he is in a place where he is well taken care of. So she can go to school and not always be around that level of stress. That's her break."

Krystal also spurred Colleen to wrack her brain for an age-appropriate way to explain Johnny's health. Her little girl, a bright and inquisitive three-year-old at the time, wanted to know why her brother was so very ill. Colleen looked to the Bible to explain why Johnny was born with such a huge set of challenges.

"Krystal was very angry at God for making her brother the way he is … I got her to understand that God is the reason Johnny is still here. Something I read in the Bible helped me to understand …"

Colleen refers to a passage of Scripture in which the Lord is asked why a child is born blind. "What did the parents do to cause this child to be punished?" The Lord answered that neither the mother nor the father had done anything but "… the child is the way he is so that the Lord's work may be manifested through him."

That notion conveys a powerful snapshot of how Colleen views Johnny. She has been entirely responsible for his care since he was quite tiny. Her husband has a new family and is not involved in Johnny's life. Her son's frailty has given unexpected purpose to Colleen's life. "Johnny can't physically advocate for himself, but he inspires me and motivates me to do what needs to be done … on behalf of so many people living with disabilities."

COMMUNITY

Becoming an activist can be very exhilarating. It can also be exhausting. In the heat of the moment, however, adrenalin runs aplenty and one feels stretched, learning new skills. Fighting for Johnny and his mates gave Colleen this rush. She discovered unknown camaraderie with the like-minded people who came together to preserve the unique program at St. Matthew's.

Colleen was ripe for this contact. From the outset of Johnny's life, she had little help dealing with her son's enormous and unrelenting need for special care. The sound of her voice hovers in zone neutral as she recounts this detail to me. Her demeanour hints no more intensity than if she were describing a neighbour trudging dutifully behind his dog on the sidewalk outside. In the short time I've spoken with Colleen, this relative deadpan is completely out of character. Like weather in a Newfoundland outpost, it doesn't last.

"You try getting ... a babysitter for a child that doctors are saying is going to die," she says. I found that the people who have been here to help me with Johnny started out as total strangers. They've become lifelong bonding friends, you know," she says, referring to the other St. Matthew's parents. "I would feel comfortable calling some of them if I really needed help." I can't help but wonder how a woman caring for two young children on her own managed to cultivate such obvious resilience. I imagine that involvement in her Church also helps solidify her stalwart inner strength, along with a deep sense of community.

"Parents like us ... we don't want our children to outlive us," says Colleen quietly. "Who is going to take care of our kids when we're not here?" This is a territory I know intimately. My son's illness threw me smack dab into this same agonizing dilemma. I felt so alone. When he went to live at his group home, his caregivers gave me invaluable support. For thirteen years, as it turned out, they provided humane care not just to my son but to our entire family.

"That's what you get from these parent groups ... because you're afraid to say these things to other people. It's not the way it's supposed to be, you know. Kids are supposed to bury their parents."

PLANNING FOR JOHNNY'S FUTURE

Johnny's future remains uncertain. He is an extremely vulnerable child; an infection that most kids would fight off could carry him away at any time. In such unsettled circumstances, many parents attempt to inject some measure of control. Concern for her son's future propels Colleen into planning mode despite the bumpy business that living for so long on red alert entails.

Taking matters in hand means canvassing all the "what ifs?" that could arise. Ironically, for Colleen, this includes the possibility that Johnny could outlive her.

As she describes this situation to me — fraught markedly with complexities few parents have to face — Colleen speaks warmly about the woman who takes Johnny some weekends to provide her with respite. Absolute trust in a caregiver is a rare possibility for mothers like Colleen. Evidently, Norma meets the test. The two women have agreed that Norma will care for young Johnny full-time in the event of Colleen's death.

While she knows that Krystal will remain involved in his life, Colleen is adamant that her daughter be free to pursue her career and her dreams. Despite the fact that Krystal cannot imagine her life without her brother, she listened carefully to her mother during our discussion and did not contradict her. For Colleen, this is absolutely not a negotiable matter.

She is determined to give her daughter wings. And it is her faith that helps Colleen persist through the demanding circumstances she faces every day. "I look at Johnny and I say, 'when God takes Johnny back, he's going back as wholesome and as pure as the day he came to me … Probably even more so because of what he's given to the world …' My hope is that Johnny will continue to touch people's lives …"

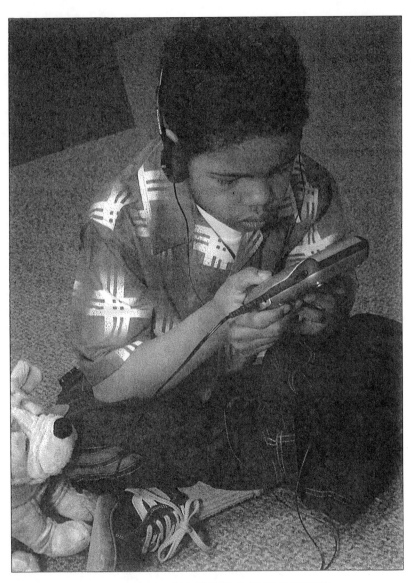

SIMON, AGE 5, DURING A QUIET MOMENT AT HOME IN TORONTO

CHAPTER TWELVE

JULIEN AND SIMON

JULIEN LEE, MOTHER OF SIX-YEAR-OLD SIMON, expects that one day she might hear him say, "My mom knows lots of blind people that go to work." And she is going to do everything in her power to make sure he does.

Julien is trained as a nurse and has worked for over fourteen years in her profession specializing in care for patients with dementia. She is now also employed by the Toronto District Canadian National Institute for the Blind (CNIB) as a vision rehabilitation worker. Her main task is to perform functional assessments for clients and encourage them to use what residual vision they have. She also educates them about the progress of their particular disease and how to use various types of assistive equipment.

I was introduced to Julien after making a cold call to the CNIB in Toronto. I explained I was writing a book and hoped to interview a mother whose child was sight-impaired. Officials at the agency were very helpful, and a day later I received a message with Julien's name and phone number, indicating that she was willing to participate. In a telephone conversation later that week, we made our initial acquaintance. I told her a bit about my research with other parents and a few details about my family and our challenges. She asked me what kinds of questions I would pose and where the book would be published. First contact made, we agreed to meet the next week.

Julien has four children, including two grown children from her first marriage who no longer live at home. In addition to Simon, she and her husband Owen are raising their older son, Jeremiah, an active nine-year-old.

SIMON'S BIRTH

On the unseasonably warm December day that I meet Julien at her office, she tells me a story. It is about a clash in attitudes between she and her mother, one that repeated itself many times following Simon's birth. Julien found her mother's perception of Simon's future prospects rather troubling. His grandmother, a native of Trinidad, called Simon "my poor child" and tended to moan about his poor health. Julien wanted her mother to accept him just as he was. She felt that her mother was not offering the kind of compassion Julien wanted for her beautiful boy.

Julien looks at me intently to check that I know the difference between empathy and the sympathy her mother tended to express lovingly at Simon's birth.

"But that is how my mom was raised to respond to a tragedy in the family," Julien explains. "She'd tell me she was praying for Simon."

"Pray more, Mom. You'll get that good spiritual connection," Julien would tell her. "But it doesn't mean his vision is going to come back tomorrow."

"You don't have faith," was her mother's retort.

"Yes I do," said Julien, "but what you don't understand is how the eye works."

And click would go the telephone.

Taking such responses in stride, Julien is raising Simon with the best possible medical and therapeutic care available.

Simon was born with bilateral cataracts, meaning the clouding of the lenses on both sides. This condition was diagnosed when he had barely reached one week old. A referral was made immediately to the Hospital for Sick Children in Toronto. By age six weeks, a brave baby Simon was in surgery to have the cataracts removed.

In fact, his mother explains, Simon was born without properly functioning pupils. One was malformed and did not contract properly; on the other side the pupil was practically non-existent, meaning that light could not get into the back of the eye, a prerequisite for ordinary vision. Simon has no natural lenses, which means that the vision he has is blurry. He has worn strong contact lenses to correct his eyesight since he was six weeks old. Julien explains that with the high strength dioptres required, Simon could not have worn glasses. Nor could he wear soft contact lenses as an infant or toddler — his prescription was so strong that he needed hard contacts. Now at six years old, his prescription is somewhat reduced and he can wear the more comfortable soft contact lenses. He also lives with a progressive condition, glaucoma, which affects his peripheral vision. During the early months of his life, Julien was aware that Simon might have other challenges to overcome besides his vision. "He was a slow child in moving ... at four and five months old, he would sit ... even with his lenses, he didn't move."

LIFE WITH SIMON

Julien has been responsible for putting in and removing the contact lenses from the beginning. "Day in and day out, it would be a battle with this baby," she says. "He would be screaming when I removed these lenses. They need to be cleansed because there is a high risk of eye infection which, of course, can lead to more complicated things." Her training as a nurse is evident.

"His dad tries, and he can manage. In an emergency situation he can manage. But Owen prefers that one person handle it ... in six years, this kid hasn't had one eye infection," Julien says with some pride. "If they weren't put in — and so much of what we learn is through visual cues — a great deal of Simon's learning would have been delayed."

Julien describes in vivid terms Simon's distressed reaction as an infant and toddler to having his contact lenses put in and removed. His high-pitched crying pierced the air. It was unremitting and of course Simon was too young to know why his mother was touching his eyes, even though she performed the procedure ever so carefully. Simon's would wail for about five minutes, until the procedure was completed. Only then could Julien comfort him.

"Imagine ... every day there would be this five minutes of loud crying in the morning and at his bedtime," she says. "I had to tell the neighbours — I had to explain the crying to them so they wouldn't be worried and call Children's Aid."

"Now they know Simon, of course, and they see him so grown-up and active. It's been such a wonderful transition to see him go down the stairs with his cane to the bus, and wanting to be on the school bus by himself."

At this point in his life, Simon has a narrow field of vision. Knowing how to use his cane allows Simon to get around safely and have some independence. His glaucoma involves increased fluid pressure within the eyeball. This damages the optic nerve and causes vision loss that can progress to blindness. Medication helps to reduce the intraocular pressure that frequently causes tearing, sensitivity to light and redness of the eye. Eventually Simon won't have any peripheral vision at all. For the moment, Julien administers medication to control the progress of the disease. Simon also uses eyedrops to reduce the discomfort that glaucoma produces.

It concerns Julien that some people do not realize that a lack of peripheral vision can be quite dangerous for a child (or anyone!). By using his cane, Simon is more able to navigate his way. A mobility specialist at his school taught him how to use it when he was in Junior Kindergarten. Julien tells me that people sometimes tussle over whether to allow their child to be seen in public with a cane. It seems that some parents and family members are afraid the cane will draw unwanted attention to their child. Julien is adamant on this point.

"The cane is absolutely necessary," she says. "It's a safety factor. He needs to be aware of where he is. The only way he can do that is to have that cane, so he knows what's beside him and what is coming up. It decreases his chance of injuring himself."

At home, his mother says, he doesn't need it; he knows every nook and cranny of the family home. "He runs around like a maniac. He tries to jump off the top of the staircase like all kids," says Julien. "That's out, but he does manage to jump from the second step to the landing and he thinks that's a great feat. I let him do that."

"Sometimes I feel like work is a relief," she says. "I'm taking care of other people's stuff. It's not as stressful." Julien mentions that she finds she has more compassion for others than she use to — and not just in "that typical nurse way," she quips.

"I've learned so much because of Simon. I don't think that learning curve would have come about without him. Before, I was so involved, and I had to finish my degree, and I had to do this and that … and I just think a big hand came down and said, 'Hold up, this is what you have to deal with now. You need to stop.'

"Now I have an understanding for what other people are going through," she says. "It could be the woman at the McDonald's window that you're barking at, 'Hey you didn't put the ketchup with my fries!' It could be that woman, or any other woman we encounter. And I say 'woman' because we women tend not to have that respect for each other sometimes."

SERVICES AND EDUCATION

When, during Simon's infancy, Julien realized Simon had other challenges than his vision, she sought assistance from the Ontario Foundation for Visually Impaired Children and other agencies. Early intervention specialists were dispatched to Simon's home. It was their role to educate the family and introduce toys, cueing skills and other techniques, known as infant stimulation, to encourage Simon's movement.[102] This therapy required Julien to carry out a range of follow-up activities to rouse her son's senses and development and fortunately Simon responded well. He also received occupational therapy in these early years to encourage him to move about and explore his environment.

"He was weaker than my other children," she says. "Simon just seemed a little floppy. I know, it's a great medical term," she chuckles. "That's how I can describe him: He was like a floppy bunny, a soft little toy. He wasn't as strong as he could be.

"He was very stubborn too. Simon had his own way of doing things. I think maybe I wasn't recognizing that he wanted to be more independent. Maybe we were helping him too much, I don't know." I am watchful as Julien says this. Of course the reflection is her truth, but so many of the mothers I interviewed expressed some doubt about their parenting skills. It seems to go with the territory, and certainly not just with special needs kids.

"Simon's speech was also delayed," she continues. "So initially we were signing to him." Julien had begun learning American Sign Language ten years earlier. It certainly came in handy. When Simon was very small, she could show him the sign for milk and they could communicate before he was able to form words.

"At first, he would make sort of grunting sounds. That's because the child isn't really close enough to see the facial expression, the animation, the lip movement and where the sound is coming from — all these little things I wish I knew more about then … in retrospect, these things would be helpful to a mom …" I know Julien is passing on this information, in part, in the hope that other women in her situation will learn more about interacting with their sight-impaired children.

"Even with all my nursing and medical background, you can understand the physiological processes, but what you can expect from the child doesn't follow a textbook," she says. "In fact, should we be putting deadlines and setting goals when it's truly the child's call? Every child is different."

"Now, he won't shut up!" she says with a laugh. "On a road trip you have to say 'now it's quiet time, let's play signing.'"

Julien explains that most blind children experience difficulty related to concept development. She says it is as though there are some blank pages that have to be filled in. "The child that is born totally blind has no concept what a carrot looks like. Or a flower. At least we know Simon's been in the garden. But last year, he asked, 'what's under the grass?' He should know about soil … but he doesn't because I didn't have him in the garden when he was little. I didn't want him getting his hands dirty and getting an eye infection … but he should have this concept of soil …"

Simon has had several hospital visits in his short life. Not just his premier surgery as a newborn, but also ongoing three-monthly checks to evaluate his glaucoma. At the time of our meeting, Simon's glaucoma checks are carried out in the operating room which means he has to be anaesthetized. When he is old enough to cooperate, a simple procedure can be done quite easily in a physician's office. Most ophthalmologists administer drops in the eye for this at regular eye examinations. "But," says Julien, giving me a knowing look, "one has to be able to sit still long enough and not shriek!"

When I ask what might help her deal with the tremendous stress she sometimes feels Julien says, "Respite care is the only thing that I could make use of that's not really available. Respite, but not too far away — maybe a granny apartment with a monitor, so I could check on them," she jokes. It's obvious that her sense of humour often carries her through tough times. I can see that Julien shares the mixed feelings we mothers often have about leaving our young children in someone else's care, even when we know we're tired and, moreover, that our son or daughter may also benefit from time spent with other caring individuals.

FAMILY RELATIONSHIPS

The two boys are inseparable, Julien tells me with a smile. "When Simon enters the room from school, his first question is, 'Is Jeremiah home?' and Jeremiah ... the same thing, 'Is Simon home yet?' They are very close. Jeremiah treats Simon no differently than any other child. They roughhouse, they wrestle, and they do whatever ... contact lenses or no contact lenses!" Cousins and frequent playmates also learn how to play with Simon safely.

When Julien and Owen first brought Simon home from the hospital, Julien told then three-year-old Jeremiah that, "Simon sees in a special way." That satisfied the young fellow's curiosity and he's grown into a big brother any boy could be proud to have.

"Now, at nine years old, Jeremiah is a strong-minded kid, a big kid. And he's also a sensitive child," says his mother. "He watches out for Simon and protects him. They've formed quite a connection."

Interestingly, although his parents never requested it, Jeremiah takes on some responsibility to ensure his younger brother's special needs are met. "He is very aware of what Simon requires in terms of allergies and his medications. Jeremiah just learns and can tell his aunt (or another adult) when the boys are visiting and I'm not there," says Julien.

In the course of our conversation, Julien voices her concern that Simon's dad still has some difficulty accepting that his youngest boy is sight-impaired. "Owen is still looking for the positive," she says. "He's a macho guy and he didn't produce a perfect specimen. In terms of the grieving we all do, he hasn't passed the first stage. He's angry. Not at anyone in particular ... just angry."

Now that Simon is old enough to participate in team sports, she feels that her husband must come to grips with this challenge. He is still reticent, she explains. "There are alternatives for low vision and blind kids. It means talking to other parents, getting interactive ... This is a big strain on our relationship for sure."

COMMUNITY

From Julien's voice and her demeanour it is evident that I am in the presence of a strong, bright woman. Occasionally, as we speak, she picks up one of the models of the eye that she uses with her clients and illustrates her remarks more fully by showing me how various parts of the eye work.

She seems to have a fairly relaxed attitude toward parenting even though her situation must be nerve-wracking at times. Perhaps the fact that she has already raised two children to adulthood accounts for her confidence with Jeremiah and Simon, or it may be a question of temperament.

I wonder how she felt at the beginning of Simon's life, since so many of us take a while to adjust to our babies' challenges and what they will mean to our lives — to all the wonderful complexities that any child brings.

The Hospital for Sick Children has support groups that run on-site and to which parents are frequently directed. The facility's social workers also help parents to link up with support networks in their community. I asked Julien if she had made any contact with these groups when Simon was tiny. She told me that while she knew a little about such groups, she had felt too drained emotionally to take that step. She also explained that she had soon returned to her nursing job after Simon's birth and found that she needed all of her energy to care for her children while also maintaining her professional mindset.

"I had to answer questions about my child, but I didn't want to give too much information," she says. "People often have misconceptions about blindness or other disabilities. They can associate them with behaviours that have nothing to do with my family. I needed my privacy too."

Although she chose not to be involved in community support groups at the time of Simon's birth or during the rather demanding, complicated first years of his life, Julien now believes that contact with other moms would have helped her. But at that time, she says with a hint of regret, she was just "in too much pain."

I recall in my own life how hard I found it to maintain my social veneer when my son was in crisis, especially near the beginning of his life. Even going to a meeting of a mothers' group run by public health in our community took great effort. It can be difficult to let anyone into your emotional life and harder to reach out, just when you need it most. And yet, many of us would counsel our friends to do exactly what we found impossible ourselves when they encounter challenging situations in their lives. Perhaps the lesson to be drawn is that we try to find that delicate balance between intruding in a friend's life and helping the person by offering to babysit other children, for example, or even by accompanying her to the support group.

As a Black woman and mother, Julien allows that she faces particular dilemmas raising her family. At the time of our meeting, the Ontario Human Rights Commission had just released its report "Paying the Price: The Human Cost of Racial Profiling."[103] It confirmed what many in her community already knew first-hand: Racial profiling exists in the city and must be addressed. The report made several recommendations regarding public institutions in general, though it highlighted the police force.

Julien and I spoke about some of her family's recent experiences of discrimination. Stereotypes and discrimination still occur in many public facilities, including health care agencies and schools. It might be assumed, for example, that a woman of colour looking for care at a doctor's office has several children with different fathers, when there is no basis to make any such assumption. A tall, sturdy Black man might be perceived as a physical threat on first meeting, when no such indication exists. Julien's family, just as those in many of the experiences documented in the December 2003 Human Rights Commission Report, is no stranger to this kind of misconception. She is clear that such stereotypes only thwart important lines of communication she (and any parent) needs to develop with her sons' teachers and doctors. As we are speaking, I have no doubt that her interaction with various agencies and public officials may often be qualitatively different from a person with white skin. However, she has felt her nurse's training has helped in her interactions with medical professionals.

ADVOCACY

Julien believes they have been quite fortunate at Toronto's Hospital for Sick Children. "Simon's physicians have been very honest with us and very efficient," she tells me. "I get full explanations, including details of the procedure, anaesthesia and any pertinent operating room details."

She feels confident that the doctors and nurses she deals with take into account her professional knowledge when discussing Simon's case with her. It is obvious to me that for this mother, being treated respectfully by medical teams is important. As she describes the extent of her son's contact with various physicians and the hospital, I sense that Julien would not tolerate anything less than a peer relationship. I suspect strongly that they know this too.

PLANNING FOR SIMON'S FUTURE

"If I educate this child, he has the capacity to overcome many challenges — and he's getting there — if he's educated in all formats; if he can read Braille quickly, he can use his computer, he can use his software, use his zoom text ... Simon will continue to be educated as long as I'm here. He knows how to blow up text on the screen. We are fortunate he is equipped.

When I ask Julien about her hopes for Simon's future, she doesn't miss a beat. "Simon is going to be awesome. Already, he wants a car that drives," she says. "Well, I tell him, there are these little remote control cars."

"No, you don't understand," he says. "I want a car that I can get in and I drive."

"That's the hard part, when you're looking at your son and imagining him as a twenty-year-old. As far as we know, glaucoma isn't reversible. It's a progressive disease and is managed. So your field of vision is reduced significantly. I'm not a doctor, but that is what we understand today in 2003. I'm very proud of Simon's accomplishments," says Julien. "The fact that he can express his needs is one of the biggest things. We weren't sure if this boy would ever verbalize." She is also pleased that Simon "... knows his limits. It's amazing that a six-year-old can say, 'I think I need some ventolin now' or 'my eyes hurt, I need drops.' He knows his needs."

"He will be able to fend for himself and he has his older brothers and sister. They will guide him. And that's why I work a lot, because I want to make sure that if he needs anything it can be provided," says Julien. "We're very fortunate here in Ontario, most of it is covered.

"Most of all, I'm happy that he doesn't see anything wrong with himself. He sees himself as perfectly normal. That I'm proud of."

JEREMIAH, AGE 7, AND ENOSH, AGE 11, KIBITZ IN THE BATH

CHAPTER THIRTEEN

CHERYL AND ENOSH

IT IS MAY 2003 AND I AM SITTING in the pleasant, modest living room of Cheryl and Tzvika Gaster's home in Toronto's East End. They have two sons, Enosh and Jeremiah. Tzvika works as an accountant and Cheryl is now a mediator with the provincial human rights commission. She is telling me about Enosh's life, his friends and the complex health challenges he confronted.

I have looked forward to this interview for some time. I know something of Cheryl's story from our few brief exchanges over the last seven or eight years. When our paths crossed on occasion at various community events we would quickly share snippets about our sons' activities and health. We certainly don't know one another well, but I am aware that Enosh lived to age twenty-four, dying in 1999. Cheryl knows about my son Jake and the writing and advocacy I've done on behalf of families like ours.

Cheryl welcomes me. She is calm, composed. Her dark hair is pulled back, wonderful wisps of silver beginning to appear. It feels to me that she wants to share her story. Our prior contact helps, fleeting though it's been; we each bring our good credentials to the table, both as mothers of severely challenged children and as politically engaged Jewish women. Cheryl's children were born several years before my own, Enosh in 1974 and Jeremiah in 1978.

This is the first time we have met purposefully for any reason and now we do so to speak about her eldest son. I fully expect our conversation to cover difficult territory, but I am also hopeful it will be infused with warmth and empathy. Cheryl and I know something of one another's emotional landscape: we have each given birth to a son who, along with his radiant smile, had a regrettable prognosis.

We are drinking tea from ceramic mugs, sitting on the comfortable sofa in the living room situated at the front of the house. Out the window I can see nearby homes, the rich spring foliage shading small yards, vines creeping up brick, just beginning to adorn exterior walls. When I first arrived Cheryl had given me a quick tour of the downstairs, showing me the area at the back of the house where Enosh's bed was situated during the last years of his life. She indicates a separate washroom cat-a-corner that allowed her young man a measure of privacy. A bank of four large windows extends across the back of the house. Looking out from his bed, Enosh could see the trees and flowers in the backyard; catch a glimpse of birds that alighted on his wooden swing. The kitchen, hub of family activity, was located just behind him.

As we make our way back to the living room, Cheryl mentions that the family is still learning to reclaim that space. I sense that Enosh's presence still lingers, a loving tribute to the fullness of his life. Even before the tape is rolling, I anticipate Cheryl's flood of memories; images sweet, tart and, occasionally, bitter to the tongue like a wild blackberry torn from the vine before it is fully ripe.

Passing through the kitchen I meet Cheryl's younger son Jeremiah, then age twenty-five, working at the kitchen table. He looks up from his university studies to nod hello. In the room where Cheryl and I begin to speak, photographs of the boys share wall space with paintings and Israeli artwork. A portrait of Enosh hangs across from us. Close to where she sits is a unit with four shelves that I only gradually realize are devoted to Enosh and tender family memories. One photo shows the brothers together, much younger and smiling brightly for the camera. Pictures, letters, photos and memories — this is the safe corner of a mother who grieves.

Enosh's Birth

As Cheryl and I begin our conversation, she tells me that there were many stages in her son's life. "First and foremost Enosh was a very wanted baby … He was adored from the moment we knew he was expected," she says. "He was very beautiful. He had these enormous blue eyes and the reddest, reddest hair, like a flame on the top of his head. And he had enormous ears that he eventually, thank goodness, grew into." Cheryl's sense of delight envelops us as she recounts her son's early infancy.

Enosh was born at the Hadassah Hospital in Jerusalem, Israel in July 1974, a seemingly healthy baby boy. The Yom Kippur War that broke out in autumn 1973 was the powerful catalyst that impelled the couple to return to Israel, a long way from British Columbia where they had been living simply on Bowen Island off the Vancouver coast. Like many Israelis living abroad, Tzvika felt compelled to rejoin his army unit for the duration of the war. When they touched down at the airport in Tel Aviv, Tzvika was met by the army and swept immediately to his unit.

Cheryl made her way to Kibbutz Negba, Tzvika's family home. Her journey took several hours, arriving at his kibbutz located near Ashkelon, south of Tel Aviv on the Mediterranean. She tells me it was never their intent to permanently leave their life in Canada, her home. She accompanied Tzvika to Israel mainly because she figured that if something happened to him, no army authority would know to inform her. While this is conveyed as a practical decision, I suspect their love for one another and commitment as life partners also figured in the equation.

Cheryl describes herself as having been an earth mother; she looked forward to nursing her babies and raising a family with Tzvika. As it turned out, several children were born on the kibbutz around the same time. As was customary on kibbutz at that time, infants and children lived primarily in separate children's houses near to their parents. Cheryl says she found "… the whole concept too foreign to accept." She says she could not bear to be separated from her baby.

Enosh was smaller than the other babies born that summer. When he didn't hold up his head or focus his gaze like the other infants, Cheryl became concerned. The *Metapelet* (Hebrew for the woman who is head caregiver for the children's houses) on the kibbutz urged her to relax, telling her that everything would turn out fine. Cheryl was reluctant to accede, conscious that from early in her son's life she had had to make quite an effort to entice Enosh to look at her directly and to focus his gaze on specific objects. She continued to breastfeed until he was about eight months old.

"Later, he started to put on weight," says Cheryl. "When he lay on his belly, he brought his legs up to his tush, with his knees out to the side, as if he were doing the frog kick." It was only much later that she and Tzvika learned that this position is a classic sign of developmental delay. At the time, no one on the kibbutz recognized it. Then, at about the same time he began plumping up, Enosh also started to focus his eyes. It was a hopeful sign.

"Once he did find Tzvika and me," she tells me, "he would track us and no one else for a long time." When Enosh was still a young infant, "… I think we learned what tones he particularly liked, what loudness he felt safe with and what speed of movement and speech he could respond to and assimilate." If people approached him too swiftly or loudly, Enosh tended to "… freeze until they proved to him they could be sensitive to his pace."

Enosh took a long time to smile, "… way past the time other babies on the kibbutz were smiling," says Cheryl. She describes encouraging him to smile over a long period of time, to no avail. "Then one day when he was still an infant, he gave it like a gift. His smile was infectious and beamed like a bright light.

"He was a joy, but he never slept," Cheryl tells me. We both roll our eyes, recognizing a refrain so familiar to young parents. "Then at six months of age Enosh became sick," says Cheryl. "At first, it looked like a cold. He lost weight. His face became heavy under his eyes and he lost ground in terms of development. He couldn't hold up his head, couldn't sit up, and by this time, all the other kids could sit. He even stopped trying to roll over."

LIFE WITH ENOSH

Just before Enosh's first birthday and after the most intense period of the war, Cheryl and Tzvika decided to return to Canada. They settled near Toronto where Cheryl's family lived. Tzvika found work as a farmhand on a dairy farm in Inglewood, northeast of Toronto. They were about forty-five minutes away from Cheryl's parents' home and one hour from the Hospital for Sick Children.

One of the first medical contacts they made in Toronto was with a geneticist at the Hospital for Sick Children. "She was so respectful," says Cheryl. "Although she had nothing but devastating news to tell us, she never once denied us our hope or right to love Enosh." The geneticist told Tzvika and Cheryl that Enosh had cytomegalovirus (CMV), then a recently identified disease. CMV-related infection is a congenital (meaning, from birth) viral infection thought to be passed from mother to baby in utero. "There was not a lot of history," says Cheryl. "Life expectancy was not great — not long or easy. There simply wasn't a lot of information then about the disease." Scientists now know that CMV can cause a range of deficits that affect mental capacity, physical coordination, sight and hearing. Each child presents in her or his own unique way. As a toddler and very young child Enosh did not walk or speak words.

"Our geneticist was wonderful. We soon learned how rare that can be. It was a very hard time ... we started on this journey," Cheryl explains. "I guess we mourned all the lost opportunity. We had no idea what was ahead for Enosh or for ourselves." Cheryl pauses for a moment and catches my eye. As we skip onto the next phase of her story I recall that initial, deep sense of loss from the moment my infant son was diagnosed with lissencephaly. Just as you grasp joy in one hand, you are seized by sorrow. Like watching a child stand atop a teeter-totter trying to find that elusive point of equilibrium, one experiences intense and contradictory feelings, never quite achieving the reassurance that balance brings.

SERVICES AND EDUCATION

Cheryl and Tzvika found a nursery school about twenty minutes from home that welcomed Enosh. The staff performed infant stimulation with him, a myriad of exercises to cue his senses and motor skills. Infant stimulation refers to a number of activities to help augment a baby's senses, for example, caressing her skin with different textures; playing music and varying sounds on tape; introducing little vials, each filled with a distinct odour for the infant to smell.

"Attending this nursery school was all arranged on an informal basis ... they loved him," says Cheryl. "I dressed him nicely; he was appealing and well-received, his appearance a kind of entrée into his new social world."

Cheryl had trained as a pre-school teacher, so she was knowledgeable about child development and the milestones one could expect. This helped her tune in to Enosh as he grew into a toddler. She took him swimming and introduced him to different activities intended to enhance his awareness of the world.

Early in 1976 the family moved into Toronto to be closer to the medical resources that Enosh needed and in order for Tzvika to study. They found an apartment not far from where Cheryl's parents lived. Unlike in a smaller community, however, she found Toronto a challenging place to hook up with the services her son needed. "Informal arrangements were much harder to find," she says.

That January, Tzvika and Cheryl had an extremely disturbing experience with a psychologist who assessed their son. She "... had no clue about loving and cherishing a child," she says. "She told us that Enosh was a vegetable and that we should not love him too much. She said we should put him in an institution ... and (essentially) that we were young, we were healthy, and should get on with our lives." Cheryl and Tzvika were appalled by this woman's professional opinion and negative attitude toward Enosh; they told her in no uncertain terms that "... she just didn't get it." Almost thirty years later, Cheryl's rage at this particular psychologist still smoulders.

Sadly they found it was not unusual to get this kind of response from some people and some professionals who encountered their son. "It was very hard for people to see past the drool, to see past the vocalizations, or see past how he moved his body or bit down on his finger," says Cheryl. "That was as far as they could go, that was all they could see. We always encouraged questions because it meant they were interested in getting past some of that superficial stuff. We would never make people feel embarrassed about asking questions — whether they were adults or children."

During the mid-sixties and early seventies there was a great deal of hope and belief in the province's evolving education system. Ontario was enjoying an economic boom. In 1965 an Ontario Provincial Committee on Aims and Objectives had begun its work on transforming the public education system to focus more on child-centred learning. The Committee was headed by two eminent individuals: Justice E. M. Hall and Lloyd A. Dennis. Its findings were reported in 1968 in an inspiring photo-filled coffee table style, soft-cover book entitled *Living and Learning*. Also known as the Hall-Dennis Report, the report was circulated widely to schools and parents and reflected the anti-traditionalist, anti-technocratic impulses typical of the 1960s.

Bill Davis, then premier of the province, had run on a platform that trumpeted the potential of Ontario's public school system to engage every child's imagination and potential. It was a period characterized by hope. For children like Enosh, however, "Everything was a struggle," Cheryl notes. The debate over inclusion and segregation for children with disabilities had not yet come to the fore. Segregation of children with disabilities was standard.

After a considerable amount of research, calling upon the expertise of other parents and professionals, Cheryl identified a nursery school located in mid-town Toronto that was geared to young children with special needs. The nursery had a very good reputation. It was the family's initiation into the segregated system. Cheryl says the teachers were great, but she believes the children were learning the wrong lessons. "There weren't high expectations. Keeping these children apart from the mainstream was sending a negative message."

Enosh remained in the segregated system until Grade 3. Cheryl devoted a lot of time to helping out in the school. But, she tells me, her frustration still evident, she continued to feel that her son was not presented with enough learning or life challenges. "At the time, I kept saying, 'I want him to live as normal a life as possible. I want him to have friends. I want him to be stimulated ...'"

While Cheryl was struggling to find a more integrated school setting for Enosh, her young son was waging an important battle on another front. From the time Enosh was two, Cheryl and Tzvika were told that he would not learn to walk or talk. Not easily deterred, their research unearthed an approach pioneered in Philadelphia called "Doman-Delecato" (D-D).

From about age three to five and a half, Enosh participated in this very specialized program, administered for several hours every day by his family and volunteers. The D-D approach was based on the principle of patterning. Used originally with stroke patients, the person who was the subject of the program would lie on his belly while three people (one on each side and one holding the head) would move the arms and legs in a pattern.

For kids like Enosh who had never crawled or moved along on the floor, the objective was to teach him how his body could work. Undertaking this approach meant periodically travelling to Philadelphia, first to learn the techniques involved and then to have Enosh's progress monitored and evaluated. Fortunately, Cheryl's parents offered to cover the cost.

It was while in the D-D program that they discovered Enosh's hearing, "...was terribly acute. It was not easy for him to distinguish between background noise and the primary noise we might want him to attend to — our voices, for example, over everyone else's or traffic, for example," Cheryl explains. "One of the exercises we did in the D-D rehabilitation program was to take Enosh into a darkened bathroom where it would be totally quiet. We would have him track a flashlight in the dark while we whispered to him." The dual purpose of this exercise was to help diminish the sensory overload Enosh experienced constantly as a result of his acute hearing. At the same time, it also assisted in training his eyes to track.

After about six to eight months in the program, the specialists in Philadelphia told Cheryl and Tzvika that the prognosis for their four-year-old son was grim: He would develop, plateau, deteriorate and then die. Cheryl would not give up. If anything, receiving this information redoubled her determination to kick-start Enosh's development in every conceivable way. Giving her son every possible opportunity to develop mobility skills became her full-time job. She wanted him to know the independence and confidence that moving his body voluntarily would bring.

It was a mammoth undertaking. Enosh had therapy six hours a day, seven days a week. Keeping up this pace required that sixty volunteers assist the family. Cheryl took Enosh to Philadelphia every two months to have his progress assessed and to receive the next steps devised for his program. Once home, they would build equipment to the doctors' specifications and continue the therapy.

Cheryl's mother signed on as "volunteer coordinator." In an animated tone Cheryl describes a beehive of activity. Setting up this innovative therapy for Enosh acquired the gusto of a mission. "My mother found volunteers at her synagogue and Jewish day schools," says Cheryl. "She even went door to door in nearby apartments looking for volunteers."

Over two and a half years, Enosh went from zero mobility to walking! He also learned to sit and to recognize words on flashcards. It was evident to his family that Enosh understood a great deal more than he could convey verbally. Then he began to communicate very effectively with gestures and signs that his family taught him. He developed some of the signals on his own. Each sign had a particular meaning. For example, Enosh made up some signs for "Jeremiah — little brother" and "the wheels on the bus," "the sun," "drink," and "music" (to name only a few), and his entourage would adopt them as well.

Cheryl made a photo book for Enosh to wear. It was attached onto his belt loop so that everyone with whom he came into contact could understand him. She takes the book from the shelving unit near the couch where we are sitting and shows me how Enosh would signal, conveying different messages. "He totally understood," she says.

The book contains several pictures of a young Enosh gesturing in different ways, with captions written in large print to explain what he is saying or needs. Cheryl is positively joyful as she shows it to me. It is made of sturdy cardboard connected by large metal rings to make it very durable. We both enjoy this moment in which she shows me action photos of her beautiful young son. He is glowing back at us during an especially healthy part of his life. The love contained in this brilliant photo book, so lovingly constructed by his mother's hands, is palpable. Enosh is with us in the room.

Until he was fourteen, he had no caregivers other than his family. Of course he had had contact with the many volunteers over the years, but none of them were entirely responsible for his care. Cheryl worked with him at home full-time. In 1987, just prior to Enosh's fourteenth birthday, she had applied to law school and was successful. She prepared to enter the demanding legal training in September.

In August 1988, just prior to this major change in the family's routines, Enosh was diagnosed with epilepsy. He had come home from summer camp with new health challenges that, after investigation, turned out to be seizures. Cheryl described them to me as "awful and constant." His physicians prescribed various medications, each with their own unpleasant set of side effects. Sadly, Enosh was allergic to these drugs. It became very difficult for him to sleep, and he lost his appetite as the convulsions took over.

Cheryl takes a breath, pausing a few moments to gather her energy. By this time, we've spent more than two hours together. She then continues, with great emphasis. "This was the demarcation point between all of this hope and light and wonderful life plans for independent living, and the curtain falling. It was just a different story from then on ... it was misery."

"Enosh slowly lost ground. Everything was subsumed by these seizures." He had no choice but to stop most, if not all, the activities he loved. His condition did not permit any more swimming, skating, skiing or going to camp. The downward spiral was quick and intense. He began to have unprecedented injuries; repeated sprains, fractures and stitches.

Enosh was seizing through the night. Tzvika and Cheryl would take turns staying up with him. "We didn't know what we were doing. We were constantly calling 911," she tells me. Exhaustion was setting in. Cheryl and Tzvika were still working outside the home; Jeremiah was at school. Trying to maintain the household and care for Enosh on their own was becoming harder. It was obvious — if not to the actors embroiled in this drama, then certainly to those looking in — that something was going to give. "That's when the caregivers started. Our friends stepped in and put an ad in the paper and hired someone." Having paid caregivers come in was a necessary step. Cheryl and Tzvika covered the bulk of the cost. The caregivers were a tremendous help to Enosh and the family, but new and unforeseen risks were also in the offing.

During our conversation Cheryl describes several incidents in which Enosh was put in compromising situations by his paid caregivers or, when he was younger, persons meant to ferry him to an activity and deliver him home safely. Cheryl explains that she and Tzvika rarely went out in the evening during the final years of Enosh's life. On one occasion that they did, they returned to find the male nurse sent by an agency drunk and passed out on their son's bed. In the morning they felt compelled to take Enosh to the doctor to check for signs of abuse. Fortunately, none were found. But the rage and sense of betrayal and powerlessness one feels when a beloved child is unable to protect himself was enormous.

In another incident Cheryl describes to me, her anger flaring just below the surface as we speak, she received a telephone call from the police. Enosh was seen sitting alone in a locked car in a dark underground parking lot at 10:00 a.m. and again at 3:00 p.m. — he had been there practically an entire day. The police were bent on pressing charges against the parents, especially as the caregiver denied having left Enosh there. Such events did not occur on a daily basis; nonetheless these episodes underline the extreme vulnerability of children and young people with severe disabilities. If a child does not have the ability to speak, to recount what has happened to her, how can an aggressor be stopped or held accountable?

At age eighteen, as his health continued to deteriorate, the circle of friends that supported Enosh and the family continued to meet, review budgets and deal with the three government ministries involved: Health, Social Services and Education. Their goal was to obtain one envelope of money to meet Enosh's various needs and to pay decent wages to the caregivers that would be involved.

By this point, care for Enosh was costing approximately $150,000 a year. His parents were paying $40,000 out of their pockets each year to cover a variety of expenses, including the training of caregivers and providing them with paid vacations and overtime for holidays and weekend work. Tzvika's insurance through his employer had provided for R.N. care but his firm told him that it had become unaffordable. Cheryl explains to me that while they could have gone to court, it did not seem wise "... to litigate oneself out of a job." Somehow they managed to offer their son the maximum in comfort care: massage treatments to help alleviate the pain, natural tinctures and herbal teas which were meant to lessen the intensity and frequency of his seizures.

"By this time, Enosh's seizures had mounted between ten and thirty per day," Cheryl says. "We needed enough changes of all his clothing, including pants, shirts, underwear, socks, and pads to cover furniture, blankets, sheets, winter jackets, shoes, sweaters, so there were always enough changes of everything. The seizures caused him to wet himself almost every time."

Cheryl kept track of every illness and medication. Her records show that between 1988 and 1999, her son suffered from aspiration pneumonia over fifty times. This pneumonia is an inflammation of the lungs and bronchial tubes caused by inhaling foreign material, most commonly food, drink, vomit or secretions from the mouth, into the lungs. The illness may progress to form a collection of pus in the lungs (lung abscess). The injured lungs then can become infected with multiple species of bacteria, causing a bacterial pneumonia, one of the most serious forms.

In January 1993, Enosh went into septic shock and was put on a respirator. Septic shock is a serious condition that occurs when an overwhelming infection leads to low blood pressure and low blood flow. Vital organs such as the brain, heart, kidneys and liver may not function properly or simply fail altogether. The family was asked by hospital staff if they wanted heroic measures performed. Cheryl was angry — she did not believe the parent of a non-disabled child would have been asked the same question. She responded resolutely, "This is the first time he is ill."

From then on, Enosh needed a feeding tube to receive nourishment. The neurologist then recommended brain surgery to lessen the seizures. Neither parent was in favour. They were afraid they would lose something of their son. After considerable discussion and debate, the doctor told them either to allow the surgery or Enosh would die. The surgery was done. In the end, it did nothing to ease the convulsions. Cheryl tells me, her bitterness evident, that Enosh did, however, lose all speech and his ability to smile.

FAMILY RELATIONSHIPS

Tzvika and Cheryl were in agreement from very early days that Jeremiah was not to carry responsibility for Enosh's care. The boys did enjoy a number of sporting activities together. "Jeremiah kind of knew instinctively at a very young age that Enosh needed help with certain things." For example, Cheryl says, as a toddler Jeremiah knew not to leave the house without his mother, so if Enosh went out, Jeremiah would be first on the scene, blocking his brother and calling their mother to come.

"On many levels, Jeremiah was like an only child," says Cheryl. "They couldn't share intimacies about 'how awful' their parents were … There were only certain ways they could play together and certain periods (of Enosh's life) when they could interact …"

One point, however, was absolutely clear from the outset. Cheryl and Tzvika did not want Jeremiah to ever feel his brother as a burden. "What eventually happened was actually quite wonderful," she says. Jeremiah ended up taking some time off after high school, and for most of Enosh's last year, Jeremiah was one of his caregivers. This was something that Jeremiah had chosen to do, and obviously no one knew that it was Enosh's last year of life. "You could see, although it was much harder for Enosh to communicate at that time. You could see that he was relieved whenever Jeremiah was his caregiver … there was so much trust between them.

"And Jeremiah learned so much in that time, being with Enosh. They were very intimate with each other, and so it was quite amazing how it worked out. That last year was a very special time for both of them."

COMMUNITY

When the family first visited the Toronto nursery school Enosh attended as a toddler, Cheryl experienced what she now describes as a pivotal moment. "The first time I walked into this nursery school, I saw that all the children were special needs kids," says Cheryl. She describes to me her first impression at seeing the room full of children with a variety of impairments. Her reaction was visceral, extremely powerful. "I was stunned, absolutely stunned. And I remember thinking, 'Oh my God, the way I'm seeing these kids is the way the world is seeing Enosh.'"

"We met other parents, we met the teachers and everything was hunky-dory," she says. She and Tzvika asked a lot of questions, felt satisfied with the program and made arrangements for Enosh to enter it. "Then I walked out with Enosh and put him in his car seat," she says. She snugged up his safety straps as always, speaking gently to her son just like so many other days. "Then without thinking, I drove down the driveway and had a car accident." No one was hurt, but for Cheryl the accident marked a moment of powerful new awareness.

Cheryl conveys the events of that day to me with great animation. "I was so blown away by my realization of how the world must be viewing my kid, because I just didn't see him like that. He was so beautiful; he was so sweet and so full of humanity. But I was only seeing those kids, the kid in the wheelchair, the kid who was blind; the kid who was ... whatever ... and it was a really important lesson."

As she is explaining her reaction, I understand fully the profound meaning of that moment. Like Cheryl, I never allowed my love and commitment to my son to be captured, wrestled down and branded no matter what diagnosis doctors offered. Not every mother feels this way (or perhaps, has the luxury of feeling this way if they already have other children to care for or are seventeen years old and don't have a supportive family they can rely upon.) For Cheryl, this realization spurred her to continue to engage in community organizing and advocacy, with a new and more inclusive sensibility.

Throughout Enosh's life, Tzvika and Cheryl arranged ways for their son to participate actively in the community. "Enosh had these fabulous middle years where he was strong," she continues. "He swam and skied and skated. When he went to the ice rink, he would hold onto a chair. His friend would push him and he, in turn, would push the chair." Cheryl is nothing short of vibrant as she tells me about her son's activities, his accomplishments. This was without a doubt a splendid, active time, in his life and hers.

Enosh participated in the Easter Seals ski program. "He knew every year as soon as it would begin to get dark early that it was going to be time for his skiing." Pre-ski conditioning was held at the Hugh MacMillan Centre,[104] a clinical facility for children with special needs in Toronto. Different equipment was available for the kids' different needs in the ski program. "Enosh's skis were set permanently in a plough position," says Cheryl. "He loved it!"

"He also swam every Sunday at the Jewish Community Centre. He took swimming lessons and could swim under water almost the entire length of the pool. He loved swimming. He always had an awkward gait, but in the water ... he could move perfectly well. He loved the water. He would go under, blowing bubbles and stay there for long periods. Then he would come up and float on his back looking up at us, giving us great big smiles."

"His life was wonderful," says his mother. "We took him to classical concerts, rock concerts and plays, whatever was going on." As we continue to speak, Cheryl is exhilarated to think of Enosh during his middle years. Her descriptions are vivid, and I can visualize an energetic, happy boy in his prime.

At age thirteen, as is the tradition in the Jewish faith, Enosh had his bar mitzvah. "He was at the peak of good health and robustness and joy and energy," Cheryl recalls. The bar mitzvah ceremony is a rite of passage, a crossover from childhood to adulthood; a significant milestone in a Jewish life. At that point the young person is no longer a child in the eyes of Jewish law. He becomes responsible for his own deeds, spiritually, ethically and morally. And then the community celebrates!

Cheryl is beaming as she shows me photographs from the event. "People had a great time," she recalls. "It was so meaningful. It was also a way for us to thank everyone who had been involved in the care circle, helping Enosh from a young age." The pride in her voice is touching; I feel honoured to share her enthusiasm for her firstborn son's considerable achievements.

ADVOCACY

When Enosh was ready to enter Junior High School, Cheryl and Tzvika had made two difficult and innovative decisions. First, they approached the school board to adopt their son as a "pilot project" within an integrated school environment. They wanted inclusion for Enosh; a study to be undertaken of the project's progress; and a facilitator to assist him. Eventually the board agreed, however they also stipulated that the family would have to bear most of the facilitator's cost. This led to the second big step.

It had become obvious to Tzvika and Cheryl that they would have to fundraise if Enosh was to enter a regular school. A facilitator was not an extra frill, but a person their son would need to rely upon. The facilitator would assist Enosh with his personal needs and help him to learn effectively in the public school system. The family decided to put together a circle of people to support and guide their efforts to integrate Enosh into public school. "This way we knew people would come with us to meetings with the board and the superintendent and help us send out newsletters to keep everyone up-to-date."

"I don't know where we got the chutzpah to ask this of our friends, but we did," says Cheryl. "We asked our friends whether they would be willing to meet with us to plan for Enosh's future and to support us in integrating him — in taking it on all together as a group. And much to our relief, people said, 'okay, sure, yeah we love the idea.'"

"We met on a regular basis, and they were dynamos," she says. "These are all really accomplished people, and they were really into it. And so that's what we did. We plotted and planned and we dreamed and we set goals and we divvied up the work and we went for it."

"Although Tzvika and I are both articulate and very political and know how to communicate, when it comes to your kid, all of that is forgotten. All you are is raw emotion. All you want is to get the right answer, the answer that you're after. You want to move ahead, you want only the best, and bureaucrats and functionaries see life very differently. They don't care, they don't understand it. They've got their little fiefdoms or little pots of money ... But our friends saw us through."

A Gentle Death

By April of 1999, Enosh had deteriorated considerably. After enjoying Passover with his family, when he was able to recognize his relatives and eat fairly well, the pattern continued unabated: aspiration pneumonia, fever, antibiotics and then feeling better for a short while. Until one day, the fever did not subside.

His pulse was weak. He threw up. He spent a couple of nights in hospital. The next morning as Cheryl was pulling on her boots to leave for St. Michael's Hospital, she received a phone call. It was the doctor. "He said, 'I'm calling to tell you that Enosh has had a full respiratory arrest.' He

repeated this three times. 'Do you understand? A full respiratory arrest.'"
Cheryl raced to the hospital where she found Enosh on a respirator. He
was being kept as comfortable as possible. It was now a question of when
he would die. The family had to face that most painful decision: Would
they keep him on life support?

"Tzvika and Jeremiah were pretty clear," says Cheryl. "Given all that
Enosh had been through, they thought it would be best to let him go. I
was much more reluctant. Their view was that the only reason not to take
Enosh off life support would really be for us. I could understand that, and
so we decided to take him off."

As Cheryl relives this painful saga, she is close to tears. So am I. The
mood has turned to sombre tones, tans and russet, the chocolate brown of
fertile life-giving soil.

"The next day, the three of us went to the hospital. We felt the most
important thing was for Enosh not to have any fear; that he not feel any
sensation of drowning, that it be as peaceful as possible."

"We were all there, two of Enosh's cousins and some close family
friends. We were all there with him. We just kept telling him that he
would always be with us and that he had brought us such joy and that we
loved him so much. It was very counterintuitive to everything, after all the
years of trying to move forward, every little step … And then the decision
to let him die."

A Legacy of Love

Cheryl, Tzvika and Jeremiah feel a need to reach out to families like their
own. Every year on the anniversary of Enosh's death, the family gives
$1000 to a family with a young adult child with special needs who lives
at home. "It is very meaningful," says Cheryl. "We've had four families
now, and it means a lot to them. This year's family just called to say the
donation will give them an additional one hundred twenty-five caregiver
support hours.

"It also means that more people are learning about Enosh, about his
life and all the things he achieved in the face of very, very difficult circumstances. That could really inspire a lot of people." In fact, a synagogue in
Toronto that heard about Enosh's bar mitzvah set up a program in which
they welcome children with special needs to come and have their bar or

bat mitzvah. "It's called the Enosh Program," Cheryl tells me. She attended the first one, a bat mitzvah for a young girl. Cheryl looks at me, and we both appreciate that another step toward inclusion is being taken, and in Enosh's name at that!

"The important thing is that he be remembered," says his mother. Before we finished our time together that evening, I wanted to ask Cheryl who she felt her son was, at his core. "He had a life going on that I didn't know of," she says. "Who he was at the end was different, very difficult to ascertain. I think he was probably very depressed.

"But to me, he was an incredible gift. The most loving. In Hebrew, Enosh means *human being*. He was so different from typical kids but every time they said his name, they were affirming his humanity.

"He was very brave. He put up with a lot of shit. I think the rest of us would have given up. There's one thing Enosh would likely say if he could get to a psychiatrist," Cheryl tells me with a twinkle in her eye, "'She gives me no peace, this mother of mine; she's always pushing me. There's no break from all this pushing!'"

I smile back at her. It's a funny image, especially to those of us who survive profound loss with a dollop of gallows humour.

"Enosh was just a bundle of joy; we used to call him Guy Smiley because everything was a 'trip' for him," Cheryl says, recalling her beautiful, good-natured son. "He loved everything. He was open to people, he was open to life, he was open to adventure. And he drew people to him.

"It gave me a lot of comfort to know that even while his struggle to be integrated and accepted and recognized for the human being he was … he had actually, without a lot of struggle, made an impact on many, many people.

"We miss his gentle, loving presence."

DAVE LEWIS AT HOME WITH HIS DAUGHTER LISA

CHAPTER FOURTEEN

SWEDEN'S DAVE AND LISA:
A HUMANE MODEL OF CARE

IN THIS CHAPTER WE STEP OUT OF the Canadian context, introducing Dave Lewis, a Canadian who lives in Sweden with his daughters Lisa, age eight, and Linn, age six. What follows is both a portrait of a family and, through that family's experience, a portrait of how Sweden has chosen to care for children living with profound challenges. As such, it provides a fascinating look at another way to organize services for children with special needs and their families.

I first "met" Dave in early January 2002, along with thousands of other radio listeners in Toronto. From his home in Stockholm, Dave had left a message on the listener talkback line at "Metro Morning," the Canadian Broadcasting Corporation's Toronto area morning show. Dave was calling in to respond to a commentary piece that had aired regarding the challenging situation facing Canadian families with severely disabled children. He explained that he lives in Sweden with his two daughters and that his older child, Lisa, lives with severe and multiple disabilities.

The "Metro Morning" commentary had focused on the inadequacies of government policy measures aimed at supporting the special needs of families who are caring for a child with profound disabilities. It came in the wake of the tragic deaths of the Baulne family of Kelowna, BC. In January 2002, Maurice and Belva Baulne had killed themselves and their thirty-four-year-old son, who lived with significant multiple disabilities including a severe form of epilepsy, after appealing for years for government financial aid to help take care of their son. The BC Ministry of Human Resources had denied Mr. and Mrs. Baulne's most recent formal request for financial assistance.[105]

At the moment Dave's talkback message aired, I was lacing up my boots, rushing to get out the door, clear the snow off the car and drive to my office. When I heard his message I stopped short and listened, positively riveted to the radio. In Ontario, a similar issue had hit the news exactly one year earlier. Families with special needs children were being told that they could not access the social and health services their children required unless they gave up custody. In essence, this meant that the province would become the child's legal guardian. The only positive effect of parents giving up custody was that children with profound and multiple disabilities could be channelled into a narrow legal category, under the Child and Family Services Act. Once a child falls into that legal category — in essence, becomes a ward of the Court — the legislation stipulates that the province must bear the cost of the various therapies and residential care he or she needs.[106]

In January 2001, a family had decided to sue the Ontario government for refusing to provide support for their child, a young person who needed a residential placement near his mother. With the help of various informal advocacy networks, a dogged journalist and a few lawyers, an ad-hoc group of parents formed and captured the media's interest. In time, plans were made to launch a class action suit against the government.

This meant that in Ontario, at least, the legal loophole that allowed the province off the hook for funding residential care for these most vulnerable infants and children was finally exposed widely. At minimum, the government would have to practise damage control and provide services to the particular families involved. Since 1994, I had been highlighting this legal issue in radio commentaries, opinion pieces in major newspapers and disability organization newsletters. Working with the research staff for the Ontario New Democratic Party at the legislature, I had also explored means of amending the law to require the provincial government to fund the care of these most vulnerable children without the necessity of a court judge's intervention.

Dave's message on the CBC described his family's starkly different experience, and his point of view as a Canadian living overseas grabbed the attention of listeners and radio producers. In his message, he spoke about the full state support Lisa received in a wide range of publicly funded programs, schooling and personal assistance. The Swedish welfare state, especially post–World War II, instituted a broad range of universal programs to support families and children. He decried the lack of programs and resources available to Canadian children with severe disabilities and their families.

CBC Radio proceeded to interview Dave during the next day or so. Through the producers at our public broadcasting corporation, I was able to secure Dave's permission to contact him by email. In time, we "cyber-connected" and I introduced myself, my writing and the challenges Jake and our family faced. We discovered that our children shared certain characteristics that necessitated special care, including seizures and mobility, speech and other sensory challenges. When I explained to Dave that I was writing a book that would include a series of interviews with parents of children like ours, he expressed a ready willingness to participate, and I was excited about the contribution he'd make. We lived in countries with profoundly different political and social contexts. It soon became crystal clear that a child such as mine who resided in Sweden with his family would be entitled to receive a comprehensive range of assistance, one that far outstrips anything Canada offers its most vulnerable children.

And so began an email correspondence. Dave was born in Hamilton, Ontario, and attended university in Toronto. He subsequently completed a Bachelor degree in Social Work in British Columbia before leaving Canada in 1991 to work and travel abroad. He was employed in Southeast Asia and also travelled widely. During this time he met a Swedish woman, and, after living briefly in Indonesia and then Alberta, they settled in Sweden. Dave completed graduate studies in Stockholm, there perfecting his command of the Swedish language, and now teaches political sociology at a university there. Dave is Lisa's legal guardian; he and Anita, the girls' mother, separated when the children were quite young. For medical reasons, Anita was unable to be fully involved in Lisa's care for several years. She now lives nearby and, at present, cares for Lisa part of each week. At the time of our interview in late 2003, Dave was forty-six years old. His story reveals a great deal both about what's lacking in the current Canadian system and what's possible when the political will is there to care well for children with severe disabilities.

LISA'S BIRTH

"There is no single name or label for Lisa's health condition, other than 'multiply disabled.' Lisa was blind at birth and is now severely sight-impaired. She is developmentally delayed in the extreme. She is unable to speak and uses a wheelchair. All of these limits have been attributed to brain damage that occurred prior to her birth," said Dave. "Lisa is epileptic, and her motor functions are severely impaired due to neurological and physiological afflictions. We learned Lisa's diagnosis ... initially at age four months, but the full scope of her condition only became known when she was twenty-four months old.

"Lisa's mother and I had been suspicious about our baby's condition a month or so after her birth. Unfortunately, district health clinic GPs as well as postnatal public health nurses dismissed our suspicions! The main symptom at the time was Lisa's inability to respond to our nurturing and affection. Nor was she able to feed from the breast, which set off alarm bells with Anita.

"It was not until we demanded to see a specialist paediatrician at one of the local children's hospitals that our concerns about Lisa's condition were validated. The paediatrician immediately referred us to a neurologist and an ophthalmologist, both specializing in children's medicine. Within two to three weeks of the latter referrals, we knew that Lisa was blind and that she was probably afflicted with severe brain damage.

"The specialists were able to provide us with relative clarity and certainty about Lisa's condition that had been lacking until then. Just knowing was something of a relief," he said. "But more importantly, the specialists gave us the assurances that we desperately needed ... that we were not going to have to contend with Lisa's condition on our own. In fact, it was thanks to the ophthalmologist that we got a flying start to the whole rehabilitation process; she initiated a number of key referrals to the National Social Insurance Board and to rehabilitation support agencies. And she did all this the very day that she examined Lisa for the first time — her last day in the office before going off on summer holidays."

Dave explained that scheduling appointments during the summer is a nightmare. The Swedish health sector essentially closes down during the five-week period from late June to late July every year. Having to wait weeks to complete a full medical work up and receive test results after receiving confirmation of Lisa's condition was very trying. Dave told me that, in fact, this period was the very worst for him and Anita.

"We endured the next five to six weeks with the emotional support of a couple of close friends and Anita's two older sisters, but no professional counselling or any other intervention from the system. Lisa, her mother and I had been scheduled to depart on a family visit to Ontario the day after our visit to the ophthalmologist, but as we were too emotionally drained and still quite worried, we cancelled the trip. It was a very difficult time, and Lisa's mother and I were both in rough shape. Anita, in particular, found it hard to come to grips with the uncertainty involved. We took care of our daughter but did not have a great deal of information about what the future held for her.

"I was on leave to be at home with Lisa those first few months, so it was usually me giving her the bottle during the nights," said Dave. In answer to a question about his feelings toward Lisa in those early days, he explained that his "... commitment grew during those first few months as I had to take on more responsibility for Lisa since Anita was less and less able to cope with the stress of not knowing ... The relatively short but intensive struggle to convince public health professionals that something was wrong during those first few months ... also increased my commitment to Lisa."

LIFE WITH LISA

"My daughter's full name is Lisa Mary Lewis; Lisa after her Swedish grandmother, Mary after her Canadian grandmother and Lewis my family name," Dave told me. "Lisa is eight years old. She has light, blondish hair and resembles both her mother and me."

Dave explained that Lisa can only see bright neon-type colours and prefers hard objects to soft ones. She also prefers materials that are warm to the touch and loves powerful classical·music and music with rhythm.

"Lisa cannot speak, but she utters an expanding range of sounds. Her voice is soft, and the range and velocity of the sounds she utters depends very much on the mood that she is in at any given time. She can express her desires, fears and pleasure with no problem at all."

I asked Dave to tell me something about Lisa's likes and dislikes. "She loves to swim/splash in the pool, pound on the piano, swat the wind chimes that hang over her place at the kitchen table, listen to music, swing out on the patio, take steps herself (with someone guiding/supporting her under the arms), throw/drop anything and everything from table top and bed to floor and play 'fetch-the-toys-from-the-floor' with her younger sister, listen to me sing her a goodnight lullaby, usually Janis Joplin's 'Mercedes,' when she is going to sleep ...

"She awakens dreadfully early in the morning and babbles happily but relentlessly to herself. She attends her special training school Monday to Friday from 8:30 a.m. to 4:00 p.m. She rides in her open trailer behind my bike, goes for walks in her wheelchair, likes to be exposed to the wind and drizzle. She enjoys eating ice cream on a stick.

"She doesn't like hot weather, sudden noises (that are not of her own making!) or having needles for blood tests," he said. "During moments of distress at the hospital, my presence and the familiar, reassuring tone of my voice calm her. And when all else fails, a quick rendition of 'Mercedes' saves the day."

I was also curious if Lisa liked to snuggle up with him, as not all children with sensory challenges enjoy such contact. "She used to like to cuddle, but seems to be growing out of it nowadays. Yet there are still times when she is not averse to it," he said. "Her favourite toys are a battery-operated piano that plays a selection of eight different nursery rhymes and a battery-operated gyrating duck that moves and hums a melody after being pounded on. She also enjoys an assortment of hand-held textile toys that are warm to the touch and 'toot' when squeezed or ring when shaken, as well as various stuffed animal toys which start out on her bed when going to sleep but are mysteriously all on the floor come morning."

Services and Education

Support, schooling, respite care and personal assistance for children with multiple and profound disabilities is funded 100 percent by the Swedish government. "Lisa has a personal assistant, Alicja, who just adores her and vice versa," said Dave. "Alicja has been with her for nearly four years now. She is everything to Lisa: a surrogate mother, best friend, teacher, day nurse and guardian. She fits into our family life. She comes home with Lisa after school every day and plays/works with Lisa at home for an hour until I arrive home from work with Linn, Lisa's younger sister. We then have a cup of tea or espresso together as we talk over the events in Lisa's day and I begin preparing supper. Occasionally Alicja stays for supper but she usually leaves between 5:00 and 5:30 p.m."

"Alicja works a full-time week, usually 8:00 a.m to 5:00 p.m. each day, Monday to Friday. Most of her work time is with Lisa at school, but she also escorts her to different places — a special play therapy centre once every other week, rehabilitation appointments and sometimes to dental or medical appointments where I will meet them. When Lisa is ill, once her condition has stabilized, Alicja spends the days with her at home while I'm at work.

"Alicja is a very, very important — central — part of Lisa's life. Lisa loves her dearly and that love is clearly reciprocated by Alicja. As a former practising social worker of many years," he told me, "I was concerned for a time about the lack of emotional boundaries between Alicja and Lisa. But I trusted Alicja and I defended her way of being with Lisa vis-à-vis other care practitioners. Alicja is able to communicate with Lisa as effectively as Lisa's mother and I, and that communication would not have been possible in a conventional caregiver–client relationship. Indeed, in Alicja's case, the professional and personal relationship has merged into one."

In Sweden, wage scales for personal assistants are set by the National Social Insurance Board and adhere to central negotiations between public sector employers and organized labour. Personal assistants are paid either directly by the National Social Insurance Board or indirectly through a municipal government agency or cooperative associations and other non-profit entities.

On a day-to-day basis "… compromises are reached and decisions made in relation to Lisa's best interests. Technically, I suppose I'm the 'boss,' but only on paper. She [Alicja] and I set the working conditions according to Lisa's needs," said Dave. "Alicja and I have a wonderful, direct style of communication, and our working relationship is 100 percent consensus driven. We (Alicja and I) are expecting that she will continue with Lisa for another two to two and a half years at which time she will have finished upgrading herself to a special education teacher and will be ready to take charge of a classroom."

Most home care in Sweden is provided by municipalities or by private (for-profit) firms that operate under contract to the municipalities. According to Dave, nearly all workers in the home care sector are unionized. Salary scales are standardized, meaning that individual families do not negotiate pay packets with the personal assistant their family requires. While the wages are not high, he says they are on par with those of similar workers (practical nurses) in hospital facilities.

It strikes me that this is a remarkably smart approach to organizing the home care sector. Not only do wages follow a pattern developed for facility settings, but in contrast to Canada, individual families are not left to carry out extensive administration themselves.

"Lisa attends a segregated special education and training school," Dave continued. "I am a firm believer in the need for the segregated option, especially after the very unfavourable experience we had in an integrated day-care program. In Sweden integration has long been the Social Democrats' mantra and while it is a wonderful goal in principle, the day-to-day reality is completely different. Indeed, in practice, it is the families of children with disabilities as well as the children themselves who are compelled to make all of the necessary compromises in the name of the goal of integration. As such, the special educational and training needs of our children are either wholly neglected or addressed in half-measure."

Lisa's right to schooling is equivalent to that of other Swedish children. She is in the first year of ten years of mandatory schooling pursuant to Sweden's Schools Act. She has access to a publicly administered and fully financed special education and training program. Lisa also stays at a respite care home for a few weekday nights on a regular basis.

How different life would be if Lisa and her family lived in Canada. The combination of supports they receive, including quality respite care and the consistent services by the same trained attendant, mean Lisa can enjoy living at home with her family. Her father is able to continue working full-time and parent his daughters with far less stress than most Canadians in a similar life situation.

"Lisa goes to a public school called Mockasinen, Stockholm's oldest specialized training school," Dave explained. "It is funded entirely by the City of Stockholm and recently relocated to new premises. Mockasinen is comprised of five classes, each with four or five children, and each with a qualified special education teacher, two qualified teaching assistants, plus one or two personal assistants. The teaching plan is pupil-centred, i.e., each student has her/his own individual plan based upon her/his particular needs as well as the particular expectations of her/his parents.

"A usual day begins with Lisa's arrival at the school at 8:15. She spends the first forty-five minutes of the day in the before-school activity program. School itself begins at 9:00. Each school day begins with a presentation of the day's activities. Once the day's planning is completed, the class comes together and forms a circle for purposes of being welcomed to class for the day and partaking in a sing-along.

"After the class get-together, each pupil goes off with an assistant to their respective activity stations (conference tables arranged in different constellations in the same classroom) to engage in their respective individual training activities for the remainder of the school day," he said. "I have requested that the two main individual training components, the cognitive and physical, be given equal weight in Lisa's teaching plan, so her individual training program is more or less equally balanced. The whole class takes lunch at 11:30 and has an afternoon snack together at 1:30. The school day comes to an end at 3:00.

"Then Lisa and her assistant participate in the school's after-school activity program for an hour before returning home or to the respite home." Dave explained that families do not pay any school fees, but a nominal monthly fee (of approximately $75 Canadian) is charged for the after-school program.

"Lisa's teacher is a professionally trained educator, with a specialization in educating children with special needs. She has twenty-five years professional teaching and administrative experience in special education. In addition, the teacher has a good range of external specialized training resources to call upon to supplement her own contributions," he said. "The most important of these external resources, in Lisa's case, are the National Special Education Resource Centre for Blind and Developmentally Handicapped Children (a state agency), the County of Stockholm's Visual Aid Consultation Agency, the municipal school board's visual aid consultant, and the municipality's music and play therapy activity centre."

Dave told me that all the services, from personal attendant to the training school (or daycare for younger children) and after-school program are available to all Swedish residents. Eligibility is based on residency, not citizenship. "I'm still a Canadian national, but fully entitled to all services." The positive results of this system can be gleaned in Dave's description of his daughter's progress.

"Lisa is generally a very happy, social and contented child. Thankfully, she has relatively recently broken out of her 'sedate self' and become more and more curious and inquisitive about what objects exist within her reach and what is happening around her. She expresses her happiness with loud, sudden spontaneous cries of joy. Likewise, when she is having a bad day, she is impatient and snarly.

"One of Lisa's favourite moments is sitting at the kitchen table when I'm entertaining a bunch of friends. We can be talking and laughing and just carrying on with one another in English and/or Swedish and, as she gets taken up in all the excitement, she lets go with several of her happy screams. Our knee-jerk responses to her shrieks of joy only cause her to bellow with laughter. It's probably Lisa's way of saying 'I got ya!'"

ACCESS TO RESPITE CARE

While in Canada, as described earlier and seen in the previous portraits, there is a paucity of respite care for families with disabled children and major gaps in social policy and practice, the Swedish model provides yet another interesting contrast. "Lisa's particular respite home has capacity — both in terms of physical/structural layout and personnel staffing — for a maximum of six children at a time," said Dave. "Each child has their own bedroom. It serves children age approximately one year up to twelve years; at age thirteen Lisa will graduate to another respite home, which will care for her until age eighteen. Each respite home serves a more or less defined geographic catchment area as well as an official client roster administered/regulated by the municipality. Respite homes are intended to provide regular or periodic relief to the families of children with profound disabilities and are intended for short-term stay only, usually not longer than a week.

"The respite home is run by the municipality and is open 360-odd days a year and operates on a reservations system basically on a first-come, first-served basis. It only closes two days over Christmas and a day or two over the year for planning and in-service training purposes," he said. "The staff is composed of a mix of qualified paediatric nurses, specialized care assistants and non-qualified assistants. It is by and large women who work in the homes. They are all unionized and earn dreadfully low salaries and wages given the high level of responsibility. Nonetheless, the rates conform to salary and wage levels in the municipal care sector."

Families pay "… a nominal administrative fee equivalent to less than $10 Canadian per twenty-four-hour day and half that for a single overnight stay which includes supper and breakfast next morning." As far as Dave is aware, waiting lists do not seem to be an issue. "Respite homes are intended for severely handicapped children. Children with any and all medical conditions are accommodated, even if that requires additional specialized training of staff."

I asked Dave to outline how services are funded. "Municipalities are generally required to fund their own public services. Their scope and organization are loosely prescribed under state (central government) legislation that confers the mandate of local government," he explained. "Municipalities enjoy extensive constitutional autonomy and generate the bulk of their own annual tax revenues — income-based as well as property tax. These locally generated tax revenues are, in turn, either topped up or reduced by the central government in Stockholm, according to a very complex national tax equalization formula.

"The central government exercises oversight of municipal implementation by way of the National Board of Health and Welfare. But given its limited mandate — primarily information gathering and comparative evaluation research — the National Board can only shame errant municipalities and praise those pursuing best practices," he said. "At the same time, the National Board is quite influential in providing essential information to the central government in the process of reforming and/or devising policy."

The practice at Lisa's respite care facility is that there is no formal rehabilitative or therapy-type programming. Activities depend upon the range of facilities that exist in the respective respite home. "Lisa's respite home, for example, has a special meditation room with waterbed, special lights, and soothing instrumental music," he said. "She loves to spend an hour in the meditation room when she returns from school. There is also a lot of special play equipment for the kids, as well as swings on the covered outer porch. On weekends and holidays there is always an outing organized by staff such as a long walk or visit to some special place. On weekdays the kids are expected to be in daycare or training school, returning to the respite home only in the late afternoon, in time for one or two pre-supper activities, supper and then getting ready for bed.

"Lisa is very happy and comfortable when spending time at the respite home and at the training school," he said. "She gets on well with the respective personnel, feels secure in both contexts and knows what to expect with regard to activities and routines in both places ... These respective programs and institutions serve to develop Lisa's confidence and emotional independence." Dave called the respite care home his lifeline.

"I have chosen to limit Lisa's stays at the respite home to three weekday nights every other week because I want her to experience as much of an ordinary home life as possible. I took the decision right from the start that she would be with me for quality time during the weekends and holidays," he explained. "On those weekends that I have the kids, for example, we go swimming and to a special play therapy centre, go for long walks, visit friends and family and receive visitors and just hang out." The girls' mother takes them every other weekend.

"The single concern I have with the respite home is what I would call a general lack of active stimulation available for the kids. Hence my decision from the start to limit her stays. I am actually eligible to receive double the time for Lisa than I utilize, but the time that I utilize is sufficient — especially now that Lisa's mother cares for her regularly."

Family Relationships

"Linn is six. She absolutely adores Lisa, while Lisa tolerates Linn," he said. "Linn is openly curious about Lisa and she is not loath to experiment with the aim of eliciting a reaction or response from Lisa. And while Lisa usually seems to enjoy the interaction with Linn, she can also be rather indifferent to Linn's overtures. Linn is always prepared to lend a helping hand and often does small things like picking up toys from the floor after Lisa has purposely dropped them, or steadying the mug for Lisa while she is drinking."

I asked if Linn ever seemed jealous of the amount of attention Lisa requires from her father and other adults such as Alicja. "From time to time, Linn can be a little envious of Lisa. It occurs sometimes when Lisa is getting the limelight. Linn can also be quite envious of Lisa's special toys and technical aides. Thankfully these episodes of jealousy are rare and very short-lived.

"Lisa can also be jealous and short-tempered when I give Linn my attention, particularly when I'm debriefing her at the kitchen table after she arrives home from school," he said. Dave explained that he tries to spend some quality time with Linn each day. "Lisa, at that moment, is usually happily occupied playing her toy piano also at the kitchen table, but still thinks that I should be directing my attention toward her, not Linn."

I asked Dave to describe the girls' bedtime routines. I was curious to know if he reads stories to both children at the same time. "A typical bedtime session usually begins in the girls' bedroom around 7:30 pm. I read stories (in English) for the two of them, but I read stretched out on Linn's bed. Lisa listens from her bed in the corner diagonally across the room from Linn. Lisa listens fairly attentively and knows some of the books pretty well — she laughs or gets excited in anticipation of when I am about to modulate my voice.

"After I've read a book, I force myself up to my feet — sometimes after being poked in the side by Linn, having nodded off myself for a few minutes — and walk the few paces over to the head of Lisa's bed where I sing a rendition of 'Mercedes' or 'You are my sunshine' for the two of them. Then it's a kiss and 'I love you' for each of them, and lights out.

"Linn falls asleep quickly and soundly. Lisa usually catches a second wind and is awake mumbling to herself and casting all of her stuffed toys to the floor for an hour after the lights go out. And some evenings it can be quite comical when Linn, having nodded off quickly and soundly, begins to snore just before or just as Lisa is about to fall asleep. Of course the sound of Linn snoring just infuriates Lisa, but Linn sleeps on, completely unaware of the stir she has caused."

Planning for Lisa's Future

I wondered how the bountiful services accessible to children with severe disabilities and their families in Sweden might affect Dave's future plans for Lisa. As with other parents interviewed in this project, I asked him what would happen at the point he is no longer able to care for her.

"I can wake up in the dead of night with thoughts of what will happen to Lisa when I'm no longer around to care for her and advocate for her," said Dave. "Although services here are much more developed and readily accessible than in Canada, the Swedish welfare state is very much in transition to a more market-oriented system. There are significant cracks appearing in the social welfare system; many commentators here speak openly about a system not so much in transition, but in crisis. It is very unclear at present how Swedish social welfare services will be organized in the future.

"It is against this backdrop of uncertainty that I am planning and preparing for Lisa's future as an adult. Lisa will likely always be dependent on the services and good graces of a caregiver, semi-independent living does not seem a realistic option given what I know of Lisa's capacities today. At the same time, I do not want Lisa to be consigned to an institution," he emphasized. "By institution I am referring to the mental institutions of old, removed from social life and complete with impersonal and arbitrary medical treatment regimes.

"Rather, I hope and expect that she will have the opportunity to live in a small group home, not unlike her respite home, where services and daily routines are more or less personalized to meet the individual's needs. Like the respite home, Lisa would spend evenings and nights at the group home, but would spend her days at external training and therapeutic programs/centres. I am assuming that by the time Lisa reaches adulthood, however, that such a facility will be (a) in great demand, (b) in short supply, (c) operated by the private sector, (d) largely unsubsidized by government and (e) relatively expensive. So I am saving like crazy for Lisa's future and Linn's as well — trust funds, life memberships in the Stockholm Cooperative Housing Association (housing is a highly prized commodity and in very short supply in Stockholm!) and the whole bit. And yes, I am beginning ever so gradually to prepare Linn to take over as Lisa's guardian and advocate." Clearly, he is planning for a time in the future when neither he nor Anita is able to care for Lisa.

Dave is the only parent I interviewed who expects that his other daughter will bear some responsibility for her severely disabled sibling. It seems to me that in the Swedish system, at least for the time being, adequate supports for families are available resulting in less isolation and personal sacrifice by family caregivers. Certainly less advocacy work is necessary since many services are already offered as a matter of course. Depending on how changes to Sweden's socio-political and economic context unfold, it seems that for Linn to act as her sister's advocate and guardian may be somewhat less demanding than it would be in Canada.

I also wondered, since so many Canadian parents I have encountered in my advocacy work and during the interviews for this book are so busy juggling their employment demands and organizing care for their children, if Dave experienced the sort of marginality that many Canadian families with special needs children experience. From his description, he seems to enjoy a life filled with family and meaningful work, without the isolation many Canadian parents face. I also wanted to know what keeps him balanced. His answers were telling:

"I do what I can for Lisa ... according to my own abilities," he said. "Knowing that I'm doing the best I can for Lisa (and for Linn as well) is important. Maintaining a positive attitude and outlook. Having accepted my family situation as it is, adjusted to it, and not letting it consume everything else."

As an outside observer it is plain that so much more is possible in a country that truly supports its people to do the best they can in challenging situations. Throughout our email conversation, Dave's strong love and commitment to each of his daughters radiated through. "I hope that Lisa continues to enjoy life; that she remains happy; that her health does not give way; that she is safe and secure; that she maintains her curiosity and wonderful sense of humour and that she remains challenged and stimulated."

At the end of our discussion I asked Dave if he could point to one thing that would show he had done his best to raise Lisa so far. His answer to my question was swift and, I found, quite tender. "That she has a good temperament," he said, "and an avid curiosity and a willingness to rise to challenges."

Swedish families are encouraged to meet their children's special needs in the context of genuine community supports and services, regardless of individual economic circumstances. In contrast to Canada, where such parents are thrust onto a racing treadmill with no *off* switch, the Swedish model makes a compelling case, and it shows unequivocally that where the political will exists, a balanced and fulfilling family life is within reach for all.

REFLECTIONS:

DRAWING SOME CONCLUSIONS

WHEN I BEGAN WRITING THIS BOOK, my son Jake was still very much alive. In all those hours that I held him in my arms, playing peekaboo to his expressive eyes, a deep truth travelled with me. My son, our entire family in fact, was privileged to receive the best quality care this country has to offer. And yet, I could never quite let myself be lulled out of the reality that most families are far less fortunate. Jake's situation spurred me to learn more about other families like my own. How did they manage? What would make their lives easier?

The starting point for my research was to pose two questions. First, what could be learned from giving a small number of Canadian families an opportunity to speak about their lives raising children with a variety of disabilities? I wanted to hear first-hand about their experiences trying to secure the health care, education and other resources their children need. I wanted to query if parents' advocacy on behalf of their child affected their general political outlook. Did the families' journeys lead them to increased political awareness and activity?

The second question I wanted to explore was how mothers (and some fathers) attempt to build community around their child, given that usual patterns of involvement in a school or daycare setting are minimized. A non-disabled child may arrive home from school with a playmate in tow. Planning Saturday night sleepovers often captures young girls' imagination. How does the child with a mobility impairment fit in? Or the child who is developmentally delayed?

But I discovered so much more. One objective of this book is to provide a window onto how families with disabled children experience their lives. Novelists have argued convincingly that in knowing one family intimately, whether through fiction or non-fiction, we can come to understand how power dynamics, like oppression, play out in a given society.[107] It is the narratives of mothers and fathers that shed light on the challenges, joys and dilemmas these families face. The insights gleaned stretch from Mary Ellen's realization that in spite of child development guidance aplenty, helping Jeremy to reach developmental milestones closer to textbook timeframes would not change the underlying chromosome-based limits of Down Syndrome; to Cheryl coming to understand, in a stunning epiphany, that her initial impression of other disabled children mirrored a stranger's view of her son, a boy she perceived as entirely beautiful. To say the least, exploring these family narratives unearthed a treasure trove of creative approaches and wisdom.

BUILDING INCLUSION

Most of the parents who have told their stories here will strive to ensure that their children live as independently as possible. Mary Ellen's son Jeremy may eventually be able to live away from home, with a significant set of community supports around him. Indeed this is precisely what his mother hopes his future will entail. In a best-case scenario, Jeremy would be in a position to make decisions about how he spends his days and time, be it paid work and/or voluntary activities.

Dave's daughter Lisa, on the other hand, will always require complex care and intensive personal support to manage her health. Her family, in partnership with the programs they access, will continue to meet her basic needs. While Dave is well aware that Swedish welfare state services are being eroded, it is evident that Lisa's access to appropriate care will always be superior to what Canadians can expect if our system forges ahead without any significant change.

Ollie will always need a great deal of personal support as well as supervision. Making practical arrangements for his future care in a harsh climate of scarcity must be daunting, even to people like Lillian and her husband who are accustomed to organizing politically and making demands upon governments.

Mathieu's children, Aude Catherine and Vincent, are now on the launching pad to independence. They are setting their own goals and pursuing them. Like many young people their age, they will continue their studies, make career decisions and no doubt, as their father hopes, find companionship during their lives. Julien expresses very similar dreams for her young son Simon. She knows that glaucoma will prevent him from doing many things, but she is making sure he learns a wide range of skills that will serve him well in adulthood.

Colleen's son Johnny attends a segregated classroom in an ordinary school. He experiences regular contact with non-disabled children through the school's Friendship Club. Cheryl's son Enosh fought hard to be included in ordinary classrooms and educational programs. At the same time, he participated in skiing and other sports activities that were geared toward the enjoyment of young people with disabilities. These two families' situations and choices speak volumes to a broad agenda for inclusion.

Why does this matter? It is significant because bringing to light deeply embedded patterns of discrimination and disadvantage has been possible in Canada through the rights-based approach adopted in Canada since Section 15 of the Charter of Rights and Freedoms came into effect in 1985. In addition, significant legal and analytical tools for remediation and redress have been utilized. Achieving gains through the Charter of Rights has brought about important improvements in the lives of people with disabilities.[108]

Yet this same culture of the individual also stands in the way of developing a broad range of practical, publicly funded services. Building inclusion is a collective project. Essentially, we in the disability community need to apply the important understanding of *difference* into how we work together politically. We need to apply principles of inclusion to our practice.

A glimpse into an ordinarily day in Lisa's life in Stockholm reflects a very different ethos than our highly individualist North American political culture produces. Swedish welfare state supports are significantly more developed than in Canada. Swedish organized labour negotiates wage rates and working conditions for support workers and personal assistants. These central negotiations with government bring about a degree of equity among workers and also partially determine standards of care. Paying decent wages encourages continuity of both employment and the care an individual receives. Canadians like to distinguish themselves from the American neighbours to the south; we say that our society draws a line below which disadvantaged persons will not to be allowed to fall. This view infuses public debates about our health care system, and yet our record in achieving social justice falls terribly short.

The Swedish model is far less reliant on trumpeting the self-sufficiency of the individual, nuclear families. Quality respite care homes and schooling support do not diminish a family's autonomy. It is the absence of such social programs in Canada that means children will continue to miss out on vital speech therapy (as Jeremy did) and more reliable and respectful caregivers (as Enosh did). In a strategic sense, it is the rhetoric of the individual and rigid positioning within the disability rights movement that stands in the way of bringing pressure to bear on civic authorities. It is that pressure precisely which would help ensure that all children live full, rewarding lives.

INTEGRATING SEGREGATION

Cheryl believed fervently that her son Enosh had the right to attend ordinary public schools. In the 1970s, before the shift toward integration had occurred substantially in this country, she and Tzvika needed to break new civic ground to prove the point. She was determined that her son spend his days in a stimulating environment. Moreover, she wanted Enosh to be treated with dignity, to live a life in which his full humanity would be recognized.

In a similar vein Mathieu and his spouse Suzanne were steadfast in their commitment that Aude Catherine and Vincent attend ordinary schools as full participants in classroom and extracurricular activities. As Mathieu's narrative suggests, seeing this objective realized has been a challenging as well as rewarding process.

Mary Ellen, on the other hand, questions whether Jeremy is better off in each of the integrated situations in which he participates. Her beliefs are not based on an ideological commitment for or against integration. She comes to her position out of experience. Some integrated situations neither helped Jeremy to learn the skills he needed, nor served to expand his self-confidence.

Julien is encouraging her son Simon to be whoever he can be and is at the same time cautiously protective of his well-being. For now, Simon attends a primary school specifically for children who are visually-impaired. He is gathering the tools, both technological and physical, to live safely and participate fully in school and other activities.

In considering the options these parents have selected for their children, I draw the conclusion that an unwavering position at either extreme of the spectrum is not very helpful. No one model fits all children or all families. Also, a child's needs may change over time and in different spheres of their lives. Parental choice is critical and, where possible, the child's desires must be part of the equation. This means that a full range of options for education and related programs is required. Moreover, some of the best experiences, according to the parents interviewed here, are those in which a balance between segregated and integrated activities is achieved. That is essentially what Colleen's (ultimately successful) community organizing in St. John's achieved. Less than three years later following a change in government, Newfoundland is planning to open new developmental delay units in other schools in the province.[109] What is painfully obvious, however, is that choice is only genuine when actual programs exist, not when made in a climate of punched-up rhetoric and scarcity.

SHIFTING ATTITUDES

Children with a variety of challenges tend not to make the same strides as their cousins or neighbours. They do, however, make progress in many ways. The baby who rolls over at fourteen months instead of three is making fabulous progress and is every bit as worthy as one that does so on schedule. Similarly, when a student at Ollie's school learns to raise herself from a sitting position to balance on her knees and reach for a colourful mobile suspended above, a celebration is in order. Expectations of what is normal are reframed; when specialized therapists break down tasks many of us take for granted into their component parts, children can learn something new. Sometimes it's the child that leads the way. Most of the parents I interviewed recognized that not only were the signposts for their child's development extraordinary, but that the child also provided cues for adults to follow.

Julien related a moment in time when she recognized she needed to rethink her expectations of Simon. When Simon was still quite young, she realized that understanding "... physiological processes ... didn't mean she could expect Simon to 'follow a textbook.'" She told me in no uncertain terms that now she questions measuring a child against usual developmental patterns, saying, "Should we be putting deadlines and setting goals when, in fact, it's the child's call? Every child is different." It was when she put these expectations aside that she was able to follow Simon's lead, finding many creative ways to help him experience the world more fully.

The attitude shift Julien experienced reveals a further insight. When a child is welcomed and embraced by members of the extended family, parents encounter more positive attitudes. Inclusion can mean invitations to family functions that makes full participation easier for both parent and child. Offering to help with transportation to an event; teaching an uncle or friend to suction a child's throat when she has difficulty breathing; encouraging young cousins to make musical tapes for an infant in hospital; carefully choosing a toy for the child who needs extra exposure to textures or sounds — these are all examples of how special needs children can be included more fully in a variety of situations such as family celebrations or community activities. When someone "gets it," great leaps of love and acceptance are possible.

Moreover, opening up to the difference these children personify is an instance teeming with potential. Rich rewards are there to be reaped if only we can strip away the fear and stigma that breed prejudice. Sadly, embracing difference is not always in the offing. As Colleen explained, some members of her immediate family have only recently found it comfortable to interact more with Johnny. Regrettably, his father is not among those making such strides. Similarly, at the beginning of Simon's life Julien experienced his grandmother's attitude, although it was clearly rooted in love, as a barrier to her acceptance of Simon as the whole and beautiful child his mother knew.

Each of the mothers and fathers I spoke with recognized that many aspects of their parenting work are universal, but that their challenges are greater. These families need a community of acceptance that, in turn, offers valorization to their children — not just good wishes but concrete actions that build inclusion and lighten the parenting load. In fact, a community that pulls together (as Cheryl and Tzvika demonstrated through the circle of support they created for Enosh and for his younger brother and themselves) can act strategically to force governments toward creating and funding the network of services special needs kids require.

Adopting an ethic of care instead of the mantra of fiscal restraint would inject a measure of collective responsibility into this fractured landscape. Embedded in the ethic of care is a notion of social responsibility that could lead to improving our children's lives. They need not face their challenges alone, but in the cradle of a nurturing community.

SIBLINGS

There are many different ways to encourage relationships between siblings, several of which parents seem to cultivate intuitively. With my kids, I took all kinds of deliberate measures to ensure that they developed a connection to one another. When we would visit Jake at his group home, a part of our ordinary routines, I would slip in first to place a little toy or treat for Emma under his blanket. When his little sister toddled in, she would find it and then give Jake a kiss on the cheek. I suspect that when she was older, she simply suspended belief, knowing her brother couldn't really have known she wanted a cuddly toy from the Lion King, much less have picked it up at the mall for her. It didn't matter. She was thrilled and felt welcomed each time we visited her brother. As she got older, we would pick up something he might like, a shiny toy or soft teddy that she could give to him as well.

We also celebrated the kids' birthdays *en famille*, often adding an extra party and cake at the group home when Jake was not well enough to travel home. A few close friends or his grandparents would trek to Belleville where Jake lived and share an afternoon with the children and caregiving staff. I see these efforts now as my own attempt to practise inclusion, although at the time I would never have called it that. When Emma was three and four, as we crept up the hill to her childcare centre and could see Lake Ontario in the distance, I would call hello to "Jake across the lake." Before long this whimsical greeting became part of our morning routine. I know now that this was my way of including them both in my embrace as well as nurturing Emma's connection to her brother.

In Sharon's family, she told me that Clarence always made a point of taking the family on long road trips to various parts of Canada and the US. Among other activities, they would visit First Nations communities as part of ensuring the children were aware of their own people and heritage. Shannon and her sister and brother all piled into the family vehicle and no doubt experienced the fun (and challenges!) of family vacations.

Interestingly, a few mothers told me that situations arise from time to time that are so ludicrous, laughter is the only answer. One mom I've met described an outing with a carload of children and members of their extended family. She was trying to ensure that all of her daughter's necessary equipment was tuned up, as well as keeping various other young ones content. Just as they arrived home and turned into the driveway, the battery charger for her daughter's feeding pump started to beep in emergency mode. As the eldest son ran to open the front door, they suddenly discovered that no-one had brought the house key. "Haven't you ever locked yourself out and had to break in to your own house through the kitchen window?" she asked me. Of course my answer is yes. In the face of such ridiculous predicaments, what better release is there than a hearty laugh?

Colleen's children, Krystal and Johnny, seem always to have had a strong connection. Krystal has grown up helping her mother care for Johnny when needed. During our interview, a couple of their cousins also came by to join our conversation. Each child was comfortable with Johnny; one very young girl told me that Johnny is her favourite cousin because "he never hits me like Cody" (another cousin). It seems that attachment, like our kids, comes in all kinds of packages.

Mothering and the Role of Community

Just as children and young people with disabilities are relegated to the outer margins of society, so too are their mothers uncomfortably perched there. Children with disabilities (like their adult counterparts) are considered different from the norm. Inclusion in groups at school, on sports teams, in access to housing and the workforce is never a given. To the extent that society is able to accept difference and, indeed, embrace it, children and adults with disabilities will be included and not get stuck on the periphery.

Mothers of children with disabilities live on the margins because the texture of their lives is different from those of other mothers. While it is true that they parent like every other parent, these mothers carry out an entire set of tasks that are not part of the original job description for which they signed on. I suspect that Colleen, for example, must run out of steam once in awhile as she cares for a little sparkplug like Johnny. Such mothers are not simply separate from the mainstream, they are socially invisible. Coordinating a multitude of appointments and having no choice but to undertake energetic advocacy efforts in caring for their children, these mothers are also frequently exhausted. Sadly, it is isolation, the marginalization of children with disabilities and their mothers, that propels the powerful winds of exclusion.

In combating marginality we must insist on telling the truth about our experiences, on stopping the self-censure that people adopt to meet what they think society expects. Mothers, in particular, need to speak the reality of how their daily lives unfold. The challenges in parenting a non-disabled child are different. Telling the truth about raising a child with disabilities means acknowledging openly that while there is plenty of love, satisfaction and joy, there is also considerably more work involved. Mothers of children with disabilities can take a step toward resisting social invisibility by sharing the genuine details of their experience. No sugar-coating should be required to meet some societal standard of self-sacrifice.

Telling the truth is not only a communications strategy but also serves to spread hope and a sense of possibility that conditions can improve. John Ralston Saul writes of

> ... 'civic storytelling' as a means of countering the public mood of discouragement and despair ... When undertaken in a thoughtful and non-sentimental way, it is critical to the public articulation of different models ... and essential to spreading 'good news' of civic work ...[110]

It is not surprising that historically, many groups seeking social justice — the women's movement, gays, lesbians, bisexuals and transgender persons, people of colour and First Nations' people — found impetus in the socio-political space they occupied (still occupy) outside the locus of power in society. That is, at the margins. Recognizing that relations of power disenfranchise equity-seeking groups allows people to name the injustice that pervades their situation. While mothers may feel this is self-indulgent and, of course, difficult to do, speaking honestly about one's reality can be liberating. It is this naming, this truth-telling, that opens the doors to strategies of resistance.[111]

ASSISTANCE AND INTRUSION

Nonetheless, even in the best-case scenario, mothering a child with disabilities occasions greater scrutiny. In the myriad of appointments with physicians and other health professionals, not to mention service agencies and government officials, the mother has to demonstrate that she is never flummoxed. Different home care workers coming in each week made me feel as if I must always be ready for inspection, as if some sergeant might suddenly arrive and bounce a dime on the beds! Spending so much time in antiseptic hospital corridors or specialists' offices, meeting social workers and physiotherapists, forces one to parent "in public" — a mode atypical of child-rearing practices in North America. There is no escaping the fact that letting all manner of strangers into one's family life can feel intrusive. I posit that one feels great pressure to be the good mother, able to handle it all, keep the home tidy and smile, because scarcity of resources structure the situation to breed a desperate gratitude, rather than a comfortable sense of entitlement.

Mathieu and Suzanne felt this scrutiny. Frequent assessments to evaluate Aude Catherine and Vincent's progress with the auditory-verbal teaching method were built into the family's relationship with the Audiology Unit at the children's hospital. Clearly, it is sensible to ensure careful follow-up. A mother's capacity and commitment to apply the method is also integral to the method's success. This notwithstanding, is it any surprise that a mother might feel more under the microscope than those in the cluster of new moms at the neighbourhood park? Imagine watching a perfectly delightful mom from down the street. She is revelling unself-consciously in her non-disabled toddler's newfound ability to scale the Mount Everest aluminium stairs of the big slide and swoosh gleefully down into the safety of her welcoming arms. Is this not one of the most superb paybacks of parenting — seeing that little person's face light up?

So-called normalcy rarely installs itself for long in homes where parents teeter on the edge of exhaustion trying to meet their children's extraordinary needs. The window on such homes suggests that where a child has multiple disabilities and experiences health crises, like Johnny, Ollie or Enosh, a climate of constant uncertainty may set in. For some, chaos reigns. So much time is spent providing care and ferrying children to appointments and assessments that ordinary social connections can wane. The woman pushing her playful child on the swing likely has no inkling of the afternoon just spent at a clinic to test a baby's brain activity, tiny electrodes taped to his head. For we other mothers, performing bowel massage, dispensing medications and monitoring side effects becomes as routine as a daily bowl of fibre-rich cereal.

Nor would the mom teaching her child to pump on the swing likely know the soul-crushing anxiety that takes up permanent residence in one's being from the moment a baby's body is wracked by seizures. The road to accepting one's child fully — including non-disabled children — is rife with potholes. Parenting isn't easy.

In the privacy of a support group and more publicly, telling the truth about the texture of our lives is a first step to getting out from under the microscope and demanding the judgement-free assistance we deserve. Only by chipping away at the confines of the ice cube tray where each individual is separated from the rest is it possible to leave the chill of isolation behind.

Doctors and Parents

Some of the parents I met described the relationships they had with their child's physicians as difficult, at least initially. Parents need the doctors' expertise but can seek to minimize the relation of power that's built in. Each child is unique and disabilities present in a variety of ways; it is usually the parents who know their child best. Most appropriate decisions about best therapies are achieved in partnership, by seeking a balance between different sets of knowledge.

Sharon faced such a challenge regarding her daughter Shannon's difficulties swallowing and digesting food. Searching for information and consulting different physicians is enervating, especially when helpful treatment is elusive. Or worse. During our conversation I could sense Sharon's pulse quicken at the memory of her daughter's degrading experiences in more than one highly recommended treatment facility. Sharon is the kind of person who asks a lot of questions. She is neither easily deflected from her path nor afraid of authority figures. In our conversation, she told me she had developed this tenacity through many taxing situations — it was a trait needed to handle the circumstances she faced. Unfortunately, mother bears on the rampage are not always well-received. Just as the medical model of disability pathologizes the individual person rather than viewing the context itself as disabling, mothers perceived as uppity or hysterical may also be pathologized.

It was with this in mind that I listened to Colleen recount the comments Johnny's neurologist made to her when she was finally able to bring her two-month-old home after his harrowing hospital stay. The physician, perhaps well-meaning or trying to buck up Colleen's morale, put the ultimate responsibility ("98 percent," he had said) for Johnny's fragile survival on her shoulders. This strikes me as cruel.and unfair. As mothers in situations like this, we listen so attentively to our children's doctors. We are virtual sponges for information, for any explanation as to why our child turned out the way he or she did. Statements made by physicians take on great meaning; we dissect them in the dark of night, turning them over in our minds as we look for answers, for solace.

In fact, Colleen's doctor loaded responsibility onto her without supplying many tools with which to carry out the monumental task ahead. When bringing home a child newly discharged from hospital, parents are thrown into an apprenticeship on fast forward; they need to know very quickly the machinations of local government, provincial health and social services and the education system. Trying to find out who is responsible for what and exactly what "what" is can be a Sisyphean task. Outside the hospital walls, lines of responsibility — save one — blur. Parents and most especially we mothers are left holding the bag; it is our responsibility to see to our children's development, to give them the care they need. Failure to do so is wrong, morally reprehensible, unnatural, unfeminine and illegal. Never did "goodbye and good luck" carry such an underlying, if unconscious, callousness.

COMMUNITY IN THE CLIMATE OF SCARCITY

For Cheryl, in her impassioned struggle to secure the supports Enosh required to live well, it was her family, their commitment to social justice and a deep sense of community that seems to have kept her going. Colleen and Mary Ellen expressed how they find strength in their faith. Sharon draws on her First Nations traditions as well as her Christian faith to weather the crises in Shannon's life.

While each individual keeps herself or himself whole in different ways, I noted an important trend in some interviews with mothers. Cheryl's insistence that Enosh leave a footprint — an appreciation of who he was and what he had taught the people around him — was critical. Colleen's approach is similar when she says, "… Johnny's given so much to the world … My hope is that he will continue to touch people's lives …" It's the flipside of community connection — the giving back.

The prayer vigil in the chapel and telephone prayer line that Sharon's extended family set up for Shannon in hospital after her cardiac arrest is not unlike the vigorous support circle that Cheryl's friends set up for her and Tzvika when it became absolutely necessary to bring in a reliable care-giver to help them manage. In the middle of a maelstrom where respond-ing to successive crises is the norm, one is not always aware that help is possible. Cheryl described how their friends grabbed the reins to bring in caregiving support from outside the family.

To have friends step in bringing a perspective from outside the home was invaluable. The circle took decisive action to ease the load that Cheryl and Tzvika were carrying. This is a powerful illustration of how commu-nity can be built around our children and their special needs. Friends pro-vided sustenance, comfort and practical supports. Shannon's community used every tool at its disposal to pray for her recovery. Native traditions and Christian prayer intermingled, reflecting the family's location in both cultures. The parallels between the two families' experience is interesting; the powerful expression of humanity in each is positively arresting.

This coming together of community helps mitigate the lack of formal public support. Most people cannot give their children all the help they need in the absence of accessible, publicly funded supports.Currently, ser-vices are fragmented and difficult to access. Mothers, in particular, must devote untold hours to finding and keeping programs that benefit their children. Mary Ellen's ongoing experience arranging a series of beneficial activities for Jeremy bears this point out. Just as a feminist analysis speaks to the executive function many women play in their families, it is usually mothers who bear the extra responsibility of coordinating appointments and specialized services for their vulnerable kids. Once services are found, fiscal constraints often undermine the continuity of care so essential to our kids. Instead of parents being provided with an opportunity to choose from a "buffet"[112] of home care supports, education programs and residential respite care, scarcity rules.

Canadian health and social services are not organized to provide the range of supports needed. Many people don't expect any better. I wonder whether their perspective would change if they could spend a day in Stockholm with Dave and Lisa. The Canada of today reflects a diminishing willingness to nurture its residents. In many jurisdictions in this country, necessary social services are victims of death by a thousand cuts.

Political and social conditions in a society affect one's expectations about such supports. In Canada, the fiscal climate and rise of neo-conservatism during the last thirty years has tamped down our expectations of the state and public agencies. While this is not the place for a comprehensive analysis of how market forces in the global economy affect what we think we may reasonably expect, it is critical to note how years of haranguing about deficits at all levels of government shapes our perspective. We often feel fortunate to receive even the most basic of supports. I have been told by mothers and fathers: "Thank heaven we got a childcare subsidy this year"; "I don't know what I'd do if the province didn't cover 75 percent of my son's wheelchair"; "At least there's one weekend a month I can stay and watch the kids' hockey game and still make it to the grocery store before it closes ..."

What is most crucial to understand is that these types of assistance are not perks. They reflect the genuine needs of our children and family members. When high quality services are available — such as the respite home where Lisa spends time, where she knows her caregivers and they know her, including which squeaky bath toy makes her laugh — there is a continuity of care vital to both parent and child.

The same is true when paid caregivers are valued in the work they do. Dave tells us that public sector wages in Sweden still fall below what human service workers should receive. Nonetheless (and Canadians should note that in most provinces parking lot attendants earn more than childcare and home care workers)[113] the Swedish system provides job security, working conditions and wages that mitigate against staff turnover. In Canada, there is ample evidence that fragmented services breed uncertainty. We cannot expect continuity of care. We cannot expect that our children will be in the company of trained individuals who can afford to stay in their jobs.[114]

The reason wages and working conditions are more stable in Sweden is that, as Dave explains, organized labour at a central level negotiates contracts that set minimum standards. These standards affect not only continuity of care in human services, but also impact directly on the standards of care consumers/clients have the right to expect. Since our sense of entitlement is influenced fundamentally by what support is genuinely available, expectations among Canadians are perpetually ratcheted down.

Social Justice and Advocacy

Among the mothers and fathers I interviewed, a few expressed views that linked their individual experience to a societal need for greater social justice. But this was not always the case. For example, although Sharon was frustrated by the inadequate allotment of respite care, she did not automatically launch into a critique of how such services are funded and organized. When I asked her about cuts that had affected her family's access to home care, she saw it as a result of decisions and/or assessments made by individual case workers.

These mothers and fathers had all developed, to varying degrees, the skill sets needed to advocate effectively on behalf of their children. It is apparent that where a particular objective was defined (i.e. Colleen organizing with other parents to save Johnny's developmental delay classroom from the cutting room floor or Lillian and Michael's work with other families to sustain Victor School for Ollie and the other children), participants did seem conscious that they were exercising their democratic rights as citizens. In my experience as an activist and organizer, such focused and explicitly political activity comes about when the opposition is clearly identified. Individuals less likely to participate in other political forums will make great efforts to achieve a goal, whether that be speed bumps or crosswalks on their streets or joining to defend the right to comprehensive health services in French in the Ottawa area.[115]

Cheryl and her husband Tzvika engaged in a very deliberate lobbying campaign to accomplish a specific set of goals. From the beginning they formulated a plan to pressure elected officials at different levels of government. As Cheryl explained, asking their friends to team up to fight for Enosh's right to participate in mainstream education took a certain amount of courage. Throughout their meetings and struggles, the circle of friends developed greater political awareness and acumen.

While many of the parents I interviewed had learned to fight City Hall on their children's behalf, it is not clear that doing so became a transformative experience in terms of their overall political views or civic participation. I suspect that the time involved in caring for and advocating on behalf of their children mitigates against broader political activism. Certainly the sheer volume of work involved in raising our high-needs kids is an enormous barrier to building a more vocal and cohesive constituency.

What was absolutely transformative, however, is how the mothers and fathers I met learned to love and experience joy with their child, to truly see their child as "a complete person in his (or her) disability," as Mary Ellen's doctor had counselled gently at Jeremy's birth. I found this characteristic most striking. Each spoke of how the child had added a previously untapped dimension to their lives. Julien, you will recall, told me she had learned to be more compassionate and, in particular, to empathize with other women she met. Colleen expressed both her devotion to Johnny and an appreciation of how his life affects others. Such observations revealed to me that these families were propelled less by overt political objectives than a desire for recognition that each child deserves to be treated in a humane manner. Some parents — Cheryl, Lillian and Colleen particularly — also urged their communities to appreciate that including children with diverse needs constitutes a shared social benefit.

THE HUB MODEL

I've argued that the current system (or lack thereof) is not working for Canadian families. We've seen the difficulties faced by parents of children with a variety of disabling conditions. In contrast, Dave's description of his situation suggests that a country can choose to organize its priorities in a way that truly supports children and their families.

One way to reconfigure services would be to adopt a hub model (picture a wheel with a central organizing body in the middle and spokes to a variety of services) to provide both services in the community and residential respite care. Facilities may be adapted, created and sustained to perform the public good; this would require a major shift in attitude and financial resources for governments to take responsibility for providing safe, high quality and affordable care. With respect to special needs kids and their families, this would mean supporting a set of integrated and flexible programs. One option is for the respite care home, staffed by trained professionals who provide high quality care, to be at the centre of the wheel. Families would make use of the residential facility on a regularly scheduled basis that ensured continuity of care to each child and correspondingly, predictable shift schedules, training and compensation for workers.

The spokes of the wheel would feature a range of therapeutic supports children may need, including, for example, nutritionists, speech therapists and physiotherapists, mobility and seating specialists, music therapists and social workers to run sibling support groups and family counselling. Another spoke of the wheel would ensure appropriate medical, nursing, dental and psychiatric care. Caregivers dispatched to in-home care locations would coordinate through central case managers to ensure an integrated, holistic approach. Links would be fostered between in-home care services, before- and after-school care, a toy lending library and a drop-in resource centre, special needs education and resources and family support services — the outer circle of the wheel. Services would need to be available in languages appropriate to the community's demographic composition, as well as English or French — encouraging diverse peoples to converse in their own tongue, an obvious contribution to forming an inclusive community centre.

As the Canadian childcare system is revamped, activists argue for integrated programs, in part so that families can access resources from one point of entry. Why not create space where non-disabled children can interact with their sisters or brothers, as well as other families like their own? Many models exist that would break down isolation and ensure that resources are available so that parents can participate in the workforce or pursue training opportunities. In one publicly funded facility I visited in the United States, elderly people (and some younger people with developmental disabilities) are picked up from their homes each morning. They spend their day in a facility where they participate in various programs, have full access to medical and nursing care and eat their lunch. In the late afternoon, several buses are dispatched to take participants home, each person supplied with a hot meal prepared in the facility's kitchen that meets their individual dietary needs.[116] No one situation is ideal, but alternative models for care do exist.

A combination of these measures would help parents to sustain their busy work and home schedules. Not only would it provide a measure of regularity, but all family members could rely on a break, adding a degree of certainty that is largely absent when one child's acute care needs dominate. A centre such as this hub would also be a place for families to learn about other activities and supports their children might enjoy. Just as moms and dads who gather at the schoolyard to pick up their non-disabled child might hear about a good soccer coach or which shop has a sale on winter boots, the respite care home could also become a point for casual information sharing between families.

How to Get There from Here

Dave's explanation of how his family's life is organized gives me pause. First, it seems such a sensible way to accommodate difference. I'm sure it's far from perfect, but each person gets what they need in the situation. Lisa's condition is not catastrophic in part because the people around her love and honour her. At a theoretical level, this reflects the social model of disability. The person with the disablement is not treated as a medical pathology. She is first and foremost a person.

At a practical level, Dave is better able to balance his life because he has confidence that both of his daughters are well looked after. Schooling, before- and after-school programs and respite are readily available. The role that Lisa's personal assistant Alicja plays is enormous, he tells us. She cares for Lisa's basic needs, accompanies her young charge to school and appointments. As Dave recognizes, Lisa will always require this kind of assistance. This is the person she is. And the family, with the support of publicly funded programs, is able to put Lisa's personhood first.

Sweden is not a panacea. We don't all have to run out and buy a plane ticket. We can force the changes here, incrementally. Every time a gain is made to improve the lives of our children and families, some progress is achieved. What Dave's story does show us, in brilliant contrast to what many Canadian families experience, is that it doesn't have to be this way. When people have a vision of how something should or could be they may be moved to use their democratic power to seek justice.

In political terms, the absence of a comprehensive web of interrelated services represents a potential contested terrain. That is, the space can be negotiated, especially if we come together to bring pressure to bear. I believe workers' associations and unions need to play a significant role in supporting families to negotiate a better deal. One aspect of a winning strategy would be for unions to insist at the bargaining table that management include establishing best practices for standards of care under the purview of collective bargaining.

Objectives for new contract language should include the braided principles of good quality service and continuity of care, including: reasonable staff-to-client ratios, workload and wages; health and safety protections for work performed in homes as well as facilities; and a dispute resolution mechanism between workers and clients when issues arise around personal care.[117] All of these measures would provide a bulwark against the instability propagated by insecure terms and conditions of employment.

Obtaining these substantive changes in social policy will require a significant reorientation. The current pace of change is slower than molasses; subtle improvements are not enough. Governments' lack of political will and refusal to shoulder the cost involved stands in the way of creating an efficient, cost-effective and high quality spectrum of supports. It's time for a significant shift in policy. Impassioned leadership harnessing bright ideas — rather than imperceptible changes creeping like tectonic plates — could bring into focus the hopes and dreams these parents hold for their children.

*

As I listened over and over to the recordings of my interviews with these mothers and fathers, a powerful image came to mind. I am standing before a massive rock face wrinkled by crevices, worn by wind and rain. Minerals crystallize and fill fissures swirling down to the ground. I am watchful. A pattern emerges and fades before my eyes, varying with angle and light. In full morning sun, the brilliant contrast between the rock and the dark, lined gaps is truly arresting. In the pitch of night, a faint trickle of water bears single witness to the wizened façade before me.

For months I worked to mine the richness of my conversations with these parents. The two most poignant topics we covered were, without exception, the unique attachment between sisters and brothers and the balance between bloody-minded determination and apprehension with which parents approach making plans for their child's future. Both issues are fraught, no beaten track to follow. We simply do our best.

Sadly, one cannot know what supports will be available in months and years to come. And yet the gems exposed in the light of our conversations were plentiful: unwavering devotion; respectful hopes and dreams; a contingency plan for the child who will never fully grow up and move out; and that stirring mix of practicality and worry that seems to filter every aspect of these families' lives.

Like flickering sunlight that alters the appearance of fragmented stone, so too does each child's future seem random. Unjustly so. The only certainty I noted is that the future is indeed a question that weighs heavily. Each family had considered their child's path long before I happened to arrive on the scene with my tape recorder.

I am honoured they allowed me to accompany them to the troubling edges of their dis/comfort. A deep sense of the familiar — my mothering sensibility in gear — recognizes in these moments an absolute clarity of purpose. We parents cling to that purpose as if to ward off the uncertainty, ignoring the fistfuls of doubt spawned as we watch our children struggle. It is our family formations — constellations in flux — that texture our vulnerable children's lives. Beyond the family hearth, initiatives that may ultimately prove counterproductive are taking root. More and more, individualistic solutions pose barriers to the public sector, not-for-profit network of programs our children need. As isolated parents committed to building a better life for all of our children, I fear we are but inadequate vessels striving to keep them from harm's way.

In my research, I came across stacks of studies presented to successive governments at all levels. There is no scarcity of good ideas and even some success stories. Some of these may be replicated. We have the expertise at hand to make meaningful improvements in health and social policy, improvements that would enrich immeasurably families such as those profiled in this book.

Replacing an ethos determined by market-driven concerns with an ethic of care would go a long way toward encouraging the paradigm shift required to bring about these changes. It must not be about profits or further privatizing the publicly funded programs that do exist. This struggle is about humane treatment and an expansive sense of possibility. It is about reaching out to the disenfranchised. It is about improving inclusion in our society and promoting active citizenship.

Achieving significant modifications in how services are dispensed would require that the constituency (families with disabled children) organize into a collective political force. Just as we care fiercely for our children, we can become a force with which to be reckoned on the public scene. Working with various caregiving groups, teachers, allied health professionals and their associations, including unions, parents could advance a powerful and hopeful vision. It is time to cast these demands centre stage in negotiations with agencies and governments.

How can I suggest parents conceivably take on even one more task? I would argue that we cannot afford not to wage this battle and further, that without parents at the forefront, positive changes will not be achieved. First, we need the high quality and accessible respite care. Once that is battened down, pursuing the rest of the goals is possible. In the humane tradition Canadians profess to support, vulnerable families are not meant to wither on the vine, or worse ... We must seize the opportunity, break the silence and organize ourselves. Together we can win just treatment for our children and transform the complexion of Canadian politics.

SOME TIPS ABOUT ADVOCACY
FINDING SERVICES AND SEEKING SUPPORT

ONE OF THE MOST HELPFUL BITS OF ADVICE I received during my son's very early days came from his paediatrician. She urged my spouse and me to consider three distinct but related sets of needs:

What did our baby need? What did his father need? What did I need? Of course we were totally focused on our son and his needs always came first. But as we moved through crises and different sorts of decisions about his care — from allowing a feeding tube to be inserted to how many weekend visits to his residential care facility we would make once his little sister was born — it made sense to apply this approach.

Locating services can be difficult and stressful. The next few pages provide some brief tips to get you started. We'll look first at strategies that can be helpful with individual families and then outline a few tips pertaining to group advocacy efforts.

INDIVIDUAL FAMILIES

It helps to be organized no matter what situation you face with your child. You will want to a) maximize the information you have about your child's needs, b) keep accurate records and c) be very persistent. Remember, you have the right to know.

Here are some general tips:

• Before you make calls, jot down a list of questions with spaces in between for answers.

• When you speak with someone from an agency, ask them about community resources such as organizations that can send you specific information on seizures or hearing impairment, for example. Almost every disability identified has an organization that works with families and also advocates on their behalf. Ask the person you contact for the names and phone numbers of such organizations or support groups in your area. Your doctor's office *may* also have this information, but don't stop there. It is in the community that you will find the most help.

• Use a notebook to record all contacts you make and what you are told. You may be referred to another person or agency. Write down names, job titles and phone numbers. Even if these don't seem helpful right away, you may need to circle back and use them later.

• If the agency you call operates in a language in which you are not fluent, ask someone else to make the call. Is there a family member or friend who can accompany you to an appointment and act as an interpreter?

• Then, tell the agency you need a language interpreter. In urban centres, some agencies keep lists of people who, for example, speak Punjabi or Italian, English or French. Often this person is a volunteer — there may be no cost involved. Ask around. Be persistent. You are entitled to assistance in the language in which you are comfortable — especially when learning about your child's diagnoses and proposed care. It is also important that you can explain your child's (and family's) needs.

• Ask if the agency or professional with whom you are meeting has any written material you can take home.

• Ask for the person's business card and keep these in your notebook or file. It helps to have a pencil case or pouch in which you can put all the different cards or scraps of paper on which you jot down information.

• As you learn about resources in the community, add these to your notebook so you can access them as required.

• Keep files with any medical records or treatment plans your child's doctor or physiotherapist, for example, develops.

• Ditto for school files such as guidance counsellors' and teachers' reports or recommendations.

• Find a way to store your files in a box or file cabinet so that you can access them when needed. You may need information about medications and therapy programs as your child grows up. If you organize these as you go, you won't need to rely on memory alone.

• The Internet is full of information about support and service organizations. "Google" is a great search engine for finding contacts and groups. But be choosy about the sites you trust; not all information is reliable.

• Find someone to help you. If you have a partner, delegate: ask them to keep the files organized, for example. Or insist that they put the child(ren) to bed a few nights each a week so you can go on-line at home or at the public library. These activities are *also* part of parenting your special needs child.

• Reach out! You will find people in similar situations who can help guide and support you.

• If you are on your own (or your partner is not as helpful as you would like), reach out to a sister or brother, a friend or workmate. You do not have to handle research and advocacy work *and* care for your child all by yourself. People are often willing to help out, they just don't know how. Tell them. Maybe someone else could go on-line or make a few calls.

When your child is in hospital:

• If your child is hospitalized, get out that notebook. Take it when you meet the various doctors, therapists and social workers. Use the same procedure: list your questions in advance and record the answers. Make sure to get clarification of anything you don't fully understand.

• You may have to be persistent with your questions. It is very likely that the people working in hospital are busy, even overloaded. Don't let that deter you from asking questions and getting answers — speaking with you is part of their job.

• Ask hospital staff if they have anything you can read on the subject of your child's condition or a medical procedure that is recommended. If the information you receive is too technical, your family doctor or the nurse practitioner at your clinic may be able to help you understand it. Do not hesitate to ask!

• You are entitled to know exactly what treatment plan your child's medical team intends to follow. Be assertive. Don't take "no" for an answer.

• Many hospitals have a patient advocate or ombudsperson. If you run into any brick walls in looking for information or answers to your questions, ask how to contact the patient advocate or ombudsperson. This does not make you a troublemaker — it makes you an informed consumer. Find that person and get the help you need.

• When you don't feel strong enough, pushing for information may just seem too hard. Get someone to help you: a friend, a member of your family, your kid's teacher. Often we are totally focused on our child and thankful when she/he gets medical attention. But you will still want to understand what is going on. When my son was an infant, for example, a girlfriend joined me at a key meeting with one of the specialists. She asked a lot of questions I had not thought of and helped me to make sense of the answers later.

• Don't be too hard on yourself. Few of us are trained to deal with stressful situations of this kind. If your sister or friend were in the same boat, wouldn't you gladly offer them help?

• When it is your child, it is natural to feel like a bundle of emotions. There is nothing wrong with your reactions or emotions. There are times we all need extra support to handle a challenging situation.

• Your family doctor or someone in your faith community may know of someone you can talk to about how *you* are feeling. Remember that you need to keep yourself well so that you can help your child over the long run.

Developing advocacy skills is not rocket science, but it may involve a new approach to problem-solving. Here are some points to help organize your approach.

1. **What is the precise problem you need to resolve?**
   If there are several, make a list. It can be daunting to figure out a plan when all the dilemmas seem related. Think of a knotted shoelace — you untie the knots one at a time. Once you have a list of issues, break them into smaller, "doable" pieces. Ask for help carrying out the ones you can delegate.

2. Develop clear, achievable objectives.

Do you want to get your child into a particular program? Do you want the program to change its rules in order to accommodate your son or daughter? Answering these questions will help you plan your next steps.

3. Who is in charge of the program?

Is it your child's school? The school board or a service agency? Is it the social service or health branch of the municipal or provincial government? Ask around. Your family doctor or agency staff should be able to give you answers. Again, once you know the answer to this question, you can figure out your next steps.

4. Who can you count on as potential allies? Are there other families that feel the same way that you do?

Try using word of mouth at your neighbourhood school, local community centre, faith group or Native friendship centre. Get your friends and family members to ask around. Some people put up a notice at a grocery store in the neighbourhood. Be creative — even a poster taped to a pole by the sidewalk might unearth a person who knows a friend who has a sister who has faced a similar issue.

5. What about your child's teachers, infant stimulation worker, daycare teacher, social worker or physiotherapist?

They may have information about programs, volunteers or support groups that can help. Never hesitate to ask. I came across services that were helpful, but never publicized. We are all entitled to whatever assistance we can find for our children. Go for it! You need to get your foot in the door to learn what services are out there.

6. Can your local elected representative(s) help?

Never hesitate to call your local elected representative's constituency office. An important part of his or her job is to assist you, the voter. Even if you did not vote for that person, they have a responsibility to try to assist you. They have paid staff to follow up on your concerns. Ask for a meeting. Be assertive about your child's needs. Eventually a door will open. Most of all, remember you are not alone.

7. Can a faith organization help?

Many faith communities are set up to help out with problems facing children and their families. Some churches have pastoral counsellors who may be able to refer you to services in the community. In the Hindu community, for example, the Pandit (congregation leader) may refer you to the resources you need. Similarly, a Muslim community will have the Imam, who will know which people in your community may be able to help you find the assistance you need. In many locations, there are Jewish and Catholic family and child services agencies.

GROUP ADVOCACY EFFORTS

In some portraits in this book, parents gave examples of how they learned to advocate on behalf of their children, sometimes on their own, sometimes with a group of people with common concerns. There are instances where only a group action will do. The following points will help your group make an initial assessment of the situation and start working together.

Here are some general tips:

• If there are other families you think might share your concerns about a program or lack of special education assistants at school, for example, you may want to call a meeting. First have coffee with one of the other parents and ask if they will help you arrange a get-together. Someone will have a kitchen or living room where a small group can meet.

• At your first gathering, after introducing yourselves, outline the issue(s) you are concerned about and ask for input from the others. It may be useful to brainstorm informally for awhile.

• While people are speaking about the problems, ask for a volunteer to take notes of items that come up. Tape a big sheet of paper on the wall (or use a flipchart page or chalk board) and use it to record these points so everyone can see them. This will help your group to stay on track.

• When it feels right, move on to possible solutions. In a similar vein, start the discussion, and on a separate sheet of paper that everyone can see, record what you might do together to change the situation.

• It works best to make your plan based on the points you seem to agree upon. Other issues can be put to one side — you don't have to agree on everything! As one parent in the Portraits section mentioned, there are some families she has advocated with who have little in common with her besides their children's needs. That's okay.

• From the points you agree upon, try to decide the order of priority.

• Break down the priority items into tasks. These should be small, manageable pieces. You almost have a plan!

• Shape the message you want to share with others into simple and understandable terms.

• Once you have agreed to a course of action, you will want to divide up the tasks.

• Take stock of the skills each person brings. Everyone will have something to offer.

Some examples:

- • Making phone calls to other families and/or to agencies or government.

- • Speaking in public.

- • Writing or doing research.

- • Taking notes at your meetings and circulating them so everyone is clear on plans and decisions, including anyone unable to attend.

- • Putting a flyer together for distribution that informs your neighbours or child's teachers of your objectives. (Often there is more support for your ideas than you might know.)

- • Sewing flags or costumes to attract media to your event or doing small scale carpentry projects for a fundraiser.

- • Choosing refreshments for your next gathering. Some groups rotate this task.

- • Contacting the media.

• Divide up the tasks and, before ending your get-together, make sure you all have one another's telephone numbers and email addresses.

• Set the date and time of your next get-together. It helps to be specific, such as 7–9 p.m. for example, so everyone knows how much time to set aside.

• Some families may need babysitters in order to participate. A couple of participants should figure out a solution; for example, if necessary, every family could throw in a few dollars so that no one is excluded.

• If more families are affected by the problems you have identified, ask each person present to try and bring just one more individual to the next meeting.

Remember that no matter how small a step forward you make, it is a victory. Few issues are solved all at once; just as you devise your plan in distinct pieces, getting one influential person or reporter on your side is a big deal. Celebrate your small victories together and then move on to the next challenge.

NOTES

INTRODUCTION

1. The word "citizen" is used in this book to denote the democratic participation in civil society by individuals in community, including those that the state may exclude, on legal grounds, from taking up full and active citizenship. In this broadest and most positive sense, citizenship denotes a way of living in a society and being of the world.

2. Saskatchewan, in 1947, was the first province to establish public, universal hospital insurance. Ten years later, the government of Canada passed legislation to allow the federal government to share in the cost of provincial hospital insurance plans. By 1961, all ten provinces and two territories had public insurance plans that provided comprehensive coverage for in-hospital care. Saskatchewan again pioneered in providing insurance for physicians' services outside hospitals, beginning in 1962. The federal government enacted medical care legislation in 1968, and by 1972, all provincial and territorial plans had been extended to include doctors' services.

3. In November 2004, British Columbia families of young children with autism were shocked by a landmark Supreme Court decision that stated the province was not obligated under the Charter of Rights and Freedoms to pay for a particularly effective — and expensive — treatment for children with autism. The higher court struck down two lower court rulings that had forced the province to cover the highly specialized treatment. "Top court: B.C. doesn't have to fund autism treatment." *CBC.ca News.* <http://www.cbc.ca/story/canada/national/2004/11/19/autism_supremecourt041119.html?>. April 24, 2005.

4. Robert F. Kennedy, Affirmation Day Speech, University of Capetown, South Africa, June 6, 1966.

5. Cynthia Garcia Coll, Janet L. Surrey and Kathy Weingarten, eds., *Mothering Against the Odds* (New York: The Guilford Press, 1998).

I: MAPPING THE TERRAIN

CHAPTER ONE

6. These terms and definitions are drawn from Medline Plus, a service of the U.S. National Library and the National Institutes of Health. <http://www.nlm.mih.gov/medlineplus/ency/article/000997>. October 14, 2004.

7. André Picard, "Segregation is not such a dirty word: Tiny school helps children with severe physical and behavioural problems to thrive," *The Globe and Mail*, 4 February 2000.

CHAPTER TWO

8. A medication inhaled in vapour that dilates the air passages (bronchial tubes) of the lungs to improve breathing.

9. The Roeher Institute, *Labour Force Inclusion of Parents Caring for Children with Disabilities* (Toronto: 1999), 18.

10. A disproportionately higher incidence of special needs exists among First Nation students compared to the general Canadian population. Aboriginal peoples are more likely than other Canadians to have hearing, sight and speech difficulties. Diabetes is epidemic, with First Nation people three times more likely to be diabetic than other Canadians. For a fuller discussion of these issues and a brief explication of the Assembly of First Nations position, see "Research Report — Governing in an Integrated Fashion: Lessons from the Disability Domain," *Canadian Policy Research Networks* (June 2001). <http://www.cprn.org/en/doc.cfm?doc=172>. January 20, 2005.

11. Mr. Justice Dennis O'Connor, *Walkerton Commission of Inquiry Report* (Ministry of the Attorney General, Government of Ontario, January 14, 2002).

12. Michael Bach, *Social Inclusion as Solidarity: Re-Thinking the Child Rights Agenda* (Toronto: Laidlaw Foundation, 2002), 15.

13. Michael J. Prince, *Research Report — Governing in an Integrated Fashion: Lessons from the Disability Domain* (Ottawa: Canadian Policy Research Networks, 2001), 65.

14. A poll conducted for the CBC by Environics Research in May 2004 indicates that health care leads the list of matters that are important for Canadians. That is consistent with polls conducted over the last few years, whether provincial or federal: more Canadians choose health care as their primary concern. "Canada Votes." CBC News. <http://www.cbc.ca/story/election/national/news/2004/05/24/healthcare_poll040524.html >. February 15, 2005.

15. Prince, *Research Report — Governing in an Integrated Fashion: Lessons from the Disability Domain*, 58.

16. The Federal-Provincial-Territorial Council of Ministers on Social Policy Renewal released a discussion paper in May 1999 that they called the first step toward developing a comprehensive, long-term strategy to improve the well-being of children. This document was entitled *A National Children's Agenda: Developing a Shared Vision*. Its stated goals were to ensure that Canada's children were a) healthy physically and emotionally, b) safe and secure, c) successful at learning and d) socially engaged and responsible. Canadian Intergovernmental Conference Secretariat. <http://www.scics.gc.ca/cinfo99/83064905_e.html>. March 19, 2005.

17. Most First Nation people in Canada live at or below the poverty line, especially in the western provinces where four times as many Aboriginal peoples as other citizens live below this level. Prince, *CPRN,* 48.

18. Fraser Valentine, *Enabling Citizenship: Full Inclusion of Children with Disabilities and their Parents* (Ottawa: Canadian Policy Research Network, June 2001), 83-85.

19. Prince, *Research Report — Governing in an Integrated Fashion: Lessons from the Disability Domain,* 38.

20. Prince, *Research Report — Governing in an Integrated Fashion: Lessons from the Disability Domain,* 60.

21. Valentine, *Enabling Citizenship: Full Inclusion of Children with Disabilities and their Parents,* 65.

22. Prince, *Research Report — Governing in an Integrated Fashion: Lessons from the Disability Domain,* 65-66.

23. Valentine, *Enabling Citizenship: Full Inclusion of Children with Disabilities and their Parents,* 66.

24. Valentine, *Enabling Citizenship: Full Inclusion of Children with Disabilities and their Parents,* 16.

25. The Ontario New Democratic Party states in a February 4, 2005 press statement that services for special needs education in the province continue to require major repairs. School boards were ordered to hand back an estimated $102 million from special education reserve accounts as of the end of 2003 and 2004. Much of that money has already been spent or earmarked for special education programs during the 2004-2005 school year. These cuts will put the pinch on programs for students in special education. In Sudbury the district school board will have to give back $2.2 million of their special education money. As a result, the board will not be able to hire special education teachers or educational assistants this year as planned.

26. *Employment Insurance Compassionate Care Benefit.* Human Resources and Skills Development Canada, Publication #IN-044-09-04.

27. National Union of Public and General Employees, *A Full Evaluation of the 2004 First Ministers' 10-year Health Action Plan.* (Ottawa: September, 2004).

28. Two new transfers, the Canada Health Transfer (CHT) and Canada Social Transfer (CST) were established by March 31, 2004, from a split in the CHST (CHT 62 percent: CST 38 percent). "Canada Health Act Federal Contributions Associated with the Canada Health Act." Health Canada. <http://www.fin.gc.ca/access/fedprov. html >. February 12, 2005.

29. Thomas Walkom, Toronto Star national issues columnist, email interview, 16 February 2005.

30. Canadian Union of Public Employees, "Health deal leaves door open for private care." <http://cupe.ca/www/p3alertoctober2004/10488>. March 13, 2005.

31. Roy J. Romanow, Q.C., *Final Report: Building on Values: The Future of Health Care in Canada* (Ottawa: Commission on the Future of Health Care in Canada, 2002).

32. Valentine, *Enabling Citizenship: Full Inclusion of Children with Disabilities and their Parents,* xiv.

33. P. Hoare, M. Harris, P. Jackson and S. Kerley, "A Community Survey of Children with Severe Intellectual Disability and Their Families: Psychological Adjustment, Carer Distress and the Effect of Respite Care," *Journal of Intellectual Disability Research* 42, no. 3 (1998), 218-227.

34. From a talk given March 20, 2004, by Francisco Rico Martinez, former President of Canadian Council of Refugees, on the occasion of the ceremony to bestow the J.S. Woodsworth Award. The Award is given annually by the Ontario New Democratic Party to an individual and/or an organization which works toward ending racial discrimination.

35. The Roeher Institute, *Beyond the Limits: Mothers Caring for Children with Disabilities* (Toronto: 2000), 20.

36. J. Good and J. Reis, *A Special Kind of Parenting* (Illinois: La Leche League International, 1985), 46.

37. Tanya Talaga, "Sick Kids faces $45M cut," *The Toronto Star,* 16 October 2004, A1, 4.

CHAPTER THREE

38. "… People who are impaired bear the burden of membership in what traditionally has been viewed as a 'weak' class, one defined as requiring heightened protection because its members are feeble or incompetent." Anita Silvers, "Introduction," in Anita Silvers, David Wasserman and Mary B. Mahowald, *Disability, Difference, Discrimination: Perspectives on Justice in Bioethics and Public Policy* (Oxford: Rowman & Littlefield, 1998), 3.

39. Canadian Institute for Children's Health, 1994. Cited in The Roeher Institute, *Labour Force Inclusion of Parents Caring for Children with Disabilities,* (Toronto: 1999), 4.

40. The Roeher Institute, *Labour Force Inclusion of Parents Caring for Children with Disabilities,* 37.

41. Haverstock, 1992; Ambert, 1992; McKeever, Angus and Spalding, 1998 in The Roeher Institute, *Beyond the Limits: Mothers Caring for Children with Disabilities,* 13.

42. Ibid.

43. Miriam Greenspan, "'Exceptional' Mothering in a 'Normal' World," in Cynthia Garcia Coll, Janet L. Surrey and Kathy Weingarten, eds., *Mothering Against the Odds: Diverse Voices of Contemporary Mothers* (New York: The Guilford Press, 1998), 42-3.

44. Haverstock, 1992; Ambert, 1992; McKeever, Angus and Spalding, 1998 in The Roeher Institute, *Beyond the Limits: Mothers Caring for Children with Disabilities*, 13.

45. Marilyn Waring, *If Women Counted: A New Feminist Economics* (California: Harper, 1988).

46. Meg Luxton, *Feminist Perspectives on Social Inclusion and Children's Well-Being* (Laidlaw Foundation: Toronto, June 2002), 5.

47. Greenspan. "'Exceptional' Mothering in a 'Normal' World," 42-3.

48. I am not claiming this to be a universal experience; of course differing contexts breed varying results. In some nomadic cultures, for example, a child that could not keep up or fulfil a purpose considered useful to the group's survival was left behind or even put to death.

49. I submit that this fact also leaves paid caregivers in many situations (e.g. group homes, small agencies and nursing homes) open to wage exploitation because the work is not highly valued. Personal support workers are stuck in a low-wage ghetto not unlike childcare workers — only worse.

50. Meg Luxton and Heather Jon Maroney, "Begetting Babies, Raising Children: The Politics of Parenting," in Jos Roberts and Jesse Vorst, eds., *Is Socialism in Crisis? Canadian Perspectives* (Fernwood Publishing: Winnipeg/Halifax, 1992).

51. Luxton, *Feminist Perspectives on Social Inclusion and Children's Well-Being*, 9.

52. Valentine, *Enabling Citizenship: Full Inclusion of Children with Disabilities and their Parents* 2001; Bach *Social Inclusion as Solidarity: Re-Thinking the Child Rights Agenda* 2002 and Sherri Torjman, *Proposal for a National Personal Supports Fund* (Ottawa: Caledon Institute for Social Policy, October 2000).

53. Weingarten, Surrey, Garcia Coll, "Introduction," Weingarten, Surrey, Garcia Goll eds, *Mothering Against the Odds*, 6-11. My use of these concepts borrows in particular from the work of bell hooks, *Talking back: Thinking Feminist, Talking Black* (Boston: South End Press, 1989) and Paulo Freire, *Pedagogy of the Oppressed* (New York: Continuum, 1989).

CHAPTER FOUR

54. Many activists and authors have contributed to the development of an alternative analysis of disability. See, for example, Len Barton ed., *Disability, Politics & the Struggle for Change* (London: David Fulton Publishers, 2001); Colin Barnes and Geof Mercer, *Disability* (Cambridge: Polity Press in association with Blackwell Publishers Ltd., 2003); Colin Barnes, Mike Oliver and Len Barton eds., *Disability Studies Today* (Cambridge: Polity Press in association with Blackwell Publishers Ltd., 2002).

55. Many parents report similar experiences. One study at the California School for the Deaf found that 50 percent of the parents were told by physicians that "nothing was

wrong with their child and not to worry." Julia Darnell Good & Joyce Good Reis, *A Special Kind of Parenting,* (Illinois: La Leche League International, 1985), 16.

56. This point was brought home to me during a week-long seminar on health care ethics I enrolled in aimed at doctors, lawyers, nurses, philosophers and clergy. The word "hysterical" was used repeatedly by some participants to describe mothers' reaction when doctors delivered troubling news regarding their ill or disabled infants. Annual Summer Seminar in Health Care Ethics. University of Washington. Seattle, Washington, USA, August, 1996.

57. Marcia Rioux, "Bending Towards Justice," in Len Barton, ed., *Disability, Politics & the Struggle for Change,* 29.

58. Moral theorists such as the German philosopher Emmanuel Kant (1724-1804) believed humans to be independent, rational, self-interested and autonomous. It is against this dominant philosophical influence that feminist scholars have developed the ethic of care. Susan Sherwin, *No Longer Patient: Feminist Ethics and Health Care* (Philadelphia: Temple University Press, 1992) and Sara Ruddick, *Maternal Thinking: Toward a Politics of Peace* (New York: Ballantine Books, 1989).

59. See, for example, Nel Noddings, *Caring: A Feminine Approach to Ethics and Moral Education* (Berkeley: University of California Press, 1984) and Susan Sherwin "Feminism and Bioethics" in Susan M. Wolf, ed., *Feminism and Bioethics: Beyond Reproduction* (New York: Oxford University Press, 1996).

60. Bach, *Social Inclusion as Solidarity,* 4.

61. "Social Inclusion, Research and Policy Papers." 2002. http://www.laidlawfdn.org/page_1213.cfm.

62. Amartya Sen, *Development as Freedom* (New York: Random House, 1999).

63. Sen, *Development as Freedom,* 87-89.

64. The major exception in Canada outside Quebec is the deaf community. American Sign Language is a distinct language. Those who "speak" it may be like other minority language groups and prefer to remain in their linguistic community. They are interested in strengthening their own cultural and community practices.

CHAPTER FIVE

65. See, for example, R.H. Bradley, S.L. Rock, L. Whiteside, B. M. Caldwell, and J. Brisby, "Dimensions of parenting in families having children with disabilities," *Exceptionality* 2, no.1 (1991), 41-61; G. Mahoney, P. O'Sullivan, and C. Robinson, "The family environments of children with disabilities: Diverse but not so different," *Topics in Early Childhood Special Education* 12, no. 3 (1992), 386-402; S. McLinden, "Mothers' and fathers' reports of the effects of a young child with special needs on the family," *Journal of Early Intervention* 14, no. 3 (1990), 249-259.

66. A fuller study would include children's own deconstruction of relationships with their siblings and consider how feelings shift over time. I did not undertake that

investigation here.

67. Ontario Ministry of Community and Social Services, "The Evolution of Services for Ontarians with a Developmental Disability," 9 September 2004, 1.

68. Helen Henderson, "Reason to Hope Liberals Will Act on Promises," *The Toronto Star,* 18 September 2004. A7.

69. Ontario Public Service Employees Union, *Centres of Excellence: Serving People with Developmental Disabilities* (Toronto: OPSEU, March 2005), 8-9.

70. Jean Vanier, *Becoming Human* (Toronto: House of Anansi, 1998), 40.

CHAPTER SIX

71. Valentine, *Enabling Citizenship: Full Inclusion of Children with Disabilities and their Parents,* xiv. I must point out that the women *are in fact* contributing to the economy through their unpaid labour.

72. Sherri Torjman, *R-E-S-P-I-T-E Spells Respect* (Ottawa: Caledon Institute of Social Policy, May 2004), 2.

73. Valentine, *Enabling Citizenship: Full Inclusion of Children with Disabilities and their Parents*, iv.

74. This is also borne out in research by the National Union of Public and General Employees. NUPGE, *A Full Evaluation of the 2004 First Ministers' 10-year Health Action Plan.*

75. NUPGE, *A Full Evaluation of the 2004 First Ministers' 10-year Health Action Plan.*

76. Sherri Torjman, *What Are the Policy-Makers Saying about Respite?* (Ottawa: Caledon Institute of Social Policy, February 2003), 11.

77. The Roeher Institute, *Labour Force Inclusion of Parents Caring for Children with Disabilities*, 1999.

78. OPSEU staff organizer, interview by author, Toronto, Ontario, 10 January 2004.

79. The Roeher Institute, *Beyond the Limits: Mothers Caring for Children with Disabilities*, 21.

80. Torjman, *What Are the Policy-Makers Saying about Respite?*, 11.

81. Valentine, *Enabling Citizenship: Full Inclusion of Children with Disabilities and their Parents*, 47.

II: Portraits

CHAPTER SEVEN

82. For a variety of reasons, Mary Ellen and I barely spoke about Jeremy and Katie's father. In conducting these interviews, I followed the parent's lead — either explicitly stated or implicit during the course of our discussion — as to what topics were out of bounds.

83. Children with Down Syndrome frequently have prominent facial features that include a flattened nose, protruding tongue and upward slanting eyes. Patterns of physical growth and mental development generally result in delayed cognitive development and social skills. Congenital heart defects are frequently present in Down Syndrome children and scientists note an increased incidence of acute leukemia. "Down Syndrome." *Medline Plus, A Service of the U.S. National Library and the National Institutes of Health.* <http://www.nlm.nih.gov/medlineplus/ency/article/000997.htm>. December 15, 2004.

84. Chromosomes are tiny threadlike structures contained in virtually every human cell. Each chromosome is made up of DNA that carries our individual genetic information in genes. In general, every human cell contains 22 pairs of chromosomes. Each cell also contains a pair of sex chromosomes. In a male, this combines an X and a Y (XY). In a female, there are two X chromosomes (XX). It is these latter two chromosomes which determine the sex of the baby. Although all of the chromosomes appear disorganized within the cell, scientific researchers have been able to identify them and thus have numbered the chromosomes from 1- 22 in order of size. "Down Syndrome." *Medline Plus, A Service of the U.S. National Library and the National Institutes of Health.* <http://www.nlm.nih.gov/medlineplus/ency/article/000997.htm>. December 15, 2004.

85. These terms and definitions are drawn from *Medline Plus,* a respected Internet-based resource. In this book I draw upon such medical definitions to give a brief outline of challenges faced by the children and families we meet. I do *not,* however, agree with reducing persons to their diagnosis nor do I use many of the value-laden, pejorative terms characteristic of such literature.

CHAPTER EIGHT

86. Cerebral palsy is a persistent qualitative motor disorder that appears during pregnancy and before age three. It is non-progressive and due to damage to the brain. The cerebral palsies of childhood are predominantly motor syndromes, not diseases, caused by a variety of pathologies. There is an abnormality of movement or posture and tone that is commonly associated with sensory abnormalities, cognitive deficits and epilepsy. "Cerebral Palsy." *Medline Plus, A Service of the U.S. National Library and the National Institutes of Health.* <http://www.nlm.nih.gov/medlineplus/ency/article/000997.htm>. December 16, 2004.

87. A weak sucking reflex sometimes indicates that a baby is at-risk. Many mothers find this a tremendously difficult and emotional time; while the baby has trouble getting

the nourishment they need, the mother's self-esteem — so wrapped in providing sustenance — may erode.
<http://www.ninds.nih.gov/disorders/amyotrophiclateralsclerosis/detail_amyotrophiclateralsclerosis.htm>.
October 2, 2004.

88. Electrolytes are minerals in the blood and other body fluids that carry an electric charge. It is important for the balance of electrolytes in the body to be maintained because they affect the amount of water in the body, blood pH, muscle action and other important processes. Shannon also underwent a tracheotomy during this crisis. "Electrolytes." *Medline Plus, A Service of the U.S. National Library and the National Institutes of Health.* <http://www.nlm.nih.gov/medlineplus/ency/article/000997.htm>. January 18, 2005.

89. Pseudobular palsy. One aspect of this palsy is a severe swallowing impairment due to an apparent weakness of the muscles used in chewing and a brisk gag reflex. When the condition is treated effectively, a speech-language pathologist first reviews the normal swallowing process with the individual. Then the person's swallowing function is tested. The speech pathologist helps the patient learn compensatory swallowing techniques to facilitate safe swallowing. Saliva control and dietary changes are reviewed as well as alternative feeding methods, if eating by mouth is no longer possible. "Cerebral Palsy: Hope through Research." *National Institute of Neurological Disorders and Stroke.* <http://www.ninds.nih.gov/disorders/cerebral_palsy/detail_cerebral_palsy.htm>. October 2, 2004. "Amyotrophic Lateral Sclerosis Fact Sheet." *National Institute of Neurological Disorders and Stroke.*

90. There was no coverage at that time for the travel expenses, as the Band did not have access to such financial resources. At present the Band covers expenses when people living there need to seek services in the city.

91. Unsung heroes are the mothers who brave snow and ice (or trolleys and then 30-step subway stairs with wee ones in strollers and backpacks in the city) in seeking care for their sick children. Do these doctors have any idea what goes on before and after the cluster of wide-eyed young ones are herded into their offices and told "shsh" in the waiting room?

92. Shannon died suddenly of a heart attack and related natural causes on March 23, 2005, just before this book went to press. The obituary printed in the *Winnipeg Sun* said, "Shannon was a spiritual person who gathered strength and courage from her faith. Although her life was often filled with pain and illness, she saw her way to make an impact on everyone that she met." A loving poem by Sharon also appeared:

A LETTER TO MY DAUGHTER

The world turned grey for us today.
Our "Sunshine" went out of our lives.
How very difficult it is to let you go,
how sad and heartbroken we are.

We had forgotten that God had only lent you to us,
never thinking that we had to give you back.
We wanted you to be with us forever.
Shan, you were one of God's chosen people, sent here on a mission.
God sent you as an example to show us all to love,
forgive and care for each other.
Shan, you were also given the task to be vocal
and to be passionate about bringing awareness
and acceptance for people with disabilities.
You worked so hard to give this message.
Shan you were so little, yet you had such a big heart.
My pain is so great, my heart so very broken,
my loneliness unbearable.
How do I go on without you?
You are my best friend, my child, my life.
My love for you will never end,
my thoughts will always be of you.
I will always look for you and give you a sign of my never-ending love.
Shannon, my heart is broken.

I love you so very much.   Love Mom.

CHAPTER NINE

93. Autism is often referred to as a "spectrum disorder," meaning that the symptoms and characteristics of autism can present themselves in a wide variety of combinations, from mild to severe. Although autism is defined by a certain set of behaviours, children and adults can exhibit any combination of the behaviours in any degree of severity. Two children, both with a diagnosis of autism, can act very differently from one another. "Autism Spectrum Disorders (Pervasive Developmental Disorders)." *National Institute of Mental Health.* <http://www.nimh.nih.gov/healthinformation/autismmenu.cfm>. January 22, 2005.

94. Picard, "Segregation is not such a dirty word: Tiny school helps children with severe physical and behavioural problems to thrive."

95. The November 2004 Supreme Court decision that ruled against the funding of the autism treatment argued that the treatment is not "medically necessary" and therefore is not covered under the Canada Health Act. Similar lower court rulings in Ontario and Newfoundland had been found in favour of similar families. Refusing to provide proven effective treatment to children with this neurological disorder

is both short-sighted and wrong. "Ontario Court Case Friend of Children with Autism." *Friends of Children with Autism.* <http://www.ont-autism.uoguelph.ca/ont-courtcase-03.html>. April 24, 2005.

Interestingly, parents in each of these provinces organized, lobbied their governments, raised funds and brought tremendous public pressure to bear on elected officials. A change of government in Ontario — in tandem with a high profile campaign by parent groups and professionals in the field — led the province to expand coverage for autism therapy in April 2004 and again in April 2005. The liberal provincial government claims that under its initiatives the number of children with autism waiting for assessment has decreased by 72 percent — from more than 1000 in March 2004 to 287 in March 2005. Clearly, organizing gets results, and yet, this narrow definition of "medically necessary" does not bode well for children in need of highly specialized services. "Ontario Providing More Autism Therapy to Young Children." *Ontario Ministry of Children and Youth Services.* <http://www.children.gov.on.ca/CS/en/newsRoom/newsReleases/050404.htm>. April 23, 2005.

CHAPTER 10

96. Some deaf individuals and families choose to communicate through American Sign Language (ASL), a distinct language and entrée into deaf culture. Those who "speak" ASL may be like other minority language groups and prefer to remain in their linguistic community. They are interested in strengthening their own cultural and community practices.

97. Interestingly, Mathieu and Suzanne found that services on the Quebec side were not as plentiful as in Ottawa. They had moved over to Hull when Aude Catherine was born. The two cities span two sides of the Ottawa River and are connected by several bridges used daily by tens of thousands of commuters. While Montreal or Quebec City may afford better opportunities for hearing-impaired children, in their estimation, Hull and Gatineau were not especially well served.

CHAPTER ELEVEN

98. Miriam Edelson, *My Journey with Jake: A Memoir of Parenting and Disability* (Toronto: Between The Lines, 2000),127-141.

99. "Trisomy 18 Facts." < http://www.trisomy.org/html/trisomy_18_facts.htm>Support Organization for Trisomy 18, 13 and Related Disorders>. July 7, 2003.

100. "Trisomy 18 Facts." *Support Organization for Trisomy 18, 13 and Related Disorders.*

101. Valentine, *Enabling Citizenship: Full Inclusion of Children with Disabilities and their Parents,* 98-105.

102. Early intervention specialists are now provided by the Canadian National Institute for the Blind.

CHAPTER TWELVE

103. Ontario Human Rights Commission, *Paying the Price: The Human Cost of Racial Profiling, Inquiry Report* (Toronto: OHRC, December 2003).

CHAPTER THIRTEEN

104. Since Enosh made use of this Centre it has merged with another facility to become Bloorview MacMillan Children's Centre. It is an academic health science centre, affiliated with the University of Toronto, dedicated to enabling children and youth with disabilities or special needs to achieve their personal best. "Defy Disability." Toronto: *Bloorview MacMillan Children's Centre.* <http://www.bloorviewmacmillan. on.ca>. October 11, 2004.

CHAPTER FOURTEEN

105. "Disabled Woman Allowed to Have Father as Caregiver: B.C. Human Rights Tribunal rules ban on hiring relatives discriminatory," *Vancouver Sun,* 30 June 2004. Reprinted in "B.R.A.I.N. Waves," *Brain Resource Advocacy Information Network* 4, no.8 (August 2004). <http://www.braininjurylaw.ca/pdf/bw-2004-08.pdf >. March 9, 2005.

106. Harry Beatty, "Comment on the Child and Family Services Act," and Miriam Edelson, "COMSOC Core Services Must be Expanded," *ARCHTYPE* (January-February 1996), 55-58.

REFLECTIONS: DRAWING SOME CONCLUSIONS

107. For example, this idea was advanced by Asne Seierstad, author of *The Bookseller of Kabul.* (London: Virago, 2004) and discussed by round table of authors: Justin Cartwright, Njabulo Ndebele, Edeet Ravel and Gillian Slovo, International Festival of Authors, Toronto, October 25, 2004.

108. Jonathan Penny, "A Constitution for the Disabled or a Disabled Constitution," *Journal of Law and Equality* 1 Spring 2002, 83-117.

109. Follow-up telephone interview, Colleen Fitzpatrick, 20 April 2004.

110. J.R. Saul, *The Unconscious Civilization* (Markham: The Free Press, 1999) quoted in Sherri Torjman,

111. bell hooks, *Teaching Community: A Pedagogy of Hope* (New York: Routledge, 2003).

112. Torjman, *What are Policy-Makers Saying about Respite?,* 10.

113. Kira Heneck, Executive Director, Ontario Coalition for Better Child Care, interviewed by author, 15 April 2005; and Jane Beach, Jane Bertrand et al., "Working for Change: Canada's Child Care Workforce," Child Care Human Resources Sector Council, (Ottawa: 2004).

Wages in licensed childcare centres are so poor that staff are taking their skills to better resourced areas. The study cited above showed that income in the childcare sector was about half the national average for all occupations. A worker with a diploma working full-time at a centre could expect an average annual salary of $22,500. Full-time staff with no diploma earn on average $16,500.

114. In research for another project, I was appalled to learn that two very competent staff at a group home decided to take jobs at Tim Hortons because the pay per hour was higher; they could not support their families on non-union caregiver wages. Those who wish to do this work may not be able to, and those who do it may not wish to be doing it.

115. When the provincial government announced in 1997 that it planned to dismantle l'hôpital Montfort, the only French-speaking teaching hospital in Ontario, a huge groundswell of resistance successfully blocked this ill-advised plan. "Ottawa - La régression du français." *Revue de presse de l'Ontario, Carrefour des francophones d'Amérique.* <http://www.cvfa.ca/Salle_Presse/Archives/Semaine-14-06-2001/S-Ontario14-06-2001/s-ontario14-06-2001.htm>. March 28, 2005, and "Drapeau franco-ontarien," *l'Association de Canadiens de Langue Francaise d'Ottawa.* <http://www.acfoottawa.ca/fr/Votre_drapeau_23.html>. March 28, 2005.

116. See David Baker, On Lok Senior Health Centre, San Francisco, California, 27 July 2004.

117. Providing personal care to vulnerable populations is a complex issue. This is true of care given in a person's home *and* in facility-based situations. Such care, by definition, is often intrusive. Neither caregiver nor client is a robot; our personalities and flaws come into play as do dynamics of power that can leave room for abuse. Any form of abuse is unacceptable.

Select Bibliography

Amaratunga, Carol ed. *Race, Ethnicity and Women's Health.* Halifax: Atlantic Centre of Excellence for Women's Health, 2002.

Barnes, Mercer and Shakespeare. *Exploring Disability: A Sociological Introduction.* Cambridge: Polity Press, 1999.

Bragg, Lois ed. *Deaf World.* New York: New York University Press, 2001.

Brill, M.T. *Keys to Parenting a Child with Down Syndrome.* New York: Barron's Educational Services, 1993.

Canadian Union of Postal Workers Special Needs Project. *Moving Mountains: Work, Family and Children with Special Needs.* Ottawa, November 2002.

Clutterbuck, Peter. *Social Inclusion and Community Participation.* Toronto: Laidlaw Foundation, 2002.

Code, Lorraine et al. "Is Feminist Ethics Possible?" Ottawa: Canadian Research Institute for the Advancement of Women, May 1991.

Eisenstein, Zillah ed. *Capitalist Patriarchy and the Case for Socialist Feminism.* London and New York: Monthly Review Press, 1979.

Friendly, Martha. *Social Inclusion through Early Childhood Education and Care.* Laidlaw Foundation: Toronto, 2002.

Golden, M. and Peacock, F.E. eds. *The Research Experience.* Itasca, Illinois: Publishers Inc., 1976.

Greaves, Lorraine et al. *A Motherhood Issue: Discourses on Mothering Under Duress.* Ottawa: Status of Women Canada, October 2002.

Hellman, Lillian. *Pentimento.* Boston: Little, Brown and Company,1973.

Holbrook, M. Cay ed. *Children with Visual Impairments: A Parents' Guide.* Bethesda Maryland: Woodbine House, 1996.

Jenson, Jane. *Research Report — Mapping Social Cohesion: The State of Canadian Research.* Ottawa: Canadian Policy Research Networks, November 27, 1998.

Longmore, Paul K. *Why I Burned My Book and Other Essays on Disability.* Philadelphia: Temple University Press, 2003.

Luxton, Meg. *More Than a Labour of Love.* Toronto: Women's Press, 1980.

Marmur, Dow. *Ethical Reflections on Social Inclusion.* Toronto: Laidlaw Foundation, 2002.

Marshall and Rossman. *Designing Qualitative Research.* London: Sage Publications, 1999.

Maynard, Mary and Purvis, June eds. *Researching Women's Lives from a Feminist Perspective.* London: Taylor & Francis Ltd, 1994.

Morris, Marika. *Participatory Research and Action.* Ottawa: Canadian Research Institute for the Advancement of Women, 2002.

Muzychka, Martha et al. *Feminist Research Ethics: A Process.* Ottawa: Canadian Research Institute for the Advancement of Women, October 1996.

Ontario Human Rights Commission. *Pay the Price: The Human Cost of Racial Profiling.* Toronto, 2003.

Peri, C. and Moses, K. eds. *Mothers Who Think: Tales of Real-Life Parenthood.* New York: Washington Square Press, 2000.

The Roeher Institute. *Disability-Related Support Arrangements, Policy Options and Implications for Women's Equality.* Ottawa: Status of Women Canada, February 2001.

Sainsbury, Diane ed. *Gendering Welfare States.* London: Sage Publications, 1994.

Salter, Pat interviewed by Margaret Dragu. "Raising Fraser: A Special Needs Child." In Margaret Dragu, Sarah Sheard and Susan Swan eds. *Mothers Talk Back.* Toronto: Coach House Press, 1991.

Thompson, Linda. "Feminist Methodology for Family Studies." *Journal of Marriage and the Family* 54 (February 1992).

Tierney and Lincoln eds. *Representation and the Text, Re-Framing the Narrative Voice.* Albany: State University of New York Press, 1997.

Tse, Catherine. "Right By Your Side: Legal Rights and Resources for Parents of Children with Disabilities." *Abilities* (Fall, 2002).

Vanier, Jean. *Becoming Human.* Toronto: House of Anansi Press, 1998.

Acknowledgements

I want first to thank the women and men who so generously shared their stories and reflections with me. Their determination is a source of inspiration.

Special thanks to sociologist Dr. Meg Luxton who critiqued an early draft and provided invaluable comments. My friend, author Jane Finlay Young, offered wise counsel throughout the birthing of this book.

Derek Fudge and John Rae helped me to clarify issues and identify prospective parents. The First Nations disAbility Association of Manitoba and Canadian National Institute for the Blind, Toronto Region were also instrumental in this process.

A warm thank you to my union sister Beverley Johnson for sharing her knowledge and gentle wisdom. My long-standing colleagues in the labour and social movements helped me to bear losing my son in the middle of this project. For their embrace, I am grateful beyond words.

Aura Aberback transcribed text and assisted me in preparing the manuscript. Shannon Roe also helped with early drafts. I am indebted to them both.

My editors Lisa Rundle and Jennifer Glossop breathed the manuscript with me to shape a far better book. I am also grateful to Sumach Press for believing in this project and bringing it to fruition.

The Canada Council for the Arts, the Canadian Research Institute for the Advancement of Women (CRIAW), the Ontario Arts Council and the Toronto Arts Council supported my work at key moments.

The Ontario Public Service Employees Union (OPSEU) Disability Rights Caucus — and other equity-seeking groups in the union — showed by example that it is possible to work politically in a manner that is respectful and honours diversity.

Finally, I wish to thank my daughter Emma-Maryse for grounding me in the world and, by her presence, always bringing me back from the safe burrow of my writing. To Andy, as always, for his insight, patience and love.

OTHER TITLES FROM SUMACH PRESS

A Recognition of Being: Reconstructing Native Womanhood
Kim Anderson

Back to the Drawing Board: African-Canadian Feminisms
Edited by Njoki Nathane Wane, Katerina Deliovsky and Erica Lawson

Doing IT: Women Working in Information Technology
Krista Scott-Dixon

Double Jeopardy: Motherwork and the Law
Lorna A. Turnbull

Gifts: Poems for Parents
Edited by Rhea Tregebov

Fuelling Body, Mind and Spirit: A Balanced Approach to Healthy Eating
Miriam Hoffer

Growing Up Degrassi: Television, Identity and Youth Cultures
Edited by Michele Byers

Madeleine Parent: Activist
Edited by Andrée Lévèsque

My Breasts, My Choice: Journeys Through Surgery
Barbara Brown, Maureen Aslin & Betsy Carey

Plots & Pans: The Book Club Cookbook
The SWIVEL Collective

Strong Women Stories: Native Vision and Community Survival
Edited by Kim Anderson and Bonita Lawrence

Turbo Chicks: Talking Young Feminisms
Edited by Allyson Mitchell, Lisa Bryn Rundle and Lara Karaian

Women in the Office: Transitions in a Global Economy
Ann Eyerman

The Women's Daybook
With images by Canadian photographers

Women's Bodies/Women's Lives: Women, Health, Well-Being and Body Image
Edited by Baukje Miedema, Janet Stoppard and Vivienne Anderson

Writing Your Way: Creating a Personal Journal
Ellen Jaffe

CHECK OUT OUR GREAT FICTION AND BOOKS FOR YOUNG ADULTS TOO AT
www.sumachpress.com